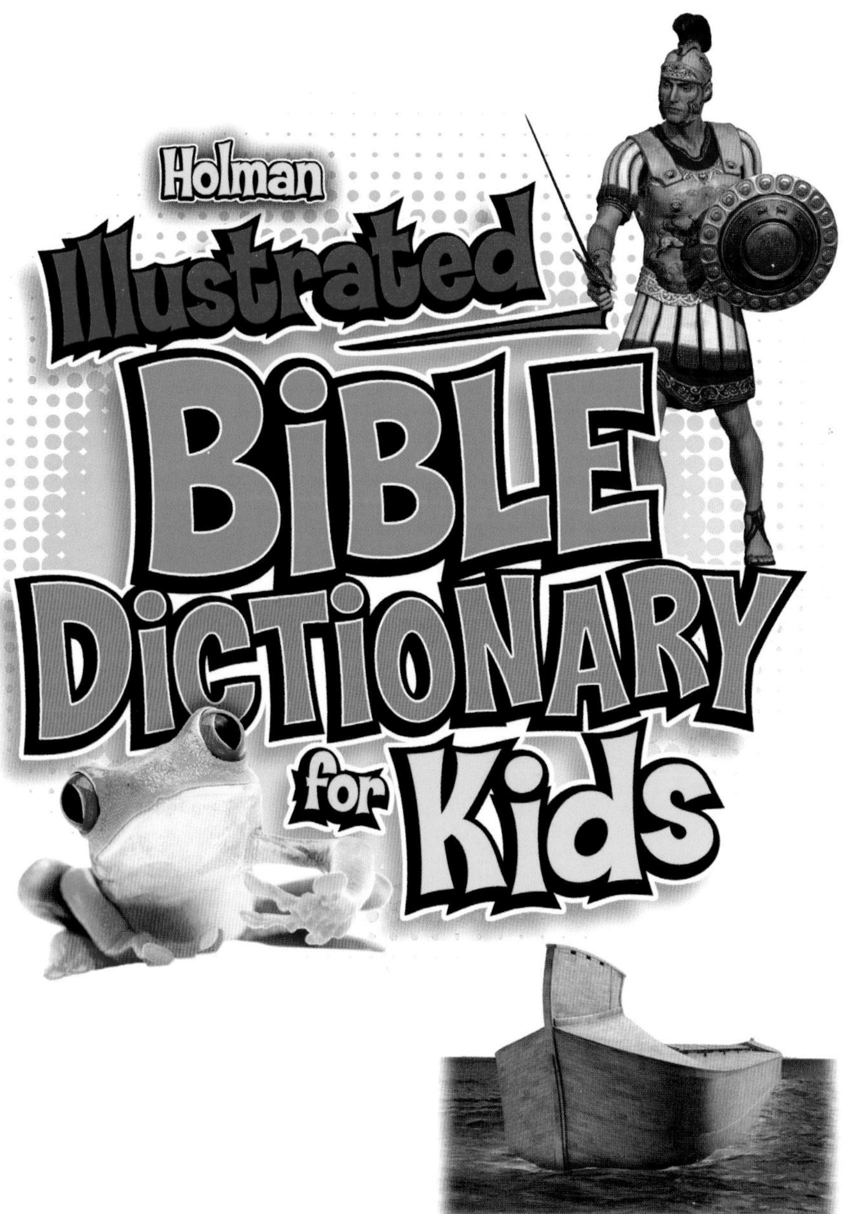

HOLMAN REFERENCE

Holman Illustrated Bible Dictionary for Kids
© 2010 by B & H Publishing Group
Nashville, Tennessee

978-0-8054-9531-7

A Holman Reference Book
Published by
B & H Publishing Group
127 Ninth Avenue, North
Nashville, TN 37234
http://www.broadmanholman.com

Dewey: 220.3
Subject Heading: BIBLE—DICTIONARIES

General Editors: Landry R. Holmes and Judy H. Latham
Stylist: Helen Owens
Art Director: Greg Pope
Cover Design: Diana Lawrence and Mark Whitaker
Design Team: Doug Powell and Jeremy Cornelius
Associate Editor: Steve Bond

The Holman editorial staff gratefully acknowledges the contributions of Trudy Gardner, Ernie Hickman, Brent Bruce, G.B. Howell, Jr., and James McLemore (retired) in providing photos and illustrations from the archives of the *Biblical Illustrator* and Church Resources Division, Childhood Ministry Publishing. We are also indebted to Sue Woodside, Steve Gateley, and Virginia Copelin of E.C. Dargan Research Library who facilitated research on this book.

Printed in China

1 2 3 4 5 6 7 15 14 13 12 11 10

DBS

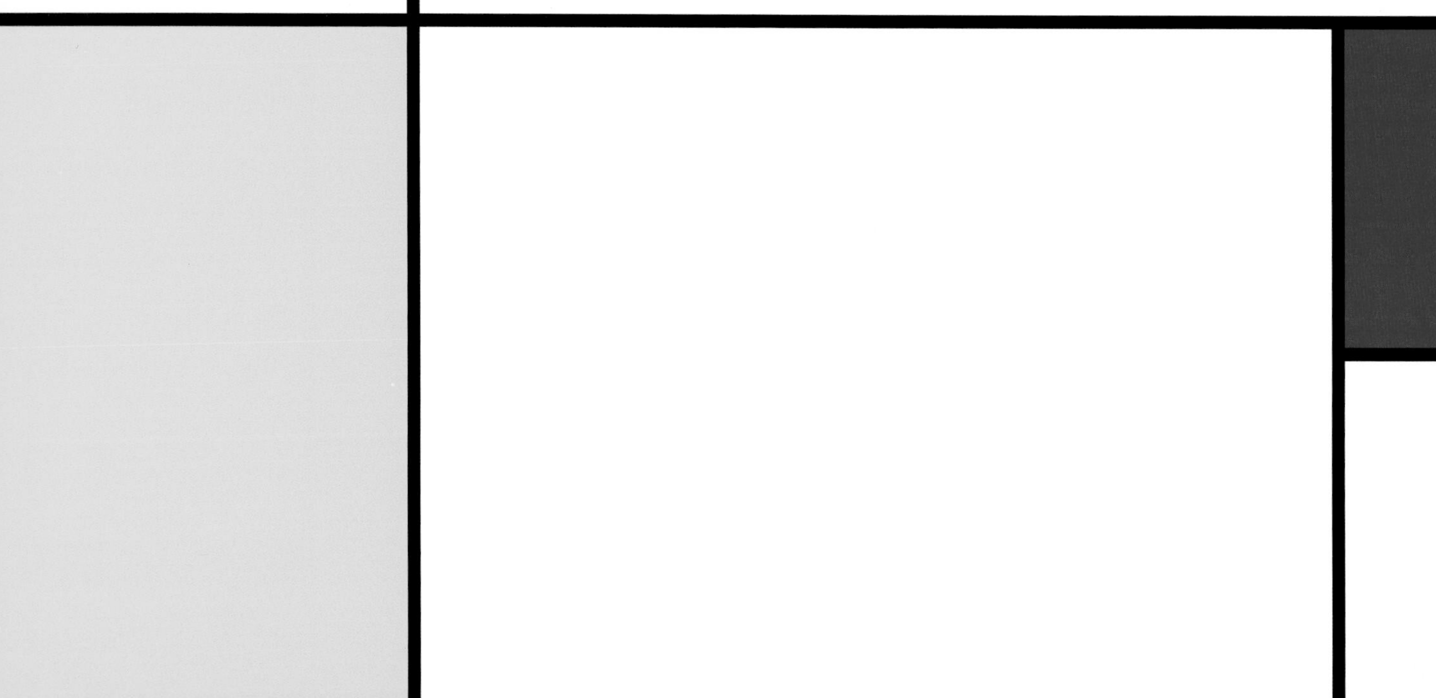

FOR PARENTS AND TEACHERS

Philip: *"Do you understand what you're reading?"*

Ethiopian Official: *"How can I, unless someone guides me?"*

God's Word.
Lamp for my feet.
Light on my path.
Sword of the Spirit.
Holy Scriptures.

All terms used to describe what we now call the Bible. In our culture, the Bible seemingly has become commonplace. We find it in multiple forms—electronic and print—and in numerous translations. The Bible is in hotel rooms, doctors' offices, churches, and homes.

One would think that with so many copies of the Bible available to us, as a society we would be extremely biblically literate. Nonetheless, quite the opposite is true. We own physical copies of God's Word, but we do not take the time to listen to God speak, try to understand His teachings, and act on and benefit from His wisdom and counsel. What can we do to change this fact? We can start with our children.

Historically, children have been fortunate to receive the rich inheritance Holy Scripture offers. When Paul wrote his last letter to his young protégé Timothy, he reminded Timothy of this heritage:

"But as for you, continue in what you have learned and firmly believed, knowing those from whom you learned, and that from childhood you have known the sacred Scriptures, which are able to instruct you for salvation through faith in Christ Jesus" (2 Timothy 3:14-15).

In a family where Timothy's father was probably not a believer, his mother and grandmother created an environment in which he came to know the sacred Scriptures.

At other times in history parents and teachers have placed top priority on leading their children to know Jesus Christ through His written word. You can continue this tradition.

However, the Bible is not an easy book because of the sheer quantity of material and the difference in time and culture in which the sixty-six books of Scripture were written. When Philip, a first-century deacon, was led by God's Spirit to a man traveling from Jerusalem to Gaza in a chariot, he saw that the man was reading a scroll. As he approach the man, Philip asked, *"Do you understand what you're reading?"* (Acts 8:30).

The Ethiopian official replied, *"How can I, unless someone guides me?"* (Acts 8:31).

You hold in your hands a resource that can enable you to help the children in your life understand what they are reading. When they do not understand the meaning of a Bible word, or when they want to know more about Bible facts, kids can look up entries and view images that help give meaning to Bible stories that are both familiar and new to them. The *Holman Bible Dictionary for Kids* is based on the popular *Holman Bible Dictionary* and *Holman Pocket Bible Dictionary*—both valuable resources for understanding the Bible.

What makes this particular dictionary unique is that it introduces kindergarteners, elementary-age children, and preteens to biblical concepts through the use of kid-friendly definitions, charts, illustrations, photographs, maps, and reconstructions. Full-color maps help kids begin to understand the importance of geography in biblical history. Almost every entry includes biblical references where the featured word

or concept can be found. Words that are difficult to pronounce include a pronunciation guide, as well. In addition, entries with King James Version words make this a "translation neutral" dictionary.

If you are a parent, keep this book accessible at home so that when you are reading the Bible with your child, you can quickly look up words he does not understand. Also, if you are telling your child a Bible story that includes a geographical location, find the map in the dictionary to help her gain a sense that the stories in the Bible are true and happened in real places. Consider challenging your child to learn a new word a week. Read the Bible verses associated with that word, and talk about the word all week.

If you are a teacher at church or Christian school, provide more than one copy of the dictionary in the classroom. As kids research Bible facts, encourage them to use this resource to give new meaning to God's Word. If they are dramatizing a Bible story, guide boys and girls to look at illustrations and photos in the dictionary to help them understand what the actual Bible scene may have looked like. Kids can also use this book as a concordance by looking up a word and then locating in the Bible some of the places where it is referenced.

Whether you are a parent or a teacher, the ways you can use this dictionary to promote biblical literacy in today's kids are numberless. Whatever you do, guide your children to develop an understanding of and a love for God's Word by modeling Bible reading and Bible study in your own life and by allowing the truths of Scripture to shape your thoughts, intentions, speech, and actions. By doing so, you not only grow in your personal relationship with God, but you lay the foundation for the next generation to know and follow Jesus Christ.

JUST FOR KIDS

God's Word is full of adventure and is for everyone, not just adults. The Bible includes exciting stories of creation, a flood, battles, good and evil kings and queens, peace, plagues, shipwrecks, love, and the birth of a King. Sometimes, the Bible has words that are hard to understand and talks about places and things that you have never seen. For example, have you ever wondered what the word *phylactery* means, or what Solomon's temple looked like? Ever thought about what kinds of insects are in the Bible, or how many Marys are in the Bible?

Now, you can find the answers to these questions and many more in the *Holman Bible Dictionary for Kids.* This dictionary is just for kids. That's right—it's just for you. Use it at home when you want to find a Bible fact that no one else in your family knows. You can also use it at church when you want to know more about the Bible. Take a quick look at some of the features of this dictionary that is just for you, then turn the page and let the adventure begin!

RECONSTRUCTIONS

show how buildings and cities may have actually looked in Bible times.

Rome (ROHM) Capital city of the Roman Empire. Paul made the trip to Rome as a prisoner and was under house arrest there for two years. **Acts 28:11-16**

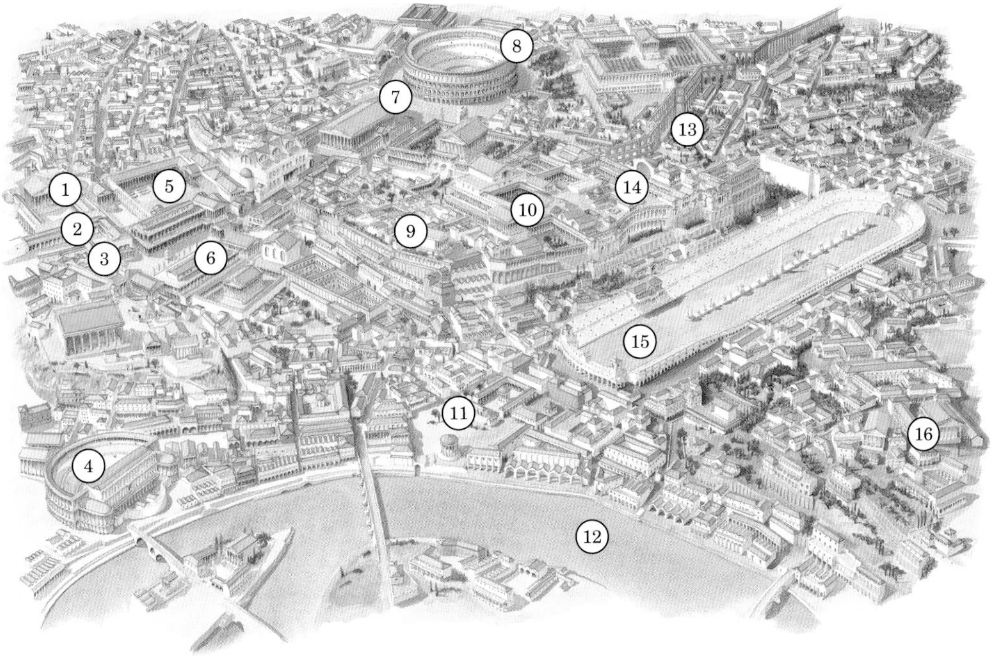

ILLUSTRATED CHARTS

with brief descriptions and biblical references provide "at-a-glance" views of Bible animals, insects, transportation, plants, and so forth.

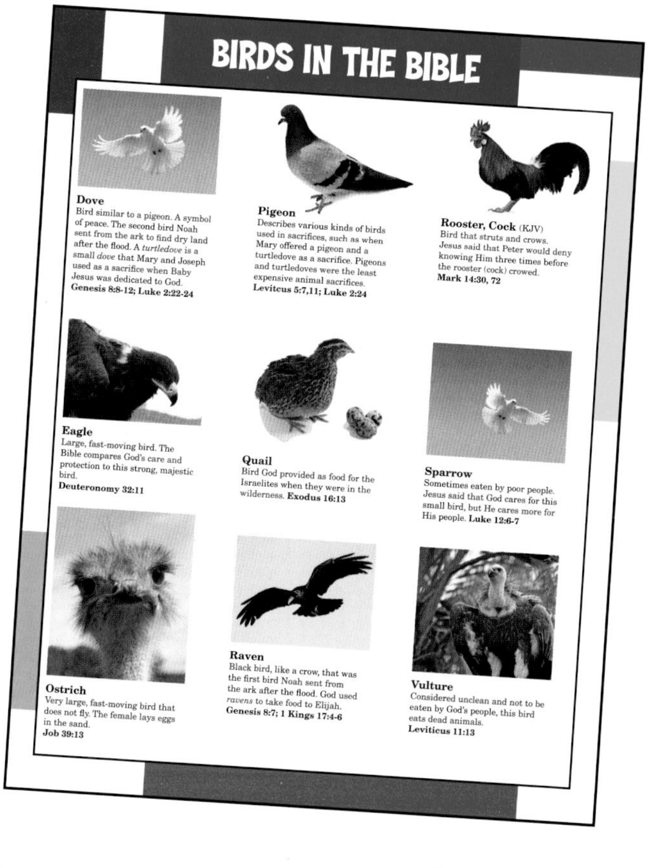

BIRDS IN THE BIBLE

Dove
Bird similar to a pigeon. A symbol of peace. The second bird Noah sent from the ark to find dry land after the flood. A *turtledove* is a small *dove* that Mary and Joseph used as a sacrifice when Baby Jesus was dedicated to God.
Genesis 8:8-12; Luke 2:22-24

Pigeon
Describes various kinds of birds used in sacrifices, such as when Mary offered a pigeon and a turtledove as a sacrifice. Pigeons and turtledoves were the least expensive animal sacrifices.
Levitcus 5:7,11; Luke 2:24

Rooster, Cock (KJV)
Bird that struts and crows. Jesus said that Peter would deny knowing Him three times before the rooster (cock) crowed.
Mark 14:30, 72

Eagle
Large, fast-moving bird. The Bible compares God's care and protection to this strong, majestic bird.
Deuteronomy 32:11

Quail
Bird God provided as food for the Israelites when they were in the wilderness. **Exodus 16:13**

Sparrow
Sometimes eaten by poor people. Jesus said that God cares for this small bird, but He cares more for His people. **Luke 12:6-7**

Ostrich
Very large, fast-moving bird that does not fly. The female lays eggs in the sand.
Job 39:13

Raven
Black bird, like a crow, that was the first bird Noah sent from the ark after the flood. God used *ravens* to take food to Elijah.
Genesis 8:7; 1 Kings 17:4-6

Vulture
Considered unclean and not to be eaten by God's people, this bird eats dead animals.
Leviticus 11:13

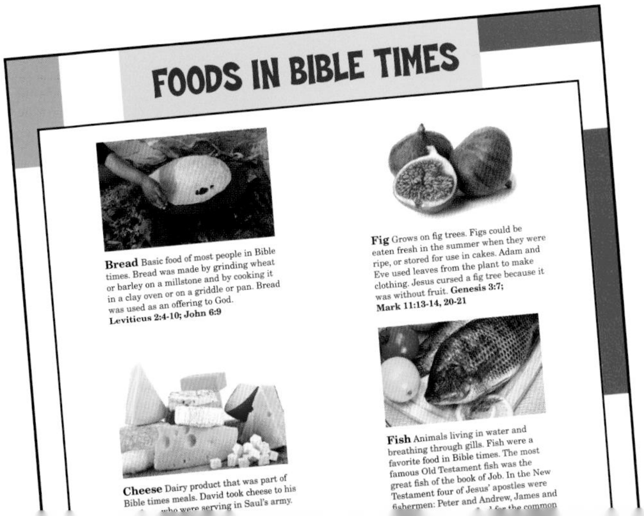

FOODS IN BIBLE TIMES

Bread Basic food of most people in Bible times. Bread was made by grinding wheat or barley on a millstone and by cooking it in a clay oven or on a griddle or pan. Bread was used as an offering to God.
Leviticus 2:4-10; John 6:9

Fig Grows on fig trees. Figs could be eaten fresh in the summer when they were ripe, or stored for use in cakes. Adam and Eve used leaves from the plant to make clothing. Jesus cursed a fig tree because it was without fruit. **Genesis 3:7; Mark 11:13-14, 20-21**

Cheese Dairy product that was part of Bible times meals. David took cheese to his ... who were serving in Saul's army.

Fish Animals living in water and breathing through gills. Fish were a favorite food in Bible times. The most famous Old Testament fish was the great fish of the book of Job. In the New Testament four of Jesus' apostles were fishermen: Peter and Andrew, James and ...

CHARTS

of names of God, names of Jesus, festivals, apostles, plagues, and so forth.

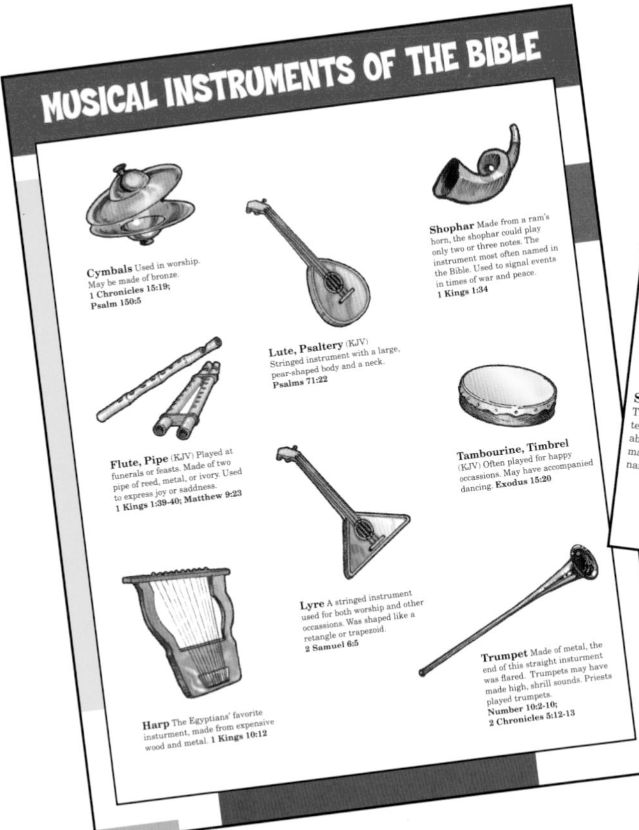

MUSICAL INSTRUMENTS OF THE BIBLE

Cymbals Used in worship. May be made of bronze. **1 Chronicles 15:19; Psalm 150:5**

Lute, Psaltery (KJV) Stringed instrument with a large, pear-shaped body and a neck. **Psalms 71:22**

Shophar Made from a ram's horn, the shophar could play only two or three notes. The instrument most often named in the Bible. Used to signal events in times of war and peace. **1 Kings 1:34**

Flute, Pipe (KJV) Played at funerals or feasts. Made of two pipe of reed, metal, or ivory. Used to express joy or saddness. **1 Kings 1:39-40; Matthew 9:23**

Tambourine, Timbrel (KJV) Often played for happy occasions. May have accompanied dancing. **Exodus 15:20**

Lyre A stringed instrument used for both worship and other occasions. Was shaped like a retangle or trapezoid. **2 Samuel 6:5**

Trumpet Made of metal, the end of this straight insturment was flared. Trumpets may have made high, shrill sounds. Priests played trumpets. **Number 10:2-10; 2 Chronicles 5:12-13**

Harp The Egyptians' favorite insturment, made from expensive wood and metal. **1 Kings 10:12**

THE APOSTLES

Andrew Andrew was a fisherman with his brother Peter on the Sea of Galilee. Jesus called Andrew to be a disciple while he was fishing (Matthew 4:18-20). Andrew brought Peter to Jesus (John 1:40-42) and told Jesus about the boy with the loaves and fishes (John 6:8).

James The Bible tells nothing about this man except his name.

James James was a fisherman on the Sea of Galilee with his father, Zebedee, and his brother John. James and John were call Boanereges, sons of thunder. Jesus called James to be a disciple while he was mending nets (Matthew 4:21-22). James was the first disciple to be killed because of his faith (Acts 12:1-2).

John John was a fisherman on the Sea of Galilee with his father, Zebedee, and his brother James. Jesus called John to be a disciple while he was mending nets (Matthew 4:21-22). John helped Peter prepare the Passover meal (Luke 22:8) and from the cross, Jesus told John to care for his Mother (John 19:26-27).

Matthew, Levi Jesus called Matthew to be a disciple while he was a tax collector in Capernaum. Matthew invited Jesus to a dinner where his friends could meet Jesus (Matthew 9:9-13).

Judas Judas was keeper of the disciples' money bag. Judas betrayed Jesus for thirty pieces of silver (Luke 22:47-48). He was sorry for what he had done and hanged himself (Matthew 27:3-5).

Nathaniel (Bartholomew) Philip introduced Nathaniel to Jesus. Jesus called him a "true Israelite" (John 1:45-51).

Philip Jesus called Philip to follow Him as a disciple (John 1:44). Philip found Nathaniel and told him about Jesus (John 1:45). Philip went with Andrew to bring some Greeks to Jesus (John 12:20-21).

Simon, Peter or Cephas (rock) Peter was a fisherman with his brother Andrew on the Sea of Galilee. Jesus called Peter to be a disciple while he was fishing (Matthew 4:18-20). Jesus helped Peter to walk on water (Matthew 14:28-33). Peter denied Jesus before His crucifixion (Luke 22:54-62) and was later forgiven by Jesus (John 21:15-19).

Simon The Bible tells nothing about this man except his name.

Thaddaeus (Judas, son of James) Thaddaeus (Judas, not Iscariot) asked Jesus how he was going to reveal Himself to the disciples and not to the world (John 14:22).

Thomas (Didymus) Thomas encouraged the disciples to go with Jesus and die with Him (John 11:16). Thomas wanted evidence that Jesus had risen from the dead (John 20:25). Jesus showed Thomas His hands and side to prove His resurrection (John 20:27-29).

ENTRiES

with King James Version words.

Self-control, Temperance (KJV)

Engaged, Espoused (KJV)

Bronze, Brass (KJV)

Broom Tree, Juniper Tree (KJV)

PRONUNCiATiON GUiDE

for those hard-to-say words.

Centurion (sen TYOOR ee uhn)

Abednego (uh BED nih goh)

Cross/crucifixion (kroo suh FIK shuhn)

Angel (AYN juhl)

Paul (PAWL, PAHL)

Bartholomew (bahr THAHL uh myoo)

PHOTOGRAPHS

to help you understand that events in the Bible happened in real places.

REALISTIC ILLUSTRATIONS

of Bible stories because the Bible is about real people who actually lived in real places.

DEFINITIONS

of people you read about in Bible stories and key bible concepts

Paul (PAWL, PAHL) Roman name of the Hebrew "Saul." Outstanding missionary and writer of the earl church. He wrote 13 letters that make up almost one-fourth of the New Testament. Paul was a Jew and a Roman citizen. He grew up in Jerusalem as a student of Gamaliel and as a Pharisee. At first Paul persecute Christians, but later became a Christian himself. He was a Christian missionary to Asia Minor, Greece, ar other countries around the Mediterranean Sea. Paul was arrested because Jewish leaders did not want him to preach about Jesus. He continued to preach and write letters from prison in Rome. **Acts 22:3, 2 Philippians 3:4-6; Acts 9:1-22**

Solomon (SAHL uh muhn) Bathsheba and David's successor He is remembered most for his wi program—including the temple in his wealth. In addition to building Solomon fortified a number of cit provide protection to Jerusalem. for keeping the materials needed built military bases for chariote wives who were princesses and from many of the kingdoms wit had treaties. He apparently all worship their own gods and ev gods built in Jerusalem. After Solomon's death, the northern tribes of Israel rebelled against Solomon's son and made their own nation known as the northern kingdom of Israel.
1 Kings 5–8; 9:15-19; 11:1-3,7-8,29-32; 12:1-19

Salvation Rescue from sin and death. A and Eve disobeyed God in the garden of Eden, si the world and separated all people from God. Thi results in physical and spiritual death. However, salvation from sin and spiritual death through th resurrection of His Son, Jesus. The Holy Spirit cor person of sin and brings about salvation.

The word *conversion* describes when a person sin (repents) to God and trusts Jesus as Savior and Salvation is a free gift from God that rescues the be sin and its consequences, renews the believer to a h and restores the believer to a right relationship wit all eternity. (See *Conversion*.) **Genesis 3:22-24; Mar Luke 19:9; Acts 4:10-12**

Aa

Aaron (EHR uhn, ER'n) Moses' brother who helped him talk to Pharaoh. His parents, Amram and Jochebed, were from the tribe of Levi, which became Israel's tribe of priests. Miriam was his sister. When the Lord sent Moses back to Egypt from the wilderness of Midian, Aaron served as Moses' spokesman before Pharaoh. At Sinai, Moses left Aaron and Hur in charge of the Israelites. When Moses' return was delayed, the people asked Aaron to make them a god. Aaron led the people in creating and worshiping a golden calf. With all his faults, Aaron was a man chosen by God. Aaron experienced the joy of being Israel's first high priest. Like his brother Moses, Aaron died before the Israelites entered the promised land.
Exodus 4:14-16; 6:16-26; 24:14; 28–29; 32; Leviticus 1–7; 8–9; Numbers 20:23-28

The garments of the high priest as prescribed in Exodus 28.

Abba
(AB buh, AH buh)
Name for God that Jesus used. Means *daddy*.
Mark 14:36

Abednego
(uh BED nih goh)
One of the three Hebrew young men who were taken from Jerusalem along with Daniel to serve in King Nebuchadnezzar's court. God delivered them from the fiery furnace. **Daniel 3**

Abel (AY buhl) Means "breath" or "vapor." Adam and Eve's second son. Abel was a shepherd, and he offered to God some of the firstborn of his flock. His brother Cain offered some of his crops to the Lord. The Lord was pleased with Abel's offering but not with Cain's. Cain became angry. His anger led him to murder Abel.
Genesis 4:1-16; Hebrews 11:4

Abraham/Abram (AY bruh ham/AY bruhm) Son of Terah. His childhood was spent in Ur of the Chaldees, an important Sumerian city. His name was Abram ("father is exalted"), but God later changed his name to Abraham ("father of a multitude"). Terah, his father, moved to Haran with the family and after some years died there. When Abram was 75, God called him to move to Canaan. God assured Abram that he would be the father of a great nation. Abram's wife was Sarai. Her name was later changed to Sarah ("princess"). When Abraham was 100 and Sarah 90, God gave them their long-promised son, Isaac ("laughter"). Abraham's faith and obedience were tested by God at Moriah when he was commanded to sacrifice Isaac. God provided an alternative sacrifice, however, saving Isaac's life. As a reward for Abraham's faithfulness, God renewed the covenant promises of great blessing and the growth of a mighty nation to father and son.
Genesis 11:31; 12:1-9; 17:5-8; 21:1-7; 22:1-18

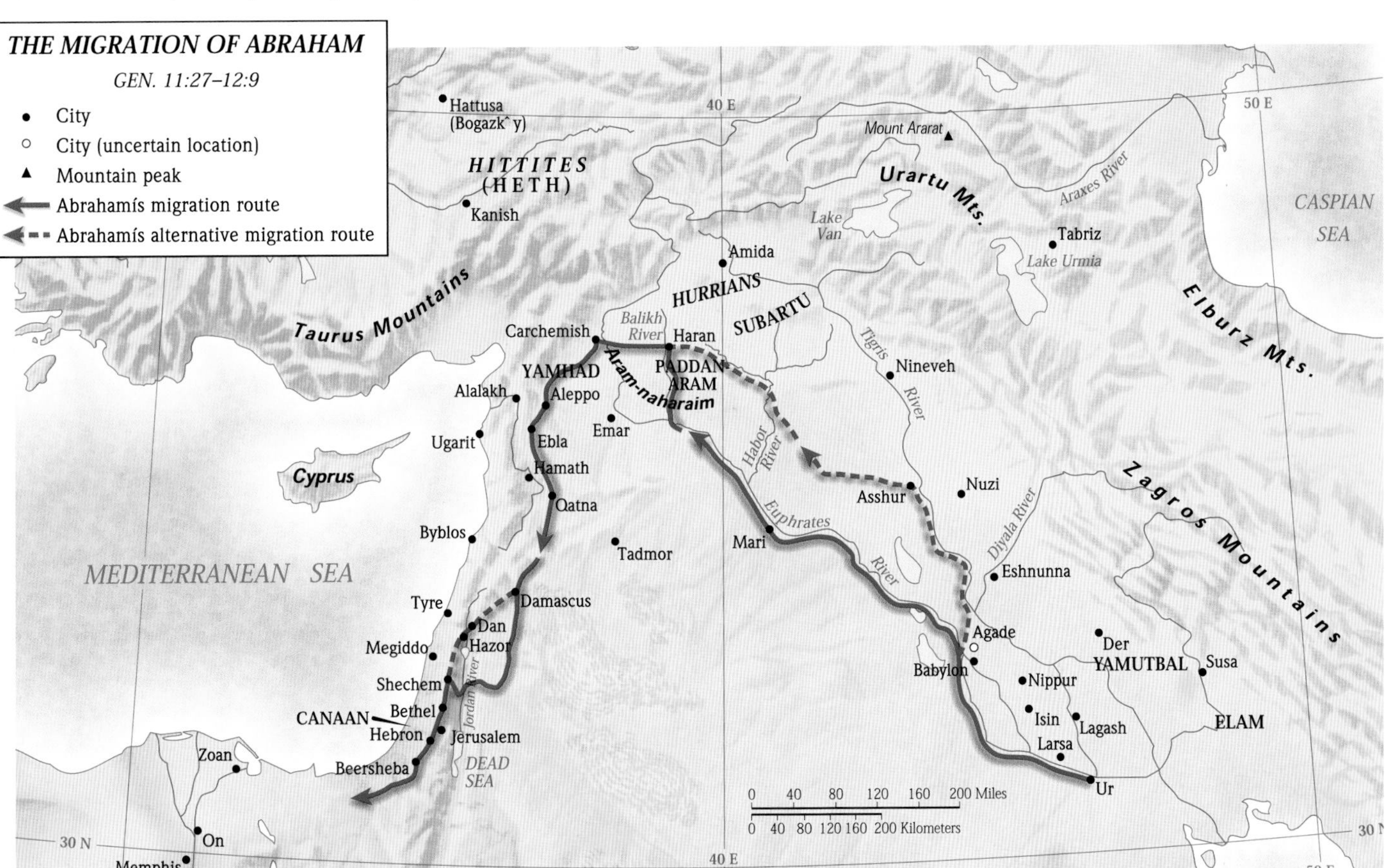

Acts (AKTS)
Only New Testament book of History; tells what the apostles did during the time after Jesus' crucifixion, resurrection, and return to heaven. Luke wrote this book and reported the coming of the Holy Spirit and the spread of the church under Peter's and Paul's leadership.
Acts 1:2-3

Adam (AD uhm) First man created by God from whom all other people come. (See *Eve*.) God placed Adam in the garden of Eden. Adam was given the privilege and responsibility of naming the animals God had created. God told Adam he could eat from any tree in the garden except the tree of the knowledge of good and evil. He was warned that if he ate from that tree, he would die. A serpent told Adam's wife, Eve, that they could become wiser if they ate the fruit God had told them not to eat. Adam and Eve believed the serpent's lie. Their act of disobedience had consequences for them and for all human beings. Adam was the father of Cain, Abel, Seth and other sons and daughters.
Genesis 2:15-25; 3:1-24; 4:1-2,25

Agabus (AG uh buhs)
Prophet from Jerusalem who visited the church at Antioch and told about a coming famine. Later, he told that the Jews would arrest Paul.
Acts 11:27-29; 21:10-11

Adoption When a child legally becomes a member of a family other than the one he was born in.

Advent
Means "coming" and often refers to the four Sundays before Christmas.

Ahab (AY hab)
Israelite king who disobeyed God more than of the previous kings of Israel. His wife Jezebel threatened to kill the prophet Elisha.
1 Kings 16:30

Almond Tree with white or pink blossoms that makes almond nuts. **Jeremiah 1:11**

Altar Place used in Bible times where people offered sacrifices and gifts to God. In Old Testament times, while animals were a common sacrifice, altars were also used to sacrifice grain, fruit, wine, and incense. The grain and fruit sacrifices were offered as a tithe of the harvest. (See *Tithe*.) Altars were made of many kinds of materials: mounds of dirt, mud-bricks, stone, bronze, and gold. In addition to being places where sacrifices were made, altars to God were places where God was present to His people. **Genesis 12:7; 26:24-25**

"Early in the morning Jacob took the stone that was near his head and set it up as a marker. He poured oil on top of it and named the place Bethel" (**Genesis 28:18-19**).

Amen (ah MEN)
Word that means "so be it." Often used at the end of prayer.
Psalm 106:48

Amorites (AM uh rights)
Often enemies of the Israelites. God caused the sun to stand still during a battle between them and the Israelites.
Joshua 10:1-15

Amos (AY mahz)
1. Shepherd from Judah who obeyed God and preached to the people of Israel. 2. Amos is the third book in the Minor Prophets division of the Old Testament. Amos called on the people of Israel to stop worshiping idols and to quit being mean to the poor.
Amos 1:1

A Middle Eastern shepherd leading his sheep

Ananias
(an uh NIGH uhs)
1. Man in Damascus whom God told to help Saul of Tarsus, who had become blind, to see again.
2. High priest of the Jewish council which tried Paul in Jerusalem. (See *Sanhedrin*.)

Acts 9:10-18; 23:1-3

Ancestor
Older family member such as a great grandparent or great-great grandparent. (See *Descendants*.)
Luke 1:55

Andrew (AN droo)
Fisherman who became a disciple of John the Baptist. Later he became an apostle of Jesus and introduced his brother, Simon Peter, to Jesus. Andrew brought the boy with his lunch to Jesus, and Jesus used the lunch to feed the 5,000. He and Philip brought some Greeks to see Jesus. He is mentioned for the last time in the first part of the Book of Acts.
Matthew 4:18; John 1:35-42; 6:8-9; 12:20-22; Acts 1:13

Angels (AYN juhlz)
Created beings whose only job is to serve and worship God. In Bible times, angels spoke messages from God to people. **Luke 1:30-33**

Anna (AN uh)
Old prophetess who recognized Jesus as the Messiah when His parents brought Him to the Temple.
Luke 2:36-38

Animals
God created birds and fish on the fifth day. On the sixth day, He created other animals and commanded man and woman to rule over all the animals.
See *Animals in the Bible*. chart on the next page.

Anoint
To pour oil or perfume on someone to show he is being set apart for a special purpose. **1 Samuel 16:12-13**

A 3500 year-old perfume jar from Judea.

Apollos
(uh PAHL uhs) Jew from Alexandria, Egypt, and student of Priscilla and Aquila. He preached powerfully about Jesus in Achaia.
Acts 18:24-28

Bear
One of the animals David killed to protect his father's sheep.
1 Samuel 17:34-36

Camel
Used for desert travel. The wise men probably rode camels on their trip to find Jesus.
Genesis 24:64

Cattle
Used for work, food, and sacrifices to God. In the Bible, *cattle* often refers to all farm animals.
Psalm 50:10

Donkey
Used for travel and for carrying heavy loads. Jesus rode a donkey into Jerusalem. **Matthew 21:7**

Fish
An important source of food. In the New Testament, the Sea of Galilee was a source of fish. Jesus blessed loaves of bread and fish and fed 5,000 people, Peter found a coin in the mouth of a fish to pay taxes, and Jesus fed fish to some of the disciples by the seaside after His resurrection.
Numbers 11:5
Matthew 4:18-22
John 6:1-15
Matthew 17:24-27
John 21:1-14

Frogs
God used frogs as a plague agains
Pharaoh and the Egyptians.
Exodus 8:1-15

Goat
Used as a source of meat, cheese, and milk; wool for clothing or tents; and sacrifices to God.
Exodus 26:7

Horse
Used for riding or for pulling chariots. **1 Kings 4:26**

Leviathan
(lih VIGH uh thuhn)
An ancient sea creature whose name means "coiled one." Isaiah described it as a serpent. Job said that it thrashed around. The psalmist said God created it.
Isaiah 27:1; Job 41:25; Psalm 104:26

Lion
God rescued Daniel from lions after the king ordered Daniel to be placed in the lions' den as punishment for praying to God.
Daniel 6:1-28

Ox/Oxen
Large cowlike animal used for farm work, carrying heavy loads, food, and sacrifices to God.
Psalm 8:6-7

Serpent
Dangerous poisonous snake. The Bible uses the names *adder, asp, cobra,* and *viper*. The serpent is used as a symbol of evil.
Psalm 58:4

Sheep
Used as a source of food and clothing. The horn of the male (ram) was used as a trumpet. (See *Shophar*.) Also offered as sacrifices to God.
Joshua 6:4

Swine
Wild pigs that, according to the Old Testament Law, were unclean and should not be eaten. In the New Testament, God showed Peter that everything He had made was clean and could be eaten.
Leviticus 11:7; Acts 10:9-16

Apostle

(uh PAHS uhl) One who is sent on a mission, especially each of the 12 men whom Jesus called and sent out to tell people about Himself. **Luke 6:12-16**

THE APOSTLES

Andrew

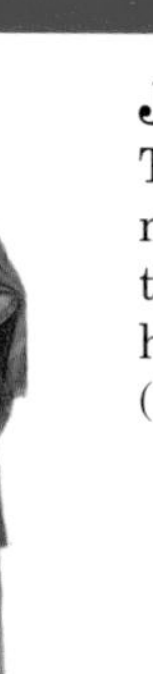

Andrew was a fisherman with his brother Peter on the Sea of Galilee. Jesus called Andrew to be a disciple while he was fishing (Matthew 4:18-20). Andrew brought Peter to Jesus (John 1:40-42) and told Jesus about the boy with the loaves and fishes (John 6:8).

Judas

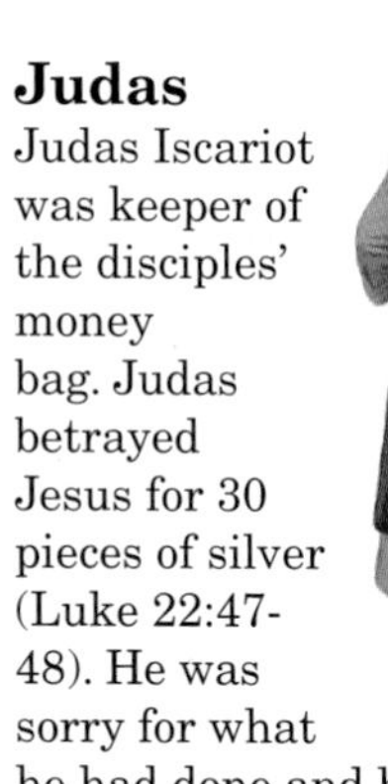

Judas Iscariot was keeper of the disciples' money bag. Judas betrayed Jesus for 30 pieces of silver (Luke 22:47-48). He was sorry for what he had done and hanged himself (Matthew 27:3-5).

Simon

The Bible tells nothing about this man except his name, Simon the Zealot (Matthew 10:4)

James

The Bible tells nothing about this man except his name. (Matthew 10:3)

Levi

Jesus called Matthew to be a disciple while he was a tax collector in Capernaum. Matthew invited Jesus to a dinner where his friends could meet Jesus (Matthew 9:9-13).

Simon, Peter or Cephas (rock)

Peter was a fisherman with his brother Andrew on the Sea of Galilee. Jesus called Peter to be a disciple while he was fishing (Matthew 4:18-20). Jesus helped Peter to walk on water (Matthew 14:28-33). Peter denied Jesus before His crucifixion (Luke 22:54-62) and was later forgiven by Jesus (John 21:15-19).

James

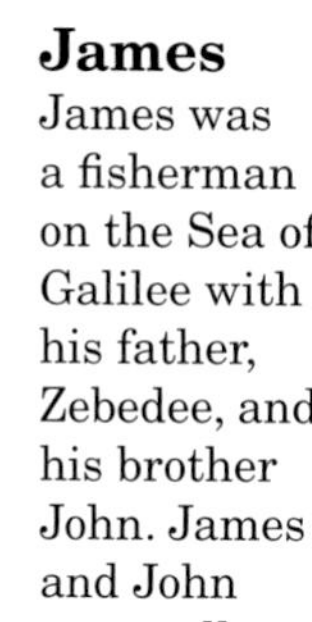

James was a fisherman on the Sea of Galilee with his father, Zebedee, and his brother John. James and John were call Boanereges, sons of thunder. Jesus called James to be a disciple while he was mending nets (Matthew 4:21-22). James was the first disciple to be killed because of his faith (Acts 12:1-2).

Nathaniel

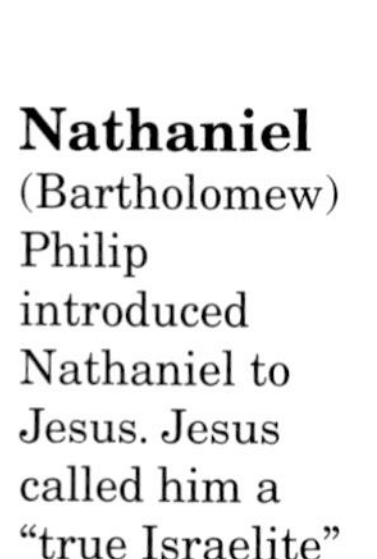

(Bartholomew) Philip introduced Nathaniel to Jesus. Jesus called him a "true Israelite" (John 1:45-51).

Thaddaeus

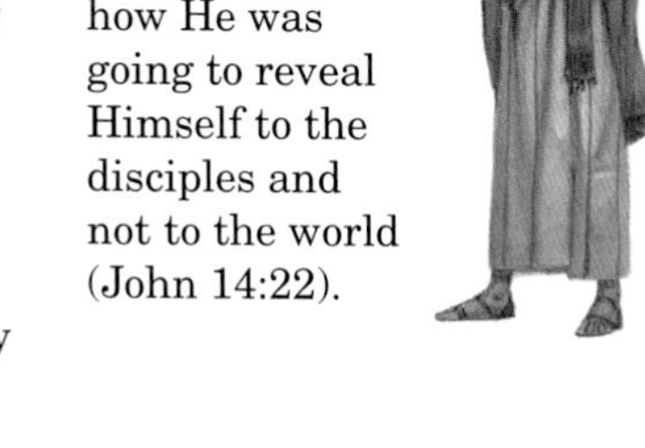

(Judas, son of James) Thaddaeus (asked Jesus how He was going to reveal Himself to the disciples and not to the world (John 14:22).

John

John was a fisherman on the Sea of Galilee with his father, Zebedee, and his brother James. Jesus called John to be a disciple while he was mending nets (Matthew 4:21-22). John helped Peter prepare the Passover meal (Luke 22:8). From the cross, Jesus told John to care for His mother (John 19:26-27).

Philip

Jesus called Philip to follow Him as a disciple (John 1:44). Philip found Nathaniel and told him about Jesus (John 1:45). Philip went with Andrew to bring some Greeks to Jesus (John 12:20-21).

Thomas

(Didymus) Thomas encouraged the disciples to go with Jesus and die with Him (John 11:16). Thomas wanted evidence that Jesus had risen from the dead (John 20:25). Jesus showed Thomas His hands and side to prove His resurrection (John 20:27-29).

Antioch (AN tih ahk) Name of two cities in the New Testament. 1. Antioch of Syria. This large city is about 300 miles north of Jerusalem. The believers in Jesus were first called Christians there. Barnabas brought Saul (Paul) to Antioch to be a teacher. The Holy Spirit told the church at Antioch to set aside Barnabas and Saul for work He called them to do. They became the first missionaries. 2. Antioch of Pisidia. Paul preached in a synagogue there on his first missionary journey (Acts 13:14) and was warmly received ((Acts 13:42-44). Some of the Jews became jealous because crowds of people were listening to what Paul said. He and Barnabas then took the good news to Gentiles. Finally, the Jews drove Paul and Barnabas from the city. These Jews followed Paul to Lystra and stirred up trouble there. Despite this, Paul returned to Antioch to strengthen the church. Paul used the experience to teach Timothy.
Acts 11:25-26; 13:1-3,14,42-44,46; 14:19,21; 2 Timothy 3:11

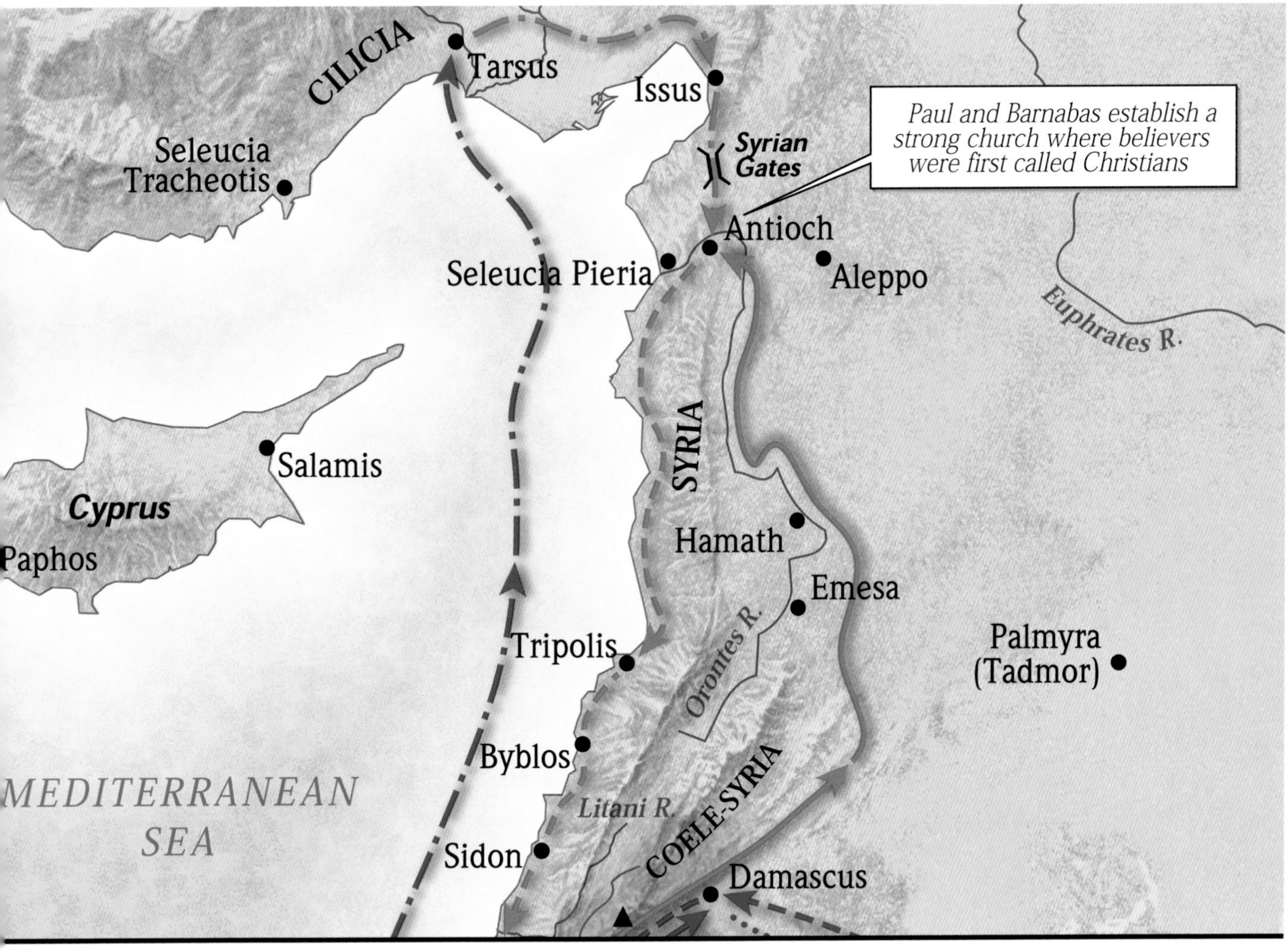

CILICIA
Tarsus
Issus
Syrian Gates
Paul and Barnabas establish a strong church where believers were first called Christians
Seleucia Tracheotis
Antioch
Seleucia Pieria
Aleppo
Euphrates R.
SYRIA
Salamis
Cyprus
Paphos
Hamath
Emesa
Tripolis
Orontes R.
Palmyra (Tadmor)
Byblos
MEDITERRANEAN SEA
Litani R.
COELE-SYRIA
Sidon
Damascus

Aquila and **Priscilla** (AK wih luh, uh KWIL uh; prih SIL uh) Married couple from Italy who were tentmakers. They became Paul's helpers in Corinth and later traveled with him to Ephesus. **Acts 18:1-3**

Archer
A person who uses a bow and arrow. **Genesis 21:20**

Arimathea (ar ih muh THEE uh), **Arimathaea** (KJV) Joseph, the disciple who claimed the body of Jesus following the crucifixion, and in whose own new tomb the body was placed, was from Arimathea; but the exact location of the city is not known.
Matthew 27:57-60

Ark

Large boat God told Noah to build. God was sad when He saw the great evil people were planning and doing on earth. Only Noah and his family pleased God, so God decided to destroy those who were doing evil. The ark was designed to save Noah's family and representatives of each kind of animal on earth. God gave Noah specific instructions about how the ark would be built: 450 feet long, 75 feet wide, and 45 feet high. The ark had one door and three floors filled with rooms. It was built of gofer wood, a kind of cypress, and covered with pitch. **Genesis 6:9-22; 1 Peter 3:20; 2 Peter 2:5; Hebrews 11:7.**

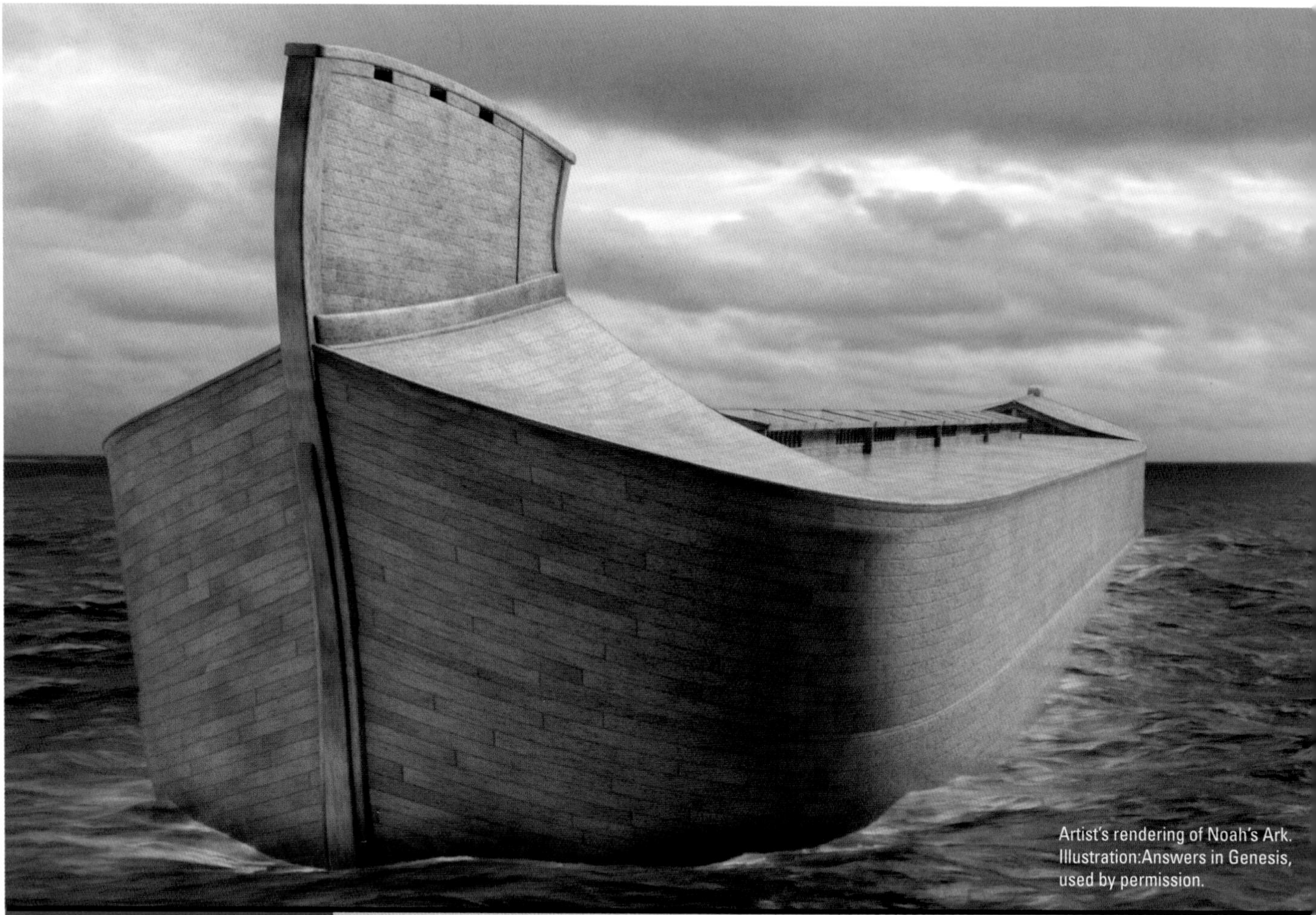

Artist's rendering of Noah's Ark. Illustration:Answers in Genesis, used by permission.

Ark of the Covenant

Wooden box covered in gold that contained the stone tablets on which the Ten Commandments were written, a jar of manna, and Aaron's rod that budded. **Hebrews 9:3-4**

Armor of God

Armor is the protective covering for the body used by soldiers in battle. Paul referred to the "armor of God" as a way for Christians to battle evil: a belt of truth, breastplate (vest) of righteousness, sandals of the gospel, shield of faith, helmet of salvation, and the sword of the Spirit, God's Word. **Ephesians 6:13-18**

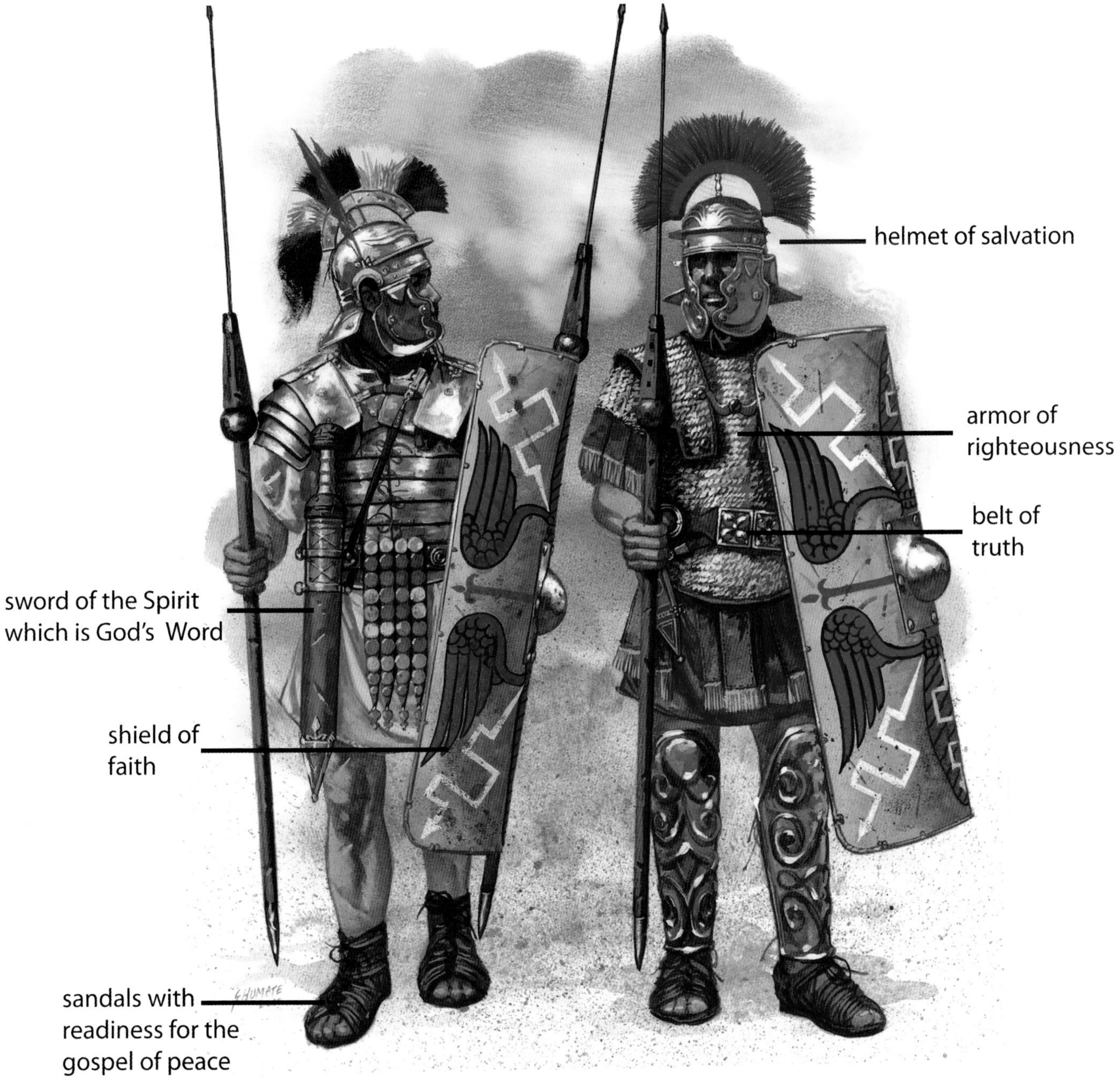

helmet of salvation

armor of righteousness

belt of truth

sword of the Spirit which is God's Word

shield of faith

sandals with readiness for the gospel of peace

Ephesians 6:14-17 (HCSB)

Ascension

(uh SEN shuhn) Act of moving upward. Jesus ascended to heaven at the end of His ministry on earth. **Acts 1:9-10**

Asia/Asia Minor

(AY zhuh; AY zhuh MIGH nuhr) Roman province whose capital was Ephesus. The cities of Asia Minor were located on the Anatolian peninsula (modern-day Turkey). They included Alexandria, Troas, Assos, Ephesus, Miletus, Patara, Smyrna, Pergamum, Sardis, Thyatira, Philadelphia, Laodicea, Colossae, Attalia, Antioch, Iconium, Lystra, Derbe, and Tarsus. **Acts 16:6**

Assyria

(uh SIHR ih uh) Nation in northern Mesopotamia in Old Testament times that became a large empire during the period of the Israelite kings. Assyrian expansion into the region of Palestine had enormous impact on the Hebrew kingdoms of Israel and Judah. **2 Kings 17:1-6**

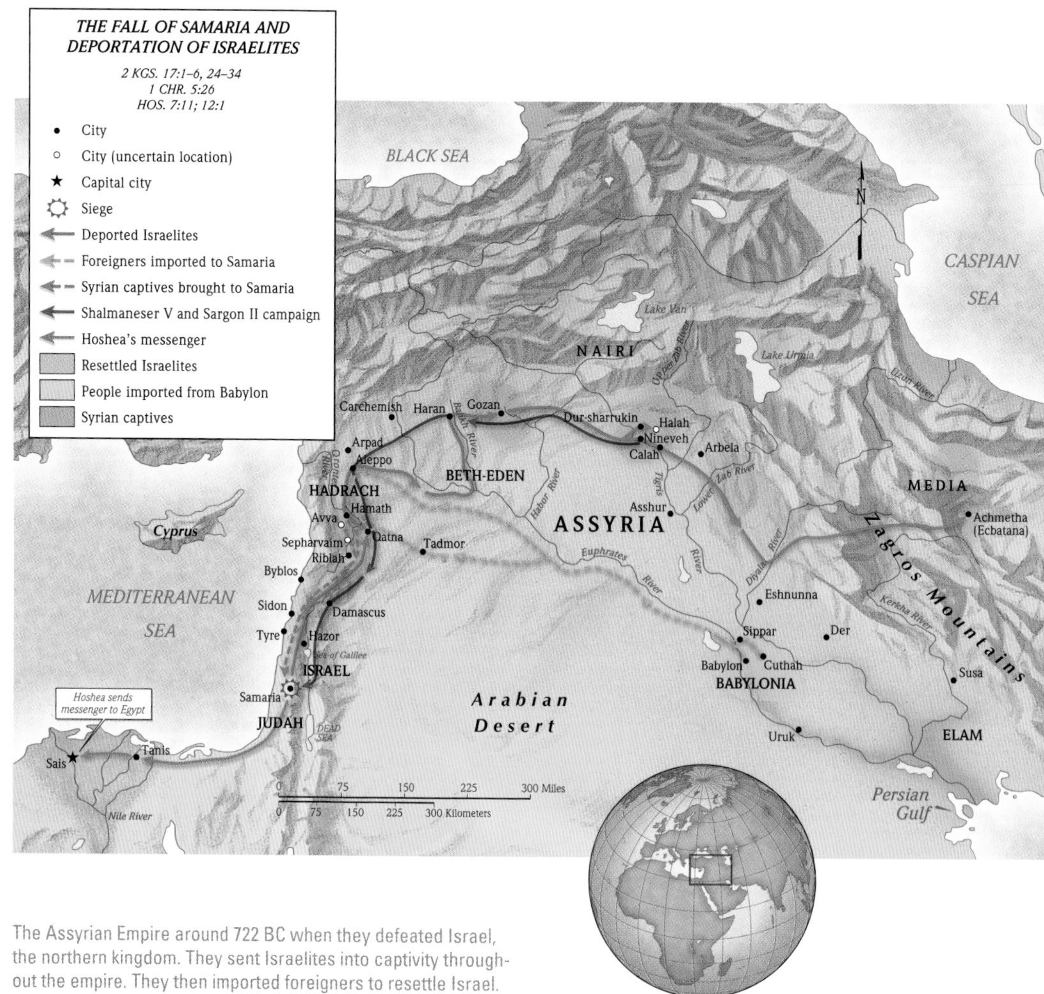

The Assyrian Empire around 722 BC when they defeated Israel, the northern kingdom. They sent Israelites into captivity throughout the empire. They then imported foreigners to resettle Israel.

Astrologer

Person who told what would happen in the future, by studying the stars. The Bible warns against this practice. **Isaiah 47:13-16**

Athens (ATH ihnz)

Capital of an ancient district of east central Greece. Paul preached to the Greek philosophers there. **Acts 17:15-34**

Atonement

Teaching from the Bible that Jesus' death on the cross has provided a way for people to have a personal relationship with God. Jesus' death and resurrection makes possible a relationship with God when people admit and repent of their sin, believe that Jesus died and that God raised Him from the dead, and confess that Jesus is their personal Savior and Lord. Without Jesus' sacrifice on the cross, people cannot have a relationship with God. A related concept is reconciliation. **Romans 5:8,11; 1 John 1:9**

Augustus

(aw GUHS tuhs) Title the Roman Senate gave to Emperor Octavian in 27 B.C. He ruled when Jesus was born. He was the adopted son of Julius Caesar. **Luke 2:1**

Augustus Caesar (44 BC - AD 14)

Awe

Refers to an emotion combining honor, fear, and respect before God. **Psalm 33:8**

Awl

Tool that makes holes. Made of flint, bone, stone, or metal. **Exodus 21:6**

Bb

Babel (BAY buhl)

Name given to the city that the disobedient descendants of Noah built so they would not be scattered over all the earth. Referred to as Babylon in some Bible translations.
Genesis 11:1-9

A ziggurat dating to the Babylonian period (605-550 B.C.)

Babylon (BAB ih lahn)

City in southern Mesopotamia that became a large empire in Old Testament times. The city of Babylon was founded on the river Euphrates, about 50 miles south of modern Baghdad in Iraq. The English names *Babylon* and *Babel* are translated from the same Hebrew word (babel). Abram, the father of the Hebrew nation, was born in this region. The Babylonians became the most powerful empire in the Middle East by 605 B.C. Under the leadership Nebuchanezzar II, the Babylonians began a series of invasions of Judah (605-586 B.C.), taking Judeans into exile with each invasion. These exiles included Daniel and Ezekiel. With the final invasion in 586 B.C., the Babylonians destroyed Jerusalem and its temple. The captivity of Judah lasted 70 years as Jeremiah had prophesied.

Apart from his military conquests, Nebuchadnezzar is responsibile for a massive rebuilding program in Babylon itself. As a part of this program, he built the world-famous Hanging Gardens, one of the seven wonders of the ancient world. In 539 B.C., the Persian Cyrus II (the Great) entered Babylon without a fight. The Persian empire replaced the Babylonian empire as the most powerful empire in the Middle East. Cyrus allowed Judeans to return to and rebuild Jerusalem. Babylon remained an important economic center and provincial capital during the period of Persian rule. For the early Christians, the city of Babylon was a symbol of human beings in rebellion against God. Christians used the name Babylon to refer to Rome.
Genesis 10:10; 11:9,27-32; 2 Kings 24:1-20; 2 Kings 25:1-30; 2 Chronicles 36:20-23; Ezra 1:1-11; Jeremiah 25:9-12; 29:10; 46:2-12; Daniel 9:1-3; 1 Peter 5:13; Revelation 14:8; 16:19; 17:5; 18:2

Lion on the glazed brick panel from Procession Way, the most important street in Babylon. Procession Way ran from the Temple of Marduk to the Ishtar Gate and the Akitu Temple.

Ancient Babylon

1. Summer Palace
2. Hanging Gardens
3. North Citadel
4. Reservoir
5. Sin Gate
6. Ishtar Gate
7. South Citadel (royal palace)
8. Emah Temple
9. Ishtar Temple
10. Nabu-sha-hare Temple
11. Marduk Gate
12. Zababa Gate
13. Elil Gate
14. Urash Gate
15. Ninurta Temple
16. Gula Temple
17. Esagila (Marduk Temple)
18. Etemananki Ziggurat
19. Processional Way
20. Lugalgirra Gate
21. Adad Gate
22. Shamash Gate
23. Shamash Temple
24. Adad Temple

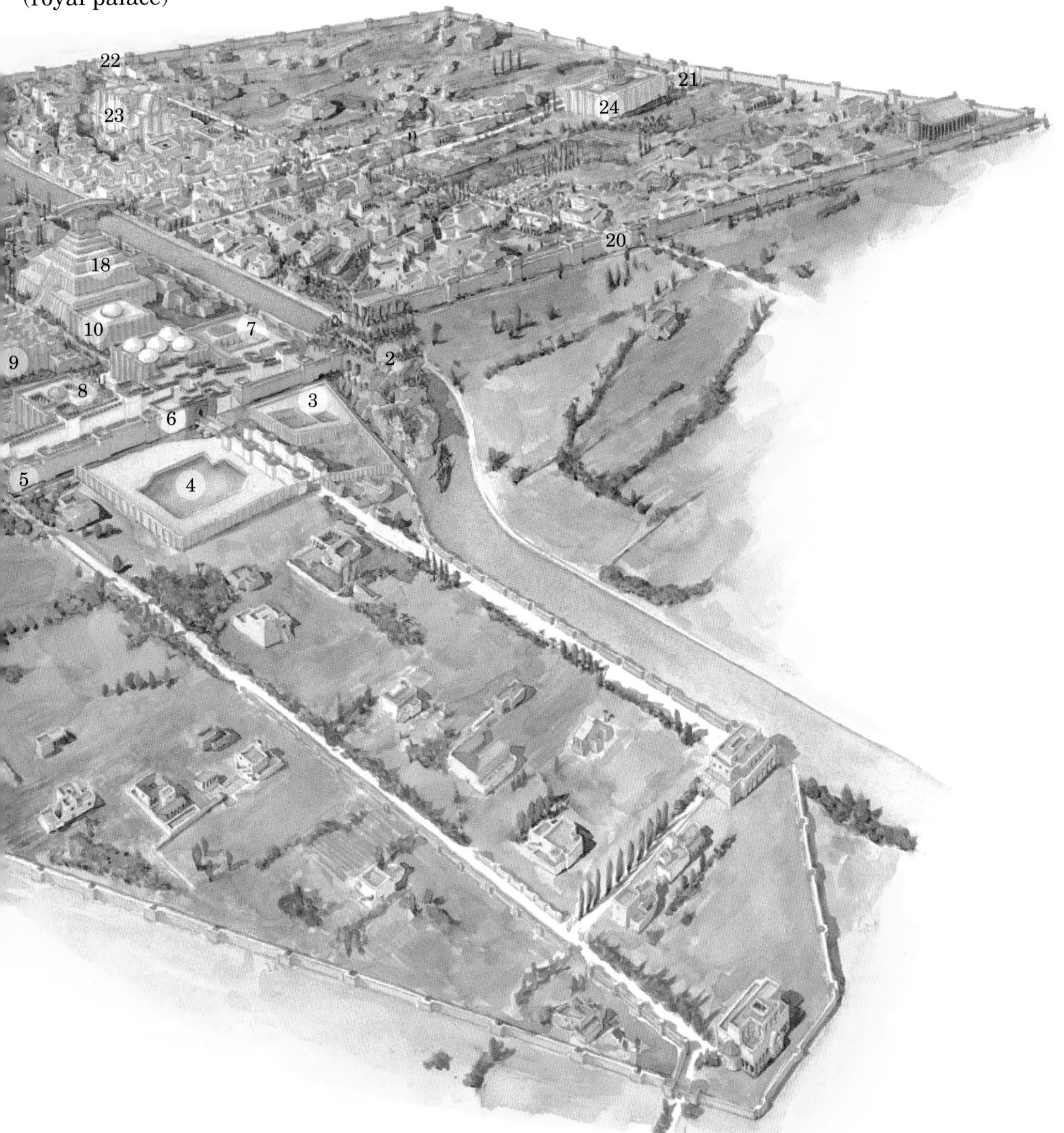

Balm Good smelling product from trees and plants used for perfume and medicine. Ancient writers refer to balm by a variety of names. **Genesis 37:25**

Banquet Large meal, sometimes called a "feast." In the Old Testament, banquets celebrated victories and other happy times. In the New Testament, Jesus told the story of a father who gave a feast when his son returned home. **Esther 1:1-4; Luke 15:22-24**

Baptism Act of baptizing. A command Jesus gave for Christians to follow. One of two church ordinances. (See *Ordinance*.) **Matthew 28:19**

Barak (BAY rak) The soldier whom Deborah asked to lead the Israelites in battle against Canaanite forces. **Judges 4:6**

Barley One of two basic grains of Palestine in Bible times. The other was wheat. Barley was the food of the poor as well as feed for horses, mules, and donkeys. **Ruth 2:15-18**

Barnabas (BAHR nuh buhs) Name means "son of encouragement." A native of Cyprus, also called Joseph. Introduced Saul (Paul) of Tarsus to the Jerusalem church. Went with Paul on the first missionary journey. **Acts 4:36-37**

Barren Describes a woman who cannot have children. **Genesis 11:30**

Baptize To lower someone in the water and bring him back up. The person who is baptized is following Jesus' example by showing others that he has confessed Jesus as Savior and Lord. **Matthew 3:13-17**

Jesus came to John to be baptized.

Bartholomew (bahr THAHL uh myoo) Apostle of Jesus. Also known as Nathanael, whom Philip introduced to Jesus. **Matthew 10:2-4; Mark 3:16-19; Luke 6:14-16; John 1:44-51**

Basket Usually refers to a food container. Also used by Moses' mother when she placed him in the reeds by the bank of the Nile River. The apostle Paul was lowered over the wall of Damascus in a basket in order to escape. **Exodus 2:3; Matthew 14:20; Acts 9:23-25**

Paul escapes from Damascus in a basket.

Bartimaeus Bartimeus (KJV) (bahr tih MEE uhs) Blind beggar who cried to Jesus for help. Jesus said that his faith had made him well. **Mark 10:46-52**

Basin, Bason (KJV) Another word for *bowl*. Jesus used a basin of water when He washed the disciples' feet. **John 13:5**

Bathsheba (bath-SHEE buh) Beautiful woman with whom King David committed adultery. Later David married her and they had a son named Solomon. **2 Samuel 11:3,27**

Beatitudes (bee A tih tyoods) Collection of blessings Jesus used in the Sermon on the Mount. They begin with the expression "blessed are," which can mean "happy are." The poor in spirit are those who know they need God. Those who mourn are sorry for their sin. The meek have a gentle kind of strength. Those who hunger and thirst for righteousness will receive what they long for. The merciful forgive and have compassion for others. The pure in heart have thoughts that are pleasing to God. Peacemakers invite others to be at peace with God and with one another. Finally, there is a blessing for those who are persecuted for following Jesus. It is normal for people who do not believe in Jesus to be against Christians. **Matthew 5:3-12; Luke 6:20-26**

Sea of Galilee from the Church of the Beatitudes built on the site where people think Jesus taught the Sermon on the Mount.

Beautiful Gate Where Peter and John healed a lame man in Jerusalem. **Acts 3:2,10**

Beautiful Gate believed by many to be the Nicanor Gate from a model of Jerusalem.

Believe To be persuaded that something is true. To trust the truth that God's Son, Jesus, died on the cross and rose from the grave to make forgiveness possible for all those who believe. **John 3:16; Acts 16:32**

Beloved Disciple (dih SIGH puhl) Another name for the Apostle John that describes Jesus' love and care for him. **John 21:7**

Benediction (BEN ih DIK shuhn) Prayer for God's blessing. **Numbers 6:24-25**

Bernice (buhr NEES) Sister of Herod Agrippa II, who heard Paul's story of his meeting Jesus on the road to Damascus. **Acts 25:13,23**

Benjamin (BEN juh min) 1. Jacob and Rachel's youngest son, the younger brother of Joseph. Benjamin's birth was difficult, and his mother named him Ben-oni, which means "son of my sorrow." She died giving him birth. His father Jacob, however, changed the child's name to Benjamin, which means "son of the right hand" or "son of the south." 2. One of the tribes of Israel. This tribe occupied the smallest territory of all the tribes. Yet, it played a significant role in Israelite history. Saul, Israel's first king, was a Benjamite. Furthermore, the city of Jerusalem, near the border between the territories of Benjamin and Judah, may have been in the territory of Benjamin originally. In the New Testament, the apostle Paul proudly proclaimed his heritage in the tribe of Benjamin.
Genesis 35:16-20; 42:1-4,33-37; 43:15-31; 44:1-34; 45:1-15; Joshua 18:21-28; Judges 1:21; 1 Samuel 9:1-2; Romans 11:1; Philippians 3:5

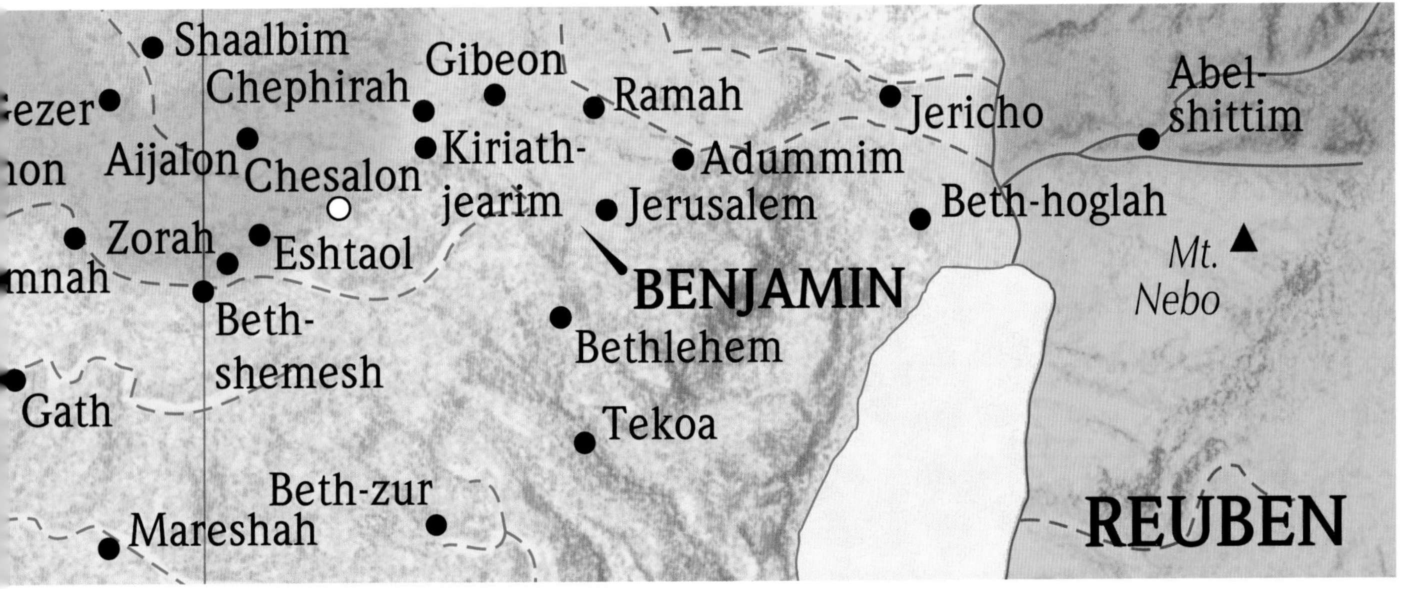

The territory alloted the tribe of Benjamin, the smallest of the twelve tribes

Beroea, Berea (KJV)

(bih REE uh) City in Macedonia to which Paul escaped after the Jews of Thessalonica rioted. The people of the city read the Scriptures for themselves to see if Paul spoke the truth.
Acts 17:10-15

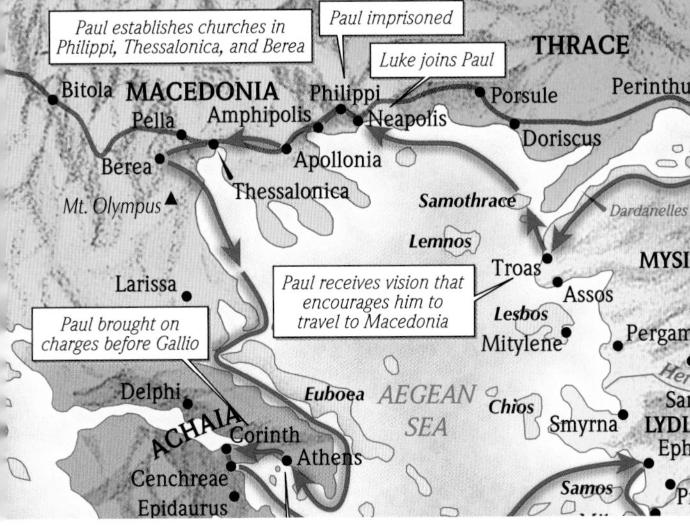

Paul preached in Beroea on his second missionary journey.

Bethany

Town where Mary, Martha, and Lazarus lived—about two miles from Jerusalem. Jesus visited Bethany often. He raised Lazarus from the dead, and Mary anointed Him there.
John 11:43-44; 12:1-3

Bethel

(BETH uhl) Means "house of God." Where Abram built an altar to God. Also, where Jacob dreamed of a ladder or stairway to heaven and built an altar.
Genesis 12:8; 28:12,18

At Bethel, God spoke to Jacob as he slept.

Bethlehem (BETH lih hem) Means "house of bread." Near Jerusalem, this town is where Ruth and Boaz lived, where David was anointed king, and where Jesus was born. **Ruth 1:22; 1 Samuel 16:1-13; Micah 5:2; Luke 2:4**

Shepherds' fields in Bethlehem

Bible The word *Bible* comes from a Greek word meaning "books." The Bible is God's Word to people to help them hear God, know God, and obey God (do what He says). The 39 books of the Old Testament and the 27 books of the New Testament make up the Bible.

Birds (See *Birds in the Bible* chart, p. 21)

Birthright Special privileges that belonged to the firstborn son in a family. He was given twice as much of his father's money and property as other sons. **Genesis 25:27-34**

Bitter Herbs Spices with a bitter taste that were eaten with the Passover meal. Bitter herbs were to help the Israelites remember their slavery in Egypt. **Exodus 12:8**

Blasphemy To speak harm; an attitude of disrespect against God. Some Jewish leaders falsely accused Jesus of blasphemy because He claimed to be the Son of God. **Matthew 26:65**

Bless/Blessing/ Blessed To honor God or a person with good words, to praise someone, to be happy. **Genesis 12:1-3; Psalm 68:19; Matthew 5:3-12**

Boaz (BOH az) A well-respected relative of Ruth's mother-in-law, Naomi. Boaz married Ruth, a young widow. **Ruth 2:1; 4:13**

Bond Rope or chains used to bind the hands and feet of prisoners or slaves. **Judges 15:14**

Book Refers to a scroll made of a long strip of parchment or papyrus and then rolled up. **1 Kings 21:8; Jeremiah 36:2**

Bow and Arrow Weapon used in combat in Bible times. The bow was made of one piece of wood and was from three to six feet long. Arrows were made of reeds with metal tips. Feathers from eagles or vultures guided the arrow to its target. **1 Samuel 18:4; 20:35-40**

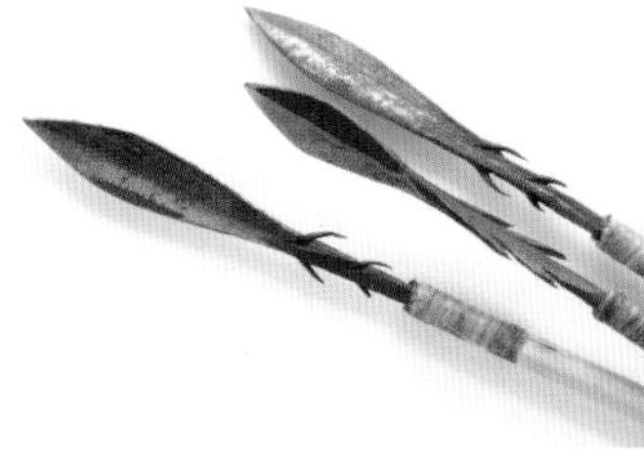

Hand-made primitive arrows

Bread The basic food of people in Bible times. Wheat or barley flour was mixed with water, salt, and yeast or olive oil. Bread was also used as an offering to God. **Leviticus 2:4; 1 Kings 17:1-16**

Breastplate 1. Part of the high priest's clothing. A 9-by-9 square piece of linen nine inches long and nine inches wide on which twelve stones were attached. Each stone represented one of the twelve tribes of Israel. 2. Defensive armor that covered the chest of a soldier. Paul used the word to describe the work of righteousness in a Christian's life. (See *Armor of God*.) **Exodus 28:15-30; Ephesians 6:13-18**

Brick Building material of clay, molded while moist into rectangular shaped blocks and hardened by the sun or fire, used to make walls or roads. The Hebrew slaves in Egypt made storehouses for Pharaoh with bricks. **Exodus 1:13-14;5:7-9**

Bronze, Brass (KJV) Combination of copper and tin used to make armor, shackles, cymbals, gates, idols, and other objects. **1 Samuel 17:5-6; 1 Chronicles 15:19**

Broom Tree, Juniper Tree (KJV) Bush that grows large enough to provide shade. Elijah sat down under a broom tree after a day's journey into the wilderness. **1 Kings 19:4-5**

BIRDS IN THE BIBLE

Dove
Bird similar to a pigeon. A symbol of peace. The second bird Noah sent from the ark to find dry land after the flood. A turtledove is a small dove that Mary and Joseph used as a sacrifice when Baby Jesus was dedicated to God.
Genesis 8:8-12; Luke 2:22-24

Pigeon
Describes various kinds of birds used in sacrifices, Mary and Joseph offered a pigeon and a turtledove as a sacrifice. Pigeons and turtledoves were the least expensive animal sacrifices.
Levitcus 5:7,11; Luke 2:24

Rooster, Cock (KJV)
Bird that struts and crows. Jesus said that Peter would deny knowing Him three times before the rooster (cock) crowed.
Mark 14:30,72

Eagle
Large, fast-moving bird. The Bible compares God's care and protection to this strong, majestic bird.
Deuteronomy 32:11

Quail
Bird God provided as food for the Israelites when they were in the wilderness. **Exodus 16:13**

Sparrow
Sometimes eaten by poor people. Jesus said that God cares for this small bird, but He cares more for His people. **Luke 12:6-7**

Ostrich
Very large, fast-moving bird that does not fly. The female lays eggs in the sand.
Job 39:13

Raven
Black bird, like a crow, that was the first bird Noah sent from the ark after the flood. God used ravens to take food to Elijah.
Genesis 8:7; 1 Kings 17:4-6

Vulture
Considered unclean and not to be eaten by God's people, this bird eats dead animals.
Leviticus 11:13

Brother

1. Male family member.
2. Fellow countryman.
3. Jesus said people who hear and do the word of God are His brothers.

Genesis 4:2; Luke 8:21

Burning Bush

Moses was caring for his father-in-law's sheep when he saw a bush on fire that did not burn up. God spoke to Moses from the bush and called him to lead the people of Israel out of slavery in Egypt.
Exodus 3:1-4

God appeared to Moses at the Burning Bush.

Burial

In Bible times, the Jews buried their dead as soon as possible, usually within 24 hours of death. Bodies were buried in caves, tombs cut from rock, or in the ground. Jesus was buried in a tomb before sundown on the day He died. **Matthew 27:57-61**

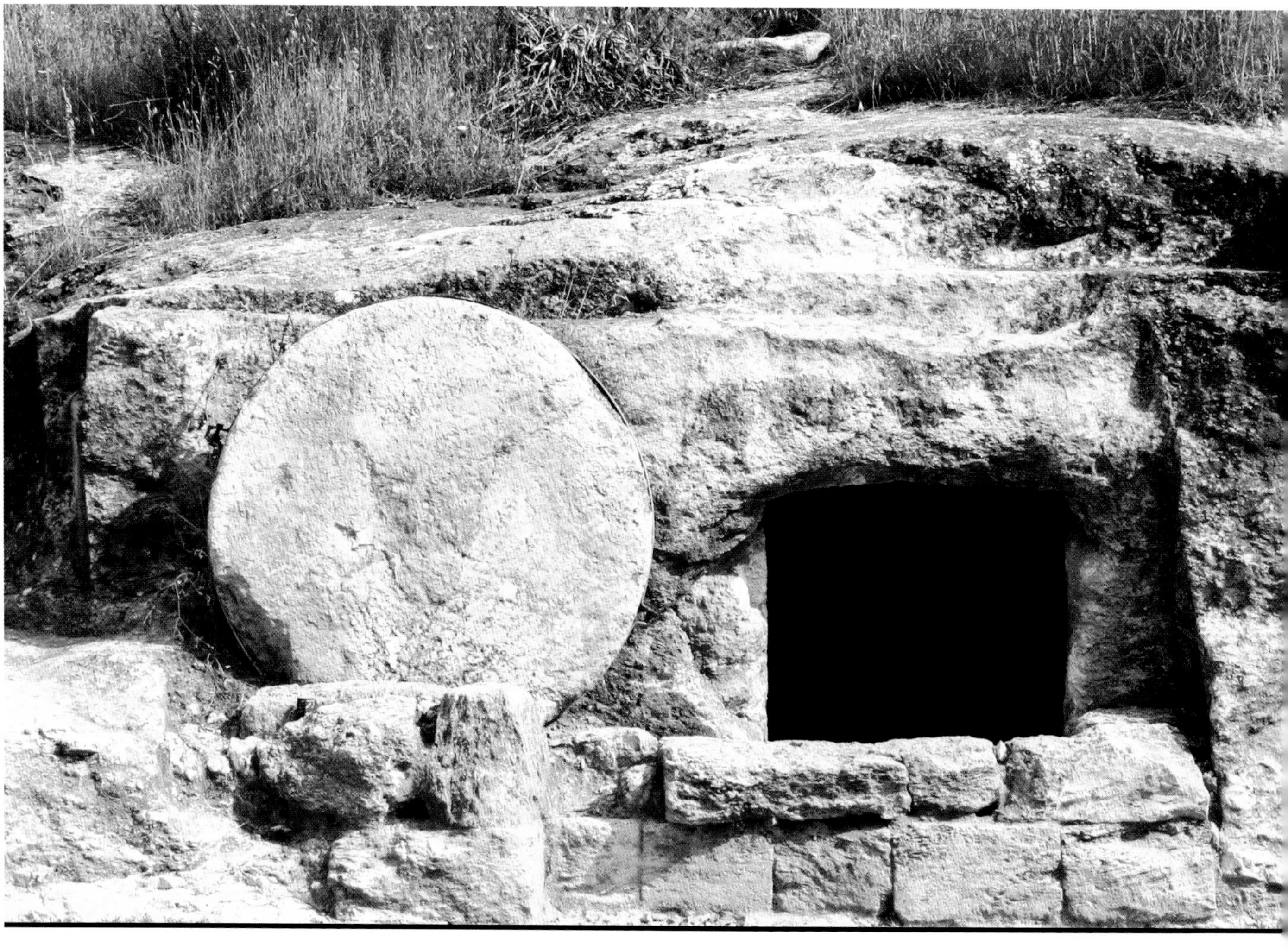

Cc

Caesar (SEE zuhr) Family name of Julius Caesar, a Roman general and politician. Later used as a title of the Roman emperors who followed him beginning with his great-nephew, Augustus. **Luke 2:1**

Statue of Gaius Julius Caesar (13 July 100 BC – 15 March 44 B.C.)

Cain (KAYN) Adam and Eve's first son. Cain was a farmer, and his brother Abel was a shepherd. As an adult, Cain became angry when God accepted Abel's offering but not his own. Cain then killed Abel. **Genesis 4:1-8**

Caldron Cooking pot used in homes and in the temple. **1 Samuel 2:12-14**

Caleb (KAY luhb) One of the 12 spies that Moses sent to scout out the territory of Canaan. He and Joshua were the only spies who brought back a positive report. Because of his obedience, God allowed Caleb to survive wandering in the wilderness for 40 years and gave him the region of Hebron as his portion in the promised land. At the age of 85, Caleb conquered Hebron. **Numbers 13:6, 30; Joshua 14:6-15**

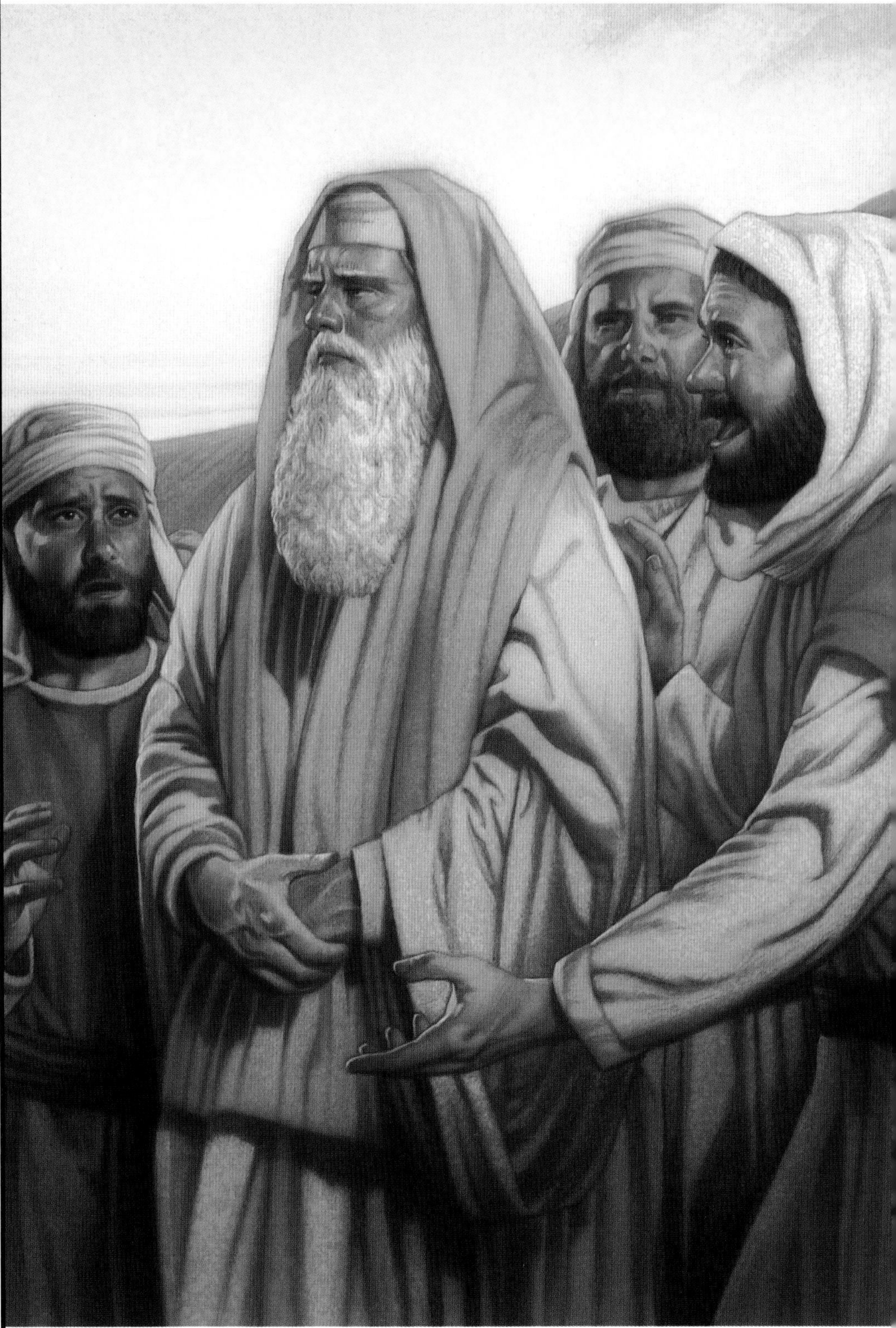

Moses (center) with Joshua (left) and Caleb (right)

Calvary (KAL vuh rih) One English name for the place where Jesus was crucified. Calvary appears only in some English translations of Luke's Gospel and comes from a Latin word that means "the skull." Matthew, Mark, and John refer to the place of Jesus' death as Golgotha, meaning "skull" or "head." Some believe the place looked like a human skull. Others think that, since this was a place of executions, skulls may have been seen there.

The Gospels indicate that Calvary was near Jerusalem, just outside the city walls, and was near a garden. Today, two different locations in Jerusalem claim to be this ancient site: (1) the Church of the Holy Sepulchre, which is within the walls of the modern city of Jerusalem, and (2) the Garden Tomb. In the 19th century, the British general Charles Gordon proposed the site of the Garden Tomb, which conforms closely to the biblical details.

Matthew 27:33; Mark 15:22; Luke 23:33; John 19:17

Gordon's Calvary is one of two sites considered to be the possible location of Jesus' crucifixion.

Camp/encampment Temporary settlement for nomadic and military people. Before the settling in the promised land, Israel was a group of tribes on the move. Hence the frequent reference to "the camp" or "the camp of Israel." The tabernacle was set at the center of the camp of Israel. The Levites were responsible for taking care of the tabernacle. Their camp was next to the tabernacle courtyard. The other twelve tribes camped in four groups of three around the Levites' camp. **Exodus 14:1-2,9; 16:13; Numbers 2:1-34**

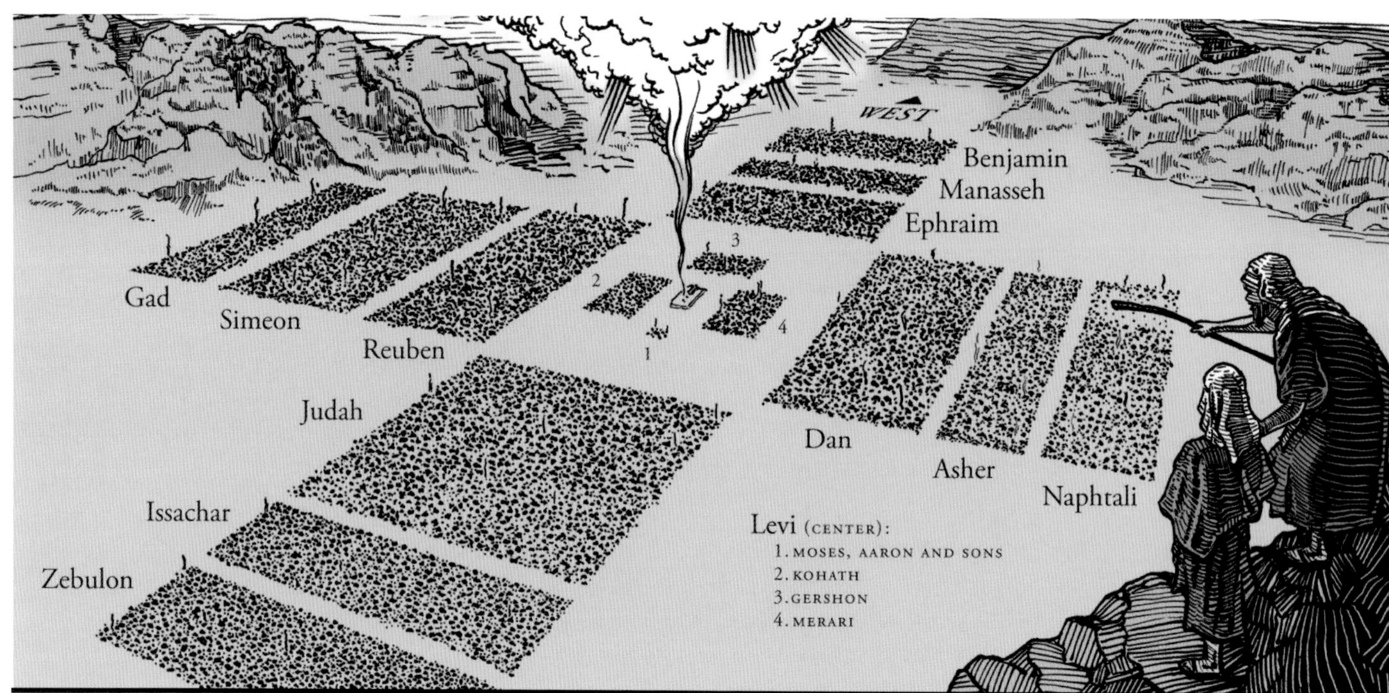

Cana (KAY nuh) The town in Galilee where Jesus changed water into wine at a wedding. Cana was also the home of Nathanael, one of Jesus' apostles. **John 2:1; 21:2**

Khirbet Cana in the Asochis Valley. Cana was where Jesus performed His first miracle (John 2:1-11).

Canaan (KAY nuhn) Large area of land that God promised to Abram and his descendants. Canaan lay between the Mediterranean Sea and the Jordan River reaching from the brook of Egypt to the area around Ugarit in Syria or to the Euphrates River. The word Canaan referred to different geographical areas at different times. Whatever the land was called, it was extremely important as the land bridge between Mesopotamia and Egypt and between the Mediterranean and the Red Sea.
Genesis 12:1- 7; 15:18; Exodus 23:20-23; Numbers 13:17-33; Deuteronomy 1:7-8; 1 Kings 4:21

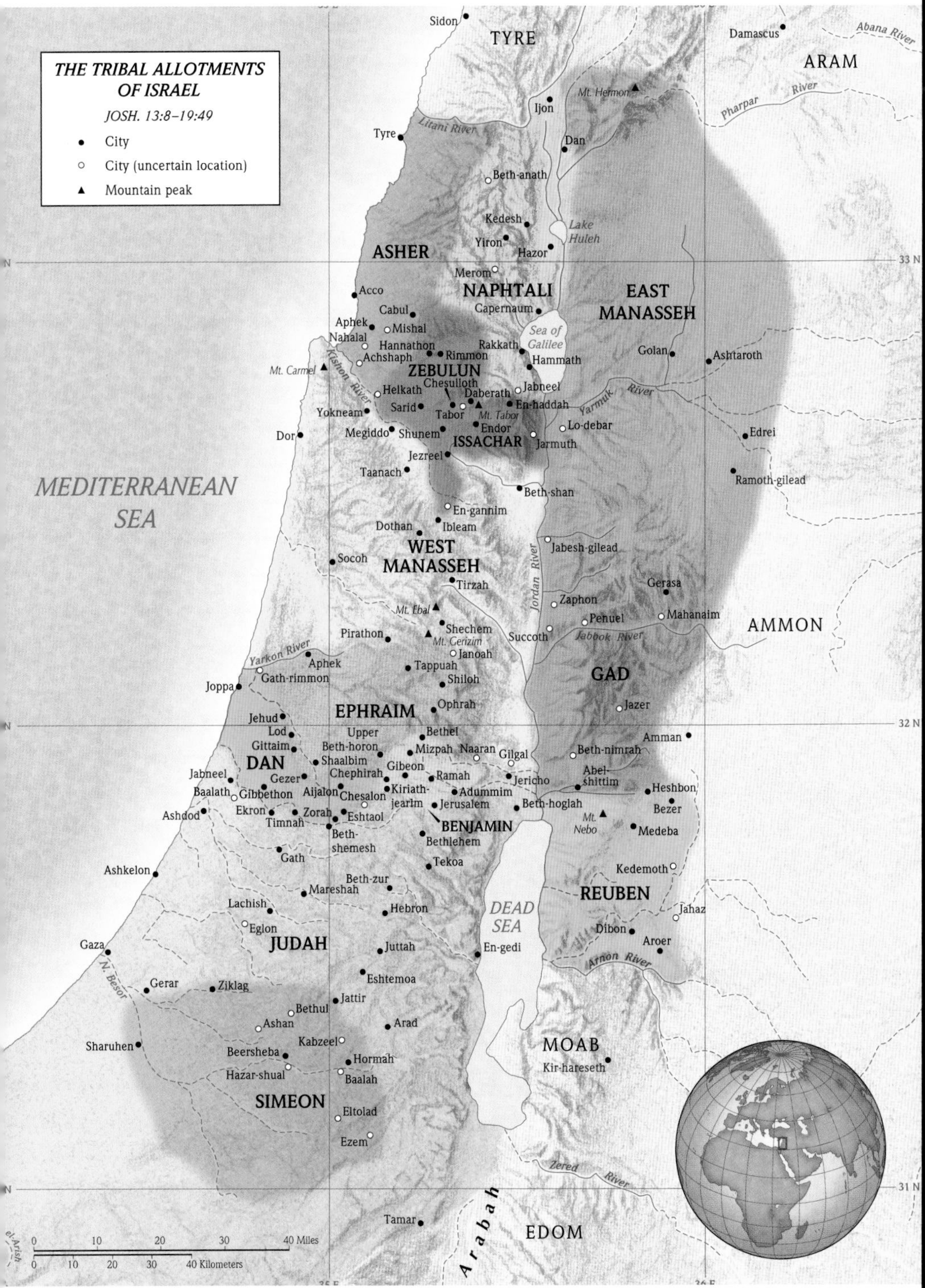

THE TRIBAL ALLOTMENTS OF ISRAEL
JOSH. 13:8–19:49
- City
- City (uncertain location)
- Mountain peak

Canaan is the territory between the Mediterranean Sea and the Jordan River. Ten of Israel's twelve tribes were given this land. The tribes of Reuben, Gad, and part of Manasseh lay outside of Canaan in the territory east of the Jordan River.

Capernaum (kuh PUHR nay uhm) Town on the northwest shore of the Sea of Galilee that Jesus considered home during His adult ministry. Capernaum is mentioned only in the Gospels. Peter, Andrew, James, and John lived there and worked as fishermen before Jesus called them to follow Him. Capernaum was located on a major trade route that connected Damascus with the Mediterranean Sea, Jerusalem, and Egypt. Matthew's (Levi's) work as a tax collector was located on this major route that passed near Capernaum. Jesus called Matthew to leave his work as a tax collector to be one of His twelve apostles.
Matthew 4:13; 8:5; John 6:17,24,59

Excavated ruins of Capernaum synagogue

Captain Usually refers to an officer or leader.
Genesis 40:1-4

Caravan Group of travelers with pack animals on a journey through desert or hostile regions.
Genesis 37:25

Centurion
(sen TYOOR ee uhn) Officer in the Roman army in command of approximately 100 soldiers.
Mark 15:39; Acts 10:1

Roman centurion

Carpenter Person who made things out of wood. Jesus was a carpenter, and Joseph, His earthly father, was a carpenter.
Matthew 13:55; Mark 6:3

Cave In Bible times, caves were used as places of burial or places to hide.
1 Samuel 22:1; John 11:38

Census Counting the people of a country for the purpose of taxing them or for finding soldiers for war.
2 Kings 12:4

Christians
(KRISS chuhns) Name given to people who have confessed Jesus as their Savior and Lord. First used in Antioch **Acts 11:26**

Cephas (SEE fuhs) Aramic word for "rock." The name given to Simon Peter by Jesus. **John 1:42**

Charity, Alms (KJV) Giving money, food, or clothing to the poor. **Acts 9:36; 10:2**

Champion A man (like Goliath) who fights a single opponent in the space of land between two armies. **1 Samuel 17:4,23**

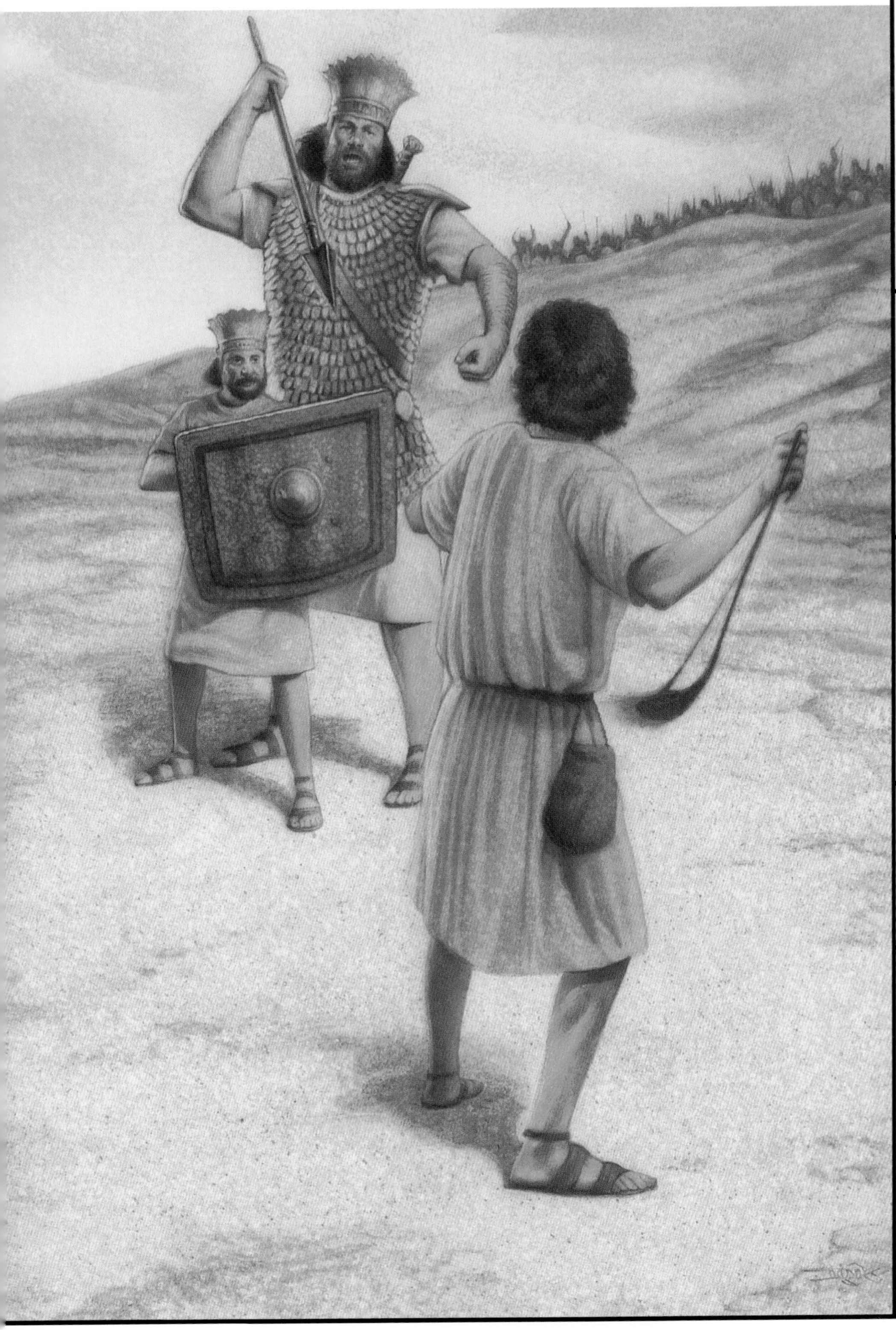

Cherub/ Cherubim (CHEHR uhb/CHEHR uh bim) Winged angels who function as guardians and who prevented Adam and Eve from returning to the Garden of Eden. Figures of cherubim were on the mercy seat of the ark of the covenant. In Solomon's temple, a pair of colossal cherubim covered the mercy seat with their wings in the holy of holies. **Genesis 3:24; Exodus 25:18; 1 Kings 6:27**

Chief priests Jewish temple officers that included the high priest, the captain of the temple, temple overseers, and treasurers. **Mark 15:11**

Children of God People who have confessed Jesus as their Savior and Lord and have a relationship with God. **Philippians 2:15**

Christ (KRIGHST) The Anointed One or Messiah, Jesus Christ, the Son of God. **Matthew 1:18**

Aa Bb Cc Dd Ee Ff Gg Hh Ii Jj Kk Ll Mm Nn Oo Pp Qq Rr Ss Tt Uu Vv Ww Xx Yy Zz

Christmas Major Christian festival. The name did not come into use until the Middle Ages. In the early part of the fourth century, Christians in Rome began to celebrate the birth of Christ. The practice spread widely and rapidly, so that most parts of the Christian world observed the new festival by the end of the century. The word is not found in the Bible.

Chronicles, First and Second

(KRAHN ih kuhls) The eighth and ninth books in the division of History of the Old Testament. Both books tell about the reigns of King David, King Solomon, and other kings of Israel and Judah.
1 Chronicles 1:1
2 Chronicles 1:1

Church Believers of all times and places. In the vision in Revelation John saw a vast multitude from every "tribe, people, and language." A local church is a group of baptized believers at a particular place, like the church at Jerusalem, Antioch, Ephesus, or Rome.

The church is God's plan for people who confess Jesus Christ as Lord and Savior. Jesus is head of the church, and the church depends on Him. Members of the church are related to each other in the same way that parts of a human body are related to each other. Each part is important for the church to be what God wants it to be. Church members work together because of their relationship with Jesus.

A local church is more than a building. A church is a group of Christians who meet together to pray, to tell other people about Jesus, to worship God, to learn from the Bible, to meet needs of others, and to encourage one another. Being a church member involves responsibilities and privileges. Church members have responsibilities to participate in worship services, to pray for their church, and to give money for the work of their church. Each believer is given one or more spiritual gifts. Believers use spiritual gifts to do God's work.

The church has two ordinances: baptism and the Lord's Supper. When people are baptized, they are telling the world that they have turned from sin and are trusting Jesus Christ as Savior and Lord. Taking the Lord's Supper reminds believers of Jesus' death for them and that He is coming again. God uses the church to accomplish His purposes in the world. Churches today are part of the movement begun by Jesus and His followers.
Matthew 16:18; Acts 2:37-47; 8:1; 13:1; Romans 6:1-14;
1 Corinthians 1:2; 11:17-26; 12:12-31; Ephesians 1:22; Revelation 7:9-10

Cistern, Dungeon (KJV)

Term that means "hole," "pit," or more often "well." The prophet Jeremiah was thrown into a cistern because he told the people that the army of Babylon would overpower Judah. **Jeremiah 38:1-13**

Citizen

Person with legal rights defined by the country where the person lives. Paul was a Roman citizen at birth because his father was a Roman citizen living in Cilicia, a Roman province in Asia Minor. **Acts 16:35-40**

City of David

In the Old Testament, the phrase refers to Jerusalem. The name was given to the city after David captured it. **2 Samuel 5:6-10, Luke 2:4-11**

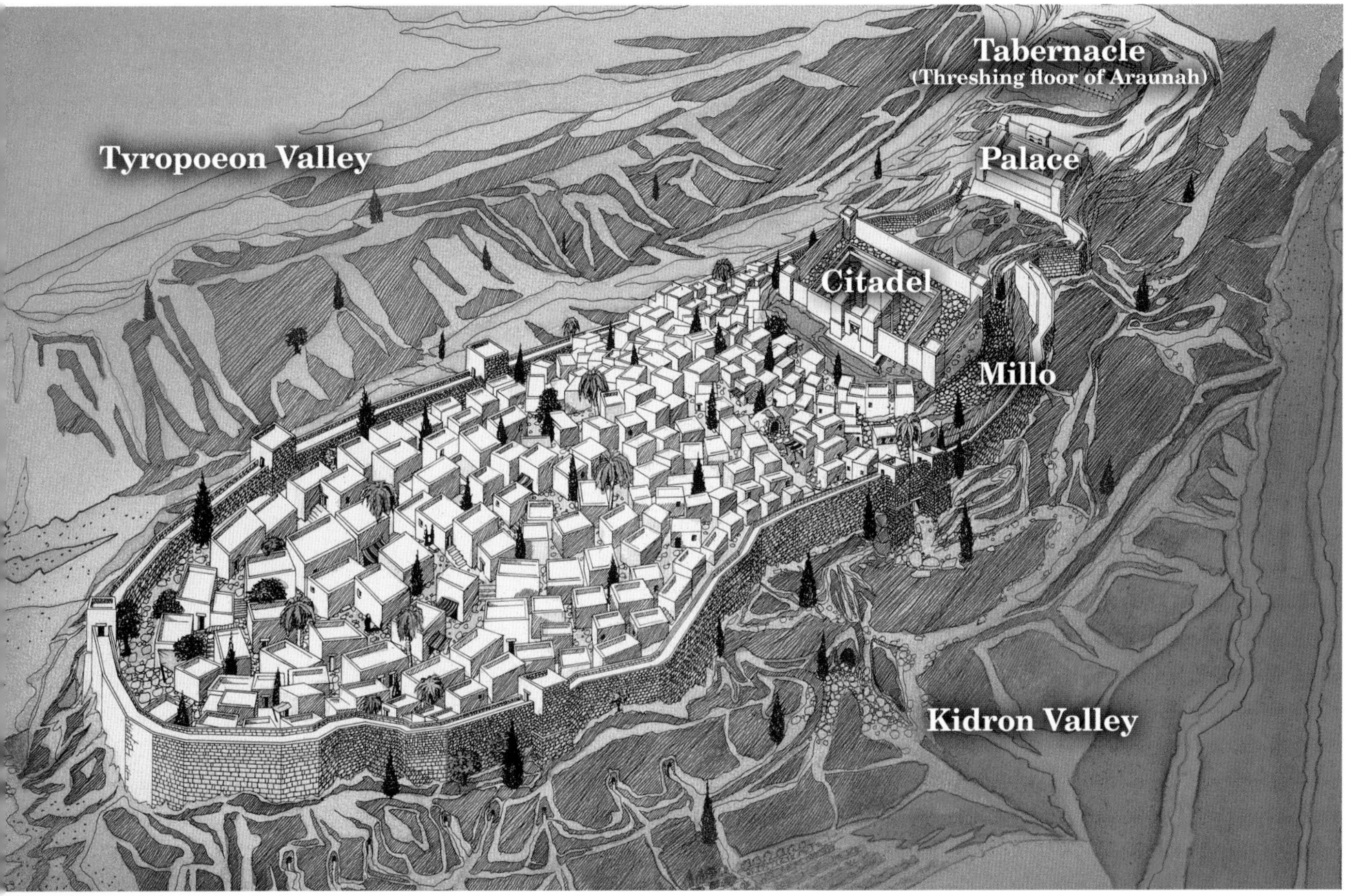

Tabernacle
(Threshing floor of Araunah)
Tyropoeon Valley
Palace
Citadel
Millo
Kidron Valley

The City of David is the most ancient part of Jerusalem on its southeast corner. The entire City of David was no more than ten acres in addition to Jerusalem, Bethlehem is called "the city of David" (**Luke 2:11**).

Clean/unclean

In the Old Testament, animals were referred to as either clean or unclean. Unclean animals had a solid hoof and could not be eaten. Sheep and cows were considered clean animals and could be eaten. Pigs were considered unclean and could not be eaten. **Genesis 7:1-3; Deuteronomy 14:3-20**

Cleopas

(KLEE oh puhs) Follower of Jesus, who was traveling with a friend toward the village of Emmaus on the day of Jesus' resurrection. A person whom they did not recognize joined them. Later, they discovered that the stranger was Jesus Himself. **Luke 24:13-35**

Cloak Outer garment worn for covering at night. Sometimes referred to as a mantle or robe. The soldiers probably draped a cloak over Jesus after He was flogged. **John 19:1-3**

Cloth Earliest clothing in Bible times was made from the hides of wild animals. Later, cloth was made from wool. Cloth was dyed in different colors. Some colors were made from sea life, plants, and insects. **Genesis 3:21; 37:3**

Cloud In the Old Testament, God led the Israelites through the wilderness by His presence. By day the Israelites saw a pillar of cloud, while by night they saw a pillar of fire. In the New Testament, Jesus ascended into heaven in a cloud. **Exodus 13:21-22; Acts 1:9-10**

God led Moses and the Israelites through the wilderness by a pillar of cloud.

Colossae, Colosse (KJV) (koh LAHS sih) City located in the Roman province of Asia (present day Turkey). City where Philemon lived. **Colossians 1:2; 4:9**

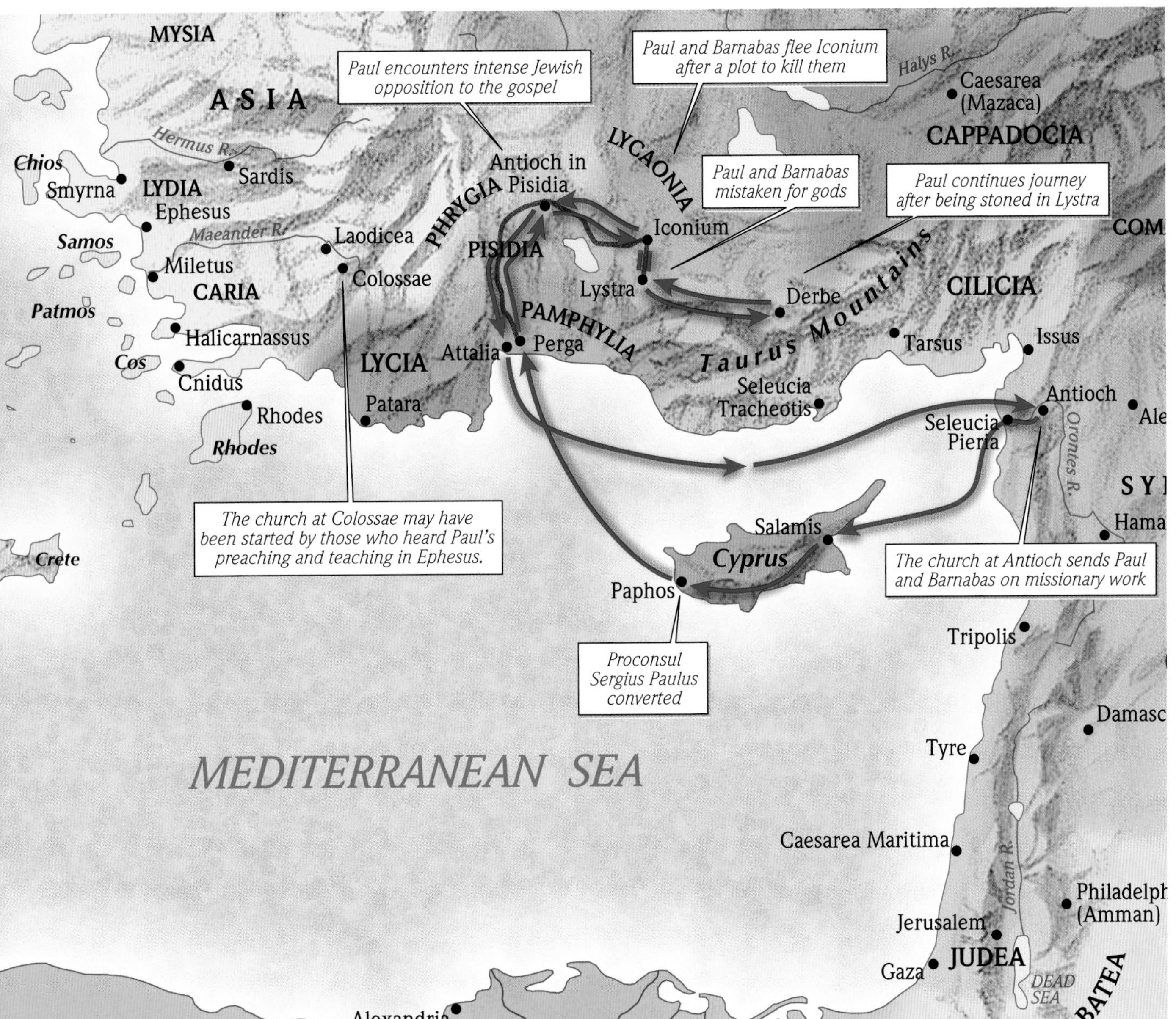

Shortly after Paul wrote Colossians (AD 61), the entire region was devasted by an earthquake.

Colossians

(kuh LAHSH uhns) Seventh book of Paul's Letters in the New Testament. This book was written while Paul was in prison. Paul wrote the church to correct false teachings that were troubling them. **Colossians 2:6-8**

Colt Young donkey, horse, camel, or other animal that can be ridden. In His triumphal entry into Jerusalem, Jesus rode on the colt of a donkey. **Zechariah 9:9; Matthew 21:1-8**

Command
Order or instruction from someone in authority. Jesus gave this command to His followers: "This is My command: love one another as I have loved you." **John 15:12**

Commander
Military person of authority with soldiers who serve under him. A commander came with his soldiers to arrest Jesus in the garden. **John 18:12-14**

Concubine
In the Old Testament, some men were married to more than one wife at a time. A concubine was a wife of lower status than a primary wife. Abram took Hagar, his wife Sarai's slave, as a concubine and she had a child named Ishmael. Later Abraham had other concubines. **Genesis 16:1-3; 25:6**

Confess To tell something that is true. Each person is invited to confess faith in Jesus as his Savior and Lord. **Romans 10:9-10**

Congregation
God's people assembled in one place. When Solomon was king, the people gathered to dedicate the temple to God. **1 Kings 8:5**

Conquer
To overcome a city, state, or government by force. Moses sent scouts into Canaan to look at the land and bring back a report; only Caleb and Joshua believed the people of Israel could conquer the land. **Numbers 13:26-33**

Conscience
Ability to think about one's behavior. For the believer, his behavior should follow the teachings of God's Word. David found King Saul in a cave and cut off a portion of his robe; later David's conscience bothered him. He decided not to do anything like that again. **1 Samuel 24:1-22**

Conversion
When a person recognizes his sin, repents, believes in Jesus, and confesses Jesus as Savior and Lord, the action is called conversion. Jesus used the term when He talked about the need for people to become like children when they come to Him. **Matthew 18:1-4**

Corinth

(KAWR inth) Important city in New Testament times. On his first visit to Corinth, Paul stayed for at least 18 months. Paul's three longest letters are associated with Corinth. First and Second Corinthians were written to Corinth, and Romans was written from Corinth. Paul, Aquila, Priscilla, Silas, Timothy, Apollos, and Titus all related to the church at Corinth.
Acts 18:1-18

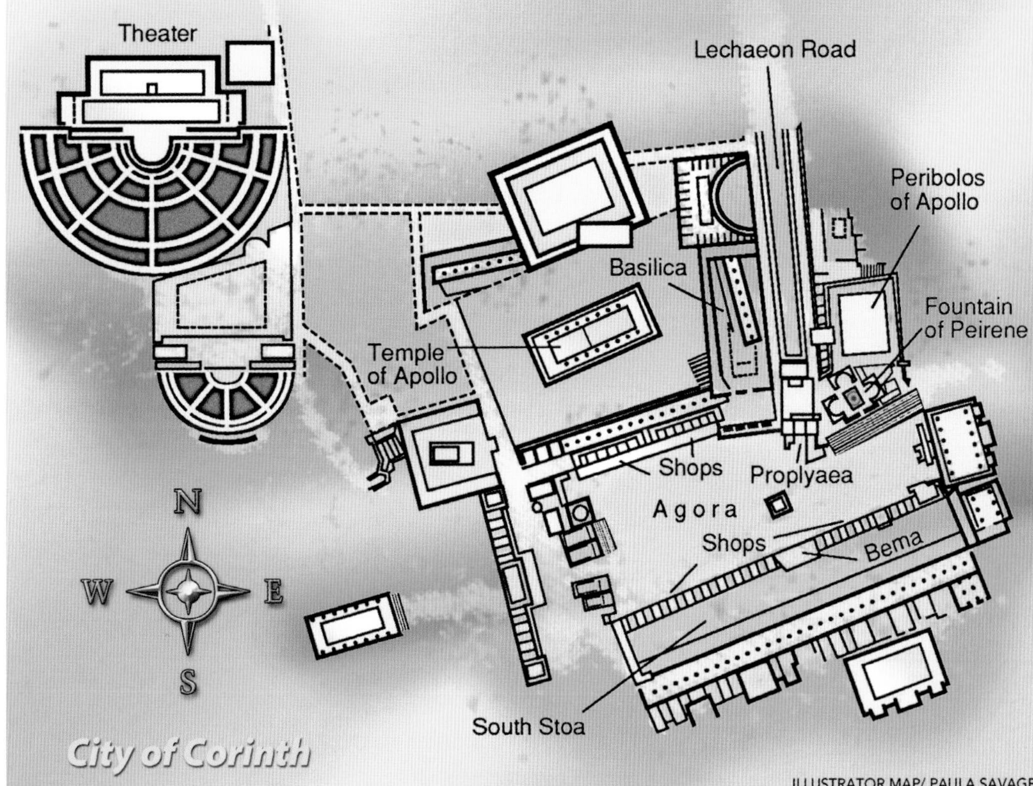

Corinth: First Century.

Corinthians (koh RIN thih uhns) First and Second Corinthians are the second and third books of Paul's Letters in the New Testament. Paul wrote First Corinthians to give the church help with problems they faced. He wrote Second Corinthians to encourage the church and to defend his own ministry. **1 Corinthians 1:1-2; 2 Corinthians 1:1-2**

A street in Corinth from the first century A. D.

Cornelius

(kawr NEE lih uhs) God-fearing centurion in the Roman army who lived in Caesarea. An angel told him to send for Peter. When Peter arrived, he preached to Cornelius and to his relatives and close friends. Cornelius and the others believed in Jesus. This was the beginning of the New Testament church's ministry to Gentiles.
Acts 10:1-48

Cornerstone

Stone laid at the corner of a building to hold two walls together and to strengthen them. After Peter and John healed the lame man, Peter spoke to the Jewish leaders. He referred to Jesus as the cornerstone because Jesus is the foundation of faith.
Acts 4:8-12

Courts, temple 1. The Court of Gentiles was as far into the temple area as people who were not Jews could go. Jesus drove out buyers and sellers from this area of the temple. 2. The Court of Women was as far into the temple as women could go. Jesus was in this area when He saw the widow give her offering. 3. The Court of Men was as far into the temple as Jewish men who were not priests could go. 4. The Court of Priests was the area outside the temple where the altar of burnt offerings and the laver (a large pot with water where priests washed their hands) were located.
Matthew 21:12-13; Luke 21:1-4

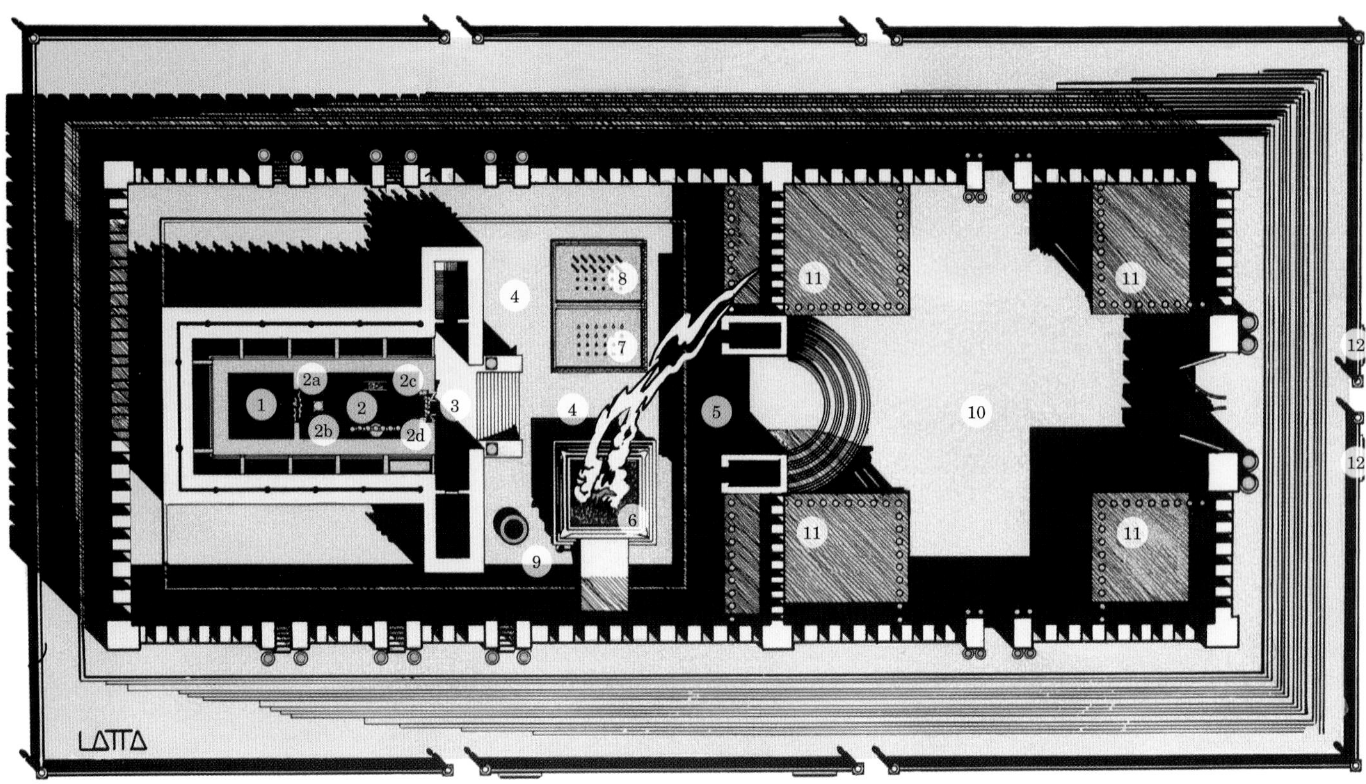

1. Holy of holies
2. Holy place
2a. Veil separating the Holy place from the Holy of holies
2b. Altar of incense
2c. Table of showbread
2d. Seven branched Lampstand (Great Menorah)
3. Temple porch
4. Court of priests
5. Court of Israel (men)
6. Altar of burnt offerings
7. Where sacrificial animals were kept
8. Where sacrificial animals were slaughtered and skinned
9. Laver
10. Court of women
11. Balconies where women view temple activities
12. Warning inscriptions to Gentiles not to go beyond this point

Covenant (KUHV uh nuhnt)
Promise between two people or between a person and God. One person promises to bless or serve another person in a specific way. Sometimes keeping the promise depends on one person's meeting conditions set by the other person. God made a covenant with Abraham to make him the father of many nations, and that covenant was renewed with Abraham's son Isaac, Isaac's son Jacob, and Jacob's sons.
Genesis 15:18-21

Creation God is the Creator of the world. He created it out of nothing. Everything that exists was created by God, who is Father, Son, and Holy Spirit. Human beings are created in the image of God. God's good creation was ruined by Adam's sin. Life became more difficult. The whole world experiences suffering and death. In spite of this, creation continues to tell all people of God's glory and greatness. Jesus came to forgive sin and to reverse the harm that was done by Adam's sin. He made the blind to see, the deaf to hear, and the lame to walk. He who was Creator came to live as a man. Although He was without sin, He experienced life in a world of pain and death. He died on the cross and was raised from death, so that those who trust Him may have eternal life. Someday the entire creation will be as good as it was before sin came into it. **Genesis 1:1,27,31; 2:15-25; 3:14-24; 19:1-6; Mark 1:23-28, 29-34,40-45; 2:1-12; 7:31-37; 10:46-52; John 1:10; Romans 1:18-20; 2 Corinthians 5:21; Colossians 1:16-17; Hebrews 1:3; 2:5-18; Revelation 4:11**

A NASA photograph showing the most distant galaxies ever seen.

Creature Animal or human having life and created by God. **Genesis 1:20,24**

Aa Bb Cc Dd Ee Ff Gg Hh Ii Jj Kk Ll Mm Nn Oo Pp Qq Rr Ss Tt Uu Vv Ww Xx Yy Zz

Cross/crucifixion (kroo suh FIK shuhn) Death on a cross. Method the Romans used to execute Jesus. The most painful and degrading form of punishment in the ancient world; the cross became the means by which Jesus died once and for all for the sins of the whole world. The cross was made from wood. The tallest piece of wood remained upright in the ground, while the person to be crucified carried the crossbeam. **Mark 15:21-25**

John the apostle with Mary, Jesus mother, at the place of Jesus crucifixion.

Cyprus (SIGH pruhs) Large island in the eastern Mediterranean Sea. Cyprus is the birthplace of Barnabas. Paul, Barnabas, and John Mark began their first missionary journey on Cyprus. They arrived at Salamis, traveled to Paphos, and preached to Sergius Paulus the proconsul. **Acts 4:36-37; Acts 13:4-12**

Ruins of Salamis, the port city where Barnabas and Paul landed on their first missionary journey

Crown Special headdress worn by royalty and other persons of high merit and honor. Most Old Testament references point to an actual headdress. In the New Testament the term *crown* is used symbolically. Paul writes about "a crown of righteousness." **Esther 2:17; 2 Timothy 4:8**

From Giza, a crown of copper overlaid with gold, gesso, and paint

Cubit (KYOO bit) Unit of measure in Bible times. The distance from a person's elbow to the tip of the middle finger, about 18 inches. **Matthew 6:27** (See *Table of Weights and Measures in the Bible*, p.117.)

Cupbearer Important official in the Ancient Near East. He served wine to the king and made sure it had not been poisoned. The king trusted the cupbearer and often sought his advice. **Nehemiah 1:11**

Golden drinking cup.

Cyrus (SIGH ruhs) King of Persia. He set free the Jewish exiles who had been taken from Jerusalem from 605 to 586 B.C. They were allowed to return to rebuild the temple and city. Cyrus restored the valuable treasures of the temple taken during the exile. **2 Chronicles 36:22-23**

Dd

Damascus

(duh MASS kuhs) Capital city of Bible-times Syria known for trading and transportation. After Paul was converted on his way to Damascus, he was taken to a house on Straight Street in the city. Later he escaped by being lowered in a basket through an opening in the city wall. (See *Basket*.) **Acts 9:22-25**

Wall from first century Damascus from which Paul escaped when his life was in danger

Dan (DAN) First son born to Jacob by Rachel's maid Bilhah. He was the ancestor of the tribe of Dan, one the twelve tribes of Israel. **Genesis 30:6**

Daniel (DAN yuhl) 1. Daniel was a young man of noble birth who was taken captive by Nebuchadnezzar, the king of Babylon in 605 B. C. He became a leader in Babylon and served three kings. His faith in God helped him when He chose to eat healthy food rather than the king's food; when Nebuchadnezzar wanted to kill all the wise men; when God wrote a message on a wall to Belshazzar, the second king; and when he was thrown in the lion's den by Darius, the third king.

2. The Book of Daniel was written by Daniel and is the last book of the Major Prophets division of the Old Testament. The book tells about the way God worked in the lives of people and nations. The first half of the book (chapters 1-6) tells stories of Daniel and his three friends after they were taken into exile. The second half of the book (chapters 7-12) is prophecies. **Daniel 1:8-16; 2:1-49; 5:1-30; 6:1-24**

David (DAY vid) Shepherd, musician, poet, warrior, King Saul's armor-bearer, and trusted friend of Jonathan, King Saul's son. David became the second king of Israel and the first to bring together the northern and southern tribes of Israel as a united kingdom. As a shepherd, David protected his sheep. As a poet he wrote many of the Psalms. As a warrior, he killed Goliath and led men into battle against the Philistines. As Saul's servant, he played the harp and carried Saul's armor. As a friend, he promised to always be loyal to Jonathan and Jonathan's family. As king, he brought the Ark of the Covenant to Jerusalem and made plans to build a temple for the worship of God. He is known as a "man after God's own heart."
Psalm 23; 1 Samuel 17:1-52; 20:1-42; 2 Samuel 5:1-3; 6:1-17; Acts 13:22

When Jonathan made a covenant of friendship with David, he gave David gifts, including his robe. **1 Samuel 18:1-4**

Deacon
(DEE kuhn) Means "servant" or "minister." In many churches, deacons help the pastor care for the members of the church.
1 Timothy 3:13

Dead Sea Lake at the southern end of the Jordan River. Water runs into the lake from the Jordan River and stays there. Because the water doesn't leave the lake, it is very salty. Also known as the Salt Sea. It is 50 miles long and 10 miles wide. The surface of the Dead Sea is 1,292 feet below sea level. At its deepest point, the Dead Sea is 1300 feet deep. The salt content of the Dead Sea makes it easy for swimmers to float above the surface. **Joshua 15:5**

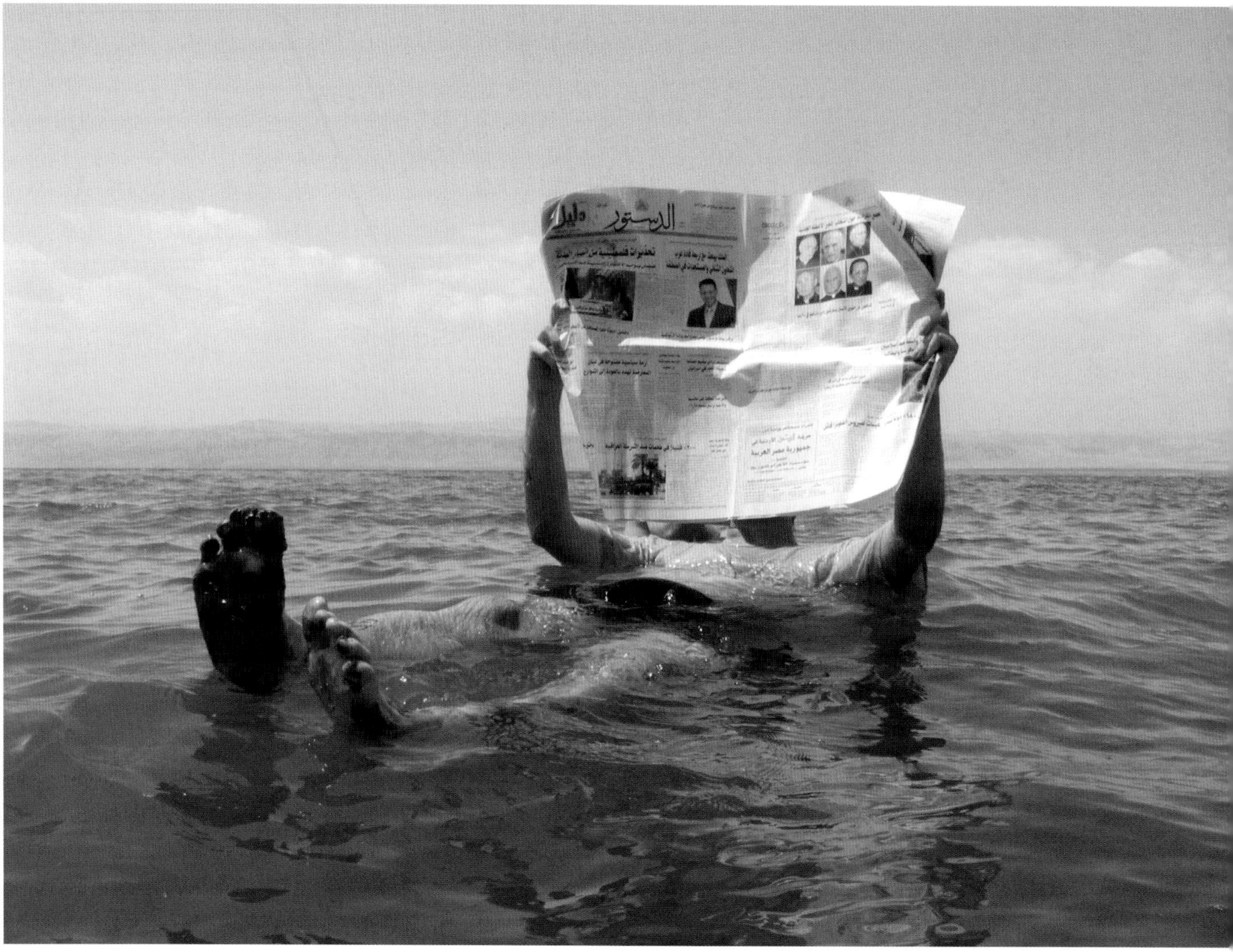

The Dead Sea's high salt content makes it virtually impossible for a person to sink in its waters.

Deborah

(DEB uh ruh) A prophetess and judge who sat under a palm tree where people came to her for help. She worked with Barak to fight against Jabin, king of Canaan, and Sisera, Jabin's commander. She is called "a mother in Israel" because of her role in delivering God's people. **Judges 4-5**

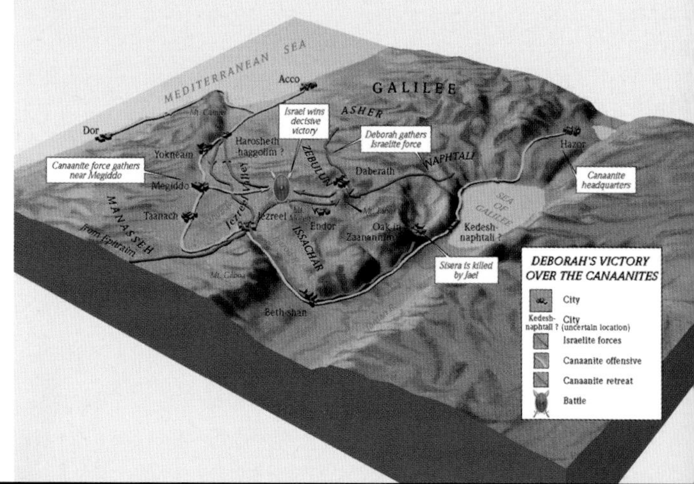

Decapolis
(dih KAP oh liss) The name for a group of 10 cities on the eastern side of the Jordan River. When Jesus healed a demon-possessed man, the man told people in Decapolis what Jesus had done for him. **Mark 5:20**

Delilah
(dih LIGH luh) A woman whom Samson loved and who betrayed him to the Philistines.
Judges 16:1-22

Demons, Devils (KJV)
Identified in Scripture as fallen angels who joined Satan in his rebellion against God. They follow Satan in doing evil, but have limited power.
Luke 8:26-39

Denarius/denarii, (dih NEHR ih uhs/dih NEHR ih igh) Penny (KJV)
Silver coin made by the Romans with the image of Caesar on one side. The daily pay for a Roman soldier and other working people. Jesus used a denarius to show the Pharisees that they should give money to Caesar and to God.
Matthew 22:15-22

Descendants
Children of a father and mother either in the first generation or in later generations. Isaac and Jesus were both descendants of Abraham.
Matthew 1:1-17

Deuteronomy
(DOO tuh RAHN uh mih) Means "second law." The fifth and last book of the division of Law in the Old Testament. Moses is the author of this book and the other books of law. The book contains speeches Moses gave to the Israelites and a second listing of the Ten Commandments.
Deuteronomy 1:1; Deuteronomy 5:6-21

Moses reminded those who were soon to enter the promised land of the Ten Commandments.

Desert Usually a rocky, dry wasteland with little rainfall. The desert to the east and south of Palestine is known as the wilderness in which the Israelites wandered for 40 years.
Exodus 16:14

Wasteland of the Negev desert in southern Israel

Aa Bb Cc Dd Ee Ff Gg Hh Ii Jj Kk Ll Mm Nn Oo Pp Qq Rr Ss Tt Uu Vv Ww Xx Yy Zz

Devil (DEV uhl) Also known as Satan and the evil one, a being who is against God and His purposes. The devil is not equal to God and he is not a threat to God's power. Jesus was tempted by the devil three times in the desert and at other times throughout His ministry. **Matthew 4:1-11; James 4:7**

Dew Moisture that forms into drops of water on the earth during a cool night. **Exodus 16:14**

Dictate To tell someone what to write. Jeremiah dictated to Baruch the words God wanted Him to write. Those words are now part of the book of Jeremiah. **Jeremiah 36**

Baruch wrote the words Jeremiah told him to write.

Disciple (dih SIGH puhl) Means "learner" or "pupil." The people Jesus called to follow Him during His earthly ministry are called disciples. One of Jesus' miracles took place when some of His disciples were in a boat with Jesus in a storm and Jesus spoke to the wind and calmed the waters. (See *Apostle*.) **Matthew 8:23-27**

Disease Physical sickness that can cause death. Jesus had the power to heal diseases. **Matthew 4:24**

Disobey To disobey is to hear God's Word and refuse to do what it says. Samuel told the people of Israel that they must not disobey God. **1 Samuel 12:15**

Divorce Legal term that describes when and a husband and wife decide not to be married any longer. (See *Engaged*.) **Matthew 1:18-19**

Divided Kingdom The nation of Israel split into two separate nations after the death of King Solomon. The Northern Kingdom was known as Israel and the Southern Kingdom was known as Judah. **1 Kings 12**

THE KINGDOMS OF ISRAEL AND JUDAH

1 KGS. 12

- • City
- ★ Capital city
- ○ City (uncertain location)
- ▲ Mountain peak
- Israel
- Judah
- International roads
- Local roads

10 20 30 40 50 Miles
10 20 30 40 50 Kilometers

Beirut
PHOENICIA
Sidon
Damascus
Mt. Hermon
Ijon
Tyre
Litani River
Abel beth-maacah
Dan
Jeroboam built a sanctuary
ARAM
Kedesh
Achzib
Hazor
Lake Huleh
Acco
Chinnereth
Sea of Galilee
GESHUR
Mt. Carmel
Gath-hepher
Aphek
Ashtaroth
Kishon River
Mt. Tabor
Yarmuk River
Edrei
Megiddo
Dor
Jezreel
Taanach
Mt. Gilboa
Ramoth-gilead
Beth-shan
Dothan
Pehel
Ibleam
Jabesh-gilead
MEDITERRANEAN SEA
Socoh
Tirzah
Samaria
Mt. Ebal
ISRAEL
Jordan River
Political capital of Israel from Omri onward
Mahanaim
Penuel
Shechem
Succoth
Jabbok River
Yarkon River
Aphek
Mt. Gerizim
Adam
Joppa
Shiloh
Jeroboam built a sanctuary
Upper Beth-horon
Rabbah (Amman)
Bethel
AMMON
Lower Beth-horon
Jericho
Mizpah
Gezer
Geba
Ashdod
Aijalon
Ramah
Heshbon
Gibeah
Ekron
Jerusalem
Mt. Nebo
Gath
Medeba
Azekah
Bethlehem
Ashkelon
Beth-zur
Mareshah
Tekoa
PHILISTIA
Lachish
Hebron
Dibon
Gaza
Adoraim
Ziph
Carmel
DEAD SEA
Arnon River
Gerar
Maon
N. Besor
JUDAH
Arad
King's Highway
International Coastal Highway
Beersheba
Kir-hareseth
Negeb
MOAB
W. el-Arish
Zered River
Tamar
Bozrah
Eastern Desert
EDOM
Kadesh-barnea
Wilderness

Doctrine Christian teaching based on the Bible. Paul told Timothy to be careful about people who would teach doctrine that was different from God's written Word and what God communicated through Jesus. **1 Timothy 6:3**

Dorcas (DAWR kuhs) Christian woman of Joppa who was known for making clothes for widows. God raised her from the dead when Peter prayed for her. **Acts 9:36-43**

Dream In Bible times, God often spoke to people in dreams. In a dream Jacob saw angels going up and down a ladder to heaven, and God made promises to him in the dream. An angel of the Lord told Joseph in a dream that the baby Mary would have should be named Jesus. **Genesis 28:12-15; Matthew 1:18-25**

"When Joseph got up from sleeping, he did as the Lord's angel commanded him." **Matthew 1:24**

Drought, Dearth (KJV)
Time when no rain falls for many months or years. God told Jeremiah that a drought would come to the land of Judah because the people did not obey Him.
Jeremiah 14:1

Dyeing Process of coloring fabric for clothes. Lydia sold cloth that had been dyed purple. She lived in Philippi and became a Christian after meeting Paul. **Acts 16:13-14**

Ee

Earth 1. God created the entire universe including planet Earth.
2. The place where people, animals, and plants live.
Genesis 1:1

Easter (EE stuhr) Annual celebration of the resurrection of Jesus from the dead. Easter is the oldest Christian festival. **Matthew 28:1-10**

Earthquake Shaking or trembling of the earth due to volcanic activity or the shifting of the earth's crusts. An earthquake in Philippi opened the doors of the prison where Paul and Silas were being kept. **Acts 16:16-34**

Damage from an earthquake in Poggioreale, Italy

Ecclesiastes (ih KLEE zih ASS teez) Fourth book of Poetry in the Old Testament. Solomon, the writer of the book, says that human beings should remember how awesome God is. They should humbly obey His commands, knowing He will judge all that is done on earth. **Ecclesiastes 12:13-14**

"When Solomon finished praying, fire descended from heaven and consumed the burnt offering and the sacrifices, and the glory of the LORD filled the temple." **2 Chronicles 7:1** Solomon wrote the book of Ecclesiastes.

Eden (EE duhn) Region in which God planted the first garden. The exact location is not known. Four rivers ran through the garden. Two of them, the Tigris and Euphrates, are in present-day Iraq. **Genesis 2:8-14**

A young Iraqi man gazing across the Euphrates River that flows through Iraq to the Persian Gulf. The Euphrates is one of the four rivers flowing from Eden.

Edict, Decree (KJV) Royal order or decision. King Darius signed an order that everyone in the kingdom could pray only to him. Daniel continued to pray to God and was thrown into the lion's den. **Daniel 6:7**

Egypt (EE jipt) Land in northeastern Africa and home to one of the world's earliest civilizations. Abraham visited Egypt when there was a famine in Canaan. Joseph was taken as a slave to Egypt and became second in command of the country. Moses led the Hebrew nation out of slavery in Egypt. Joseph took Mary and Jesus to Egypt for protection from Herod. **Genesis 12:10-20; 37–50; Exodus 1–14; Matthew 2:13-15**

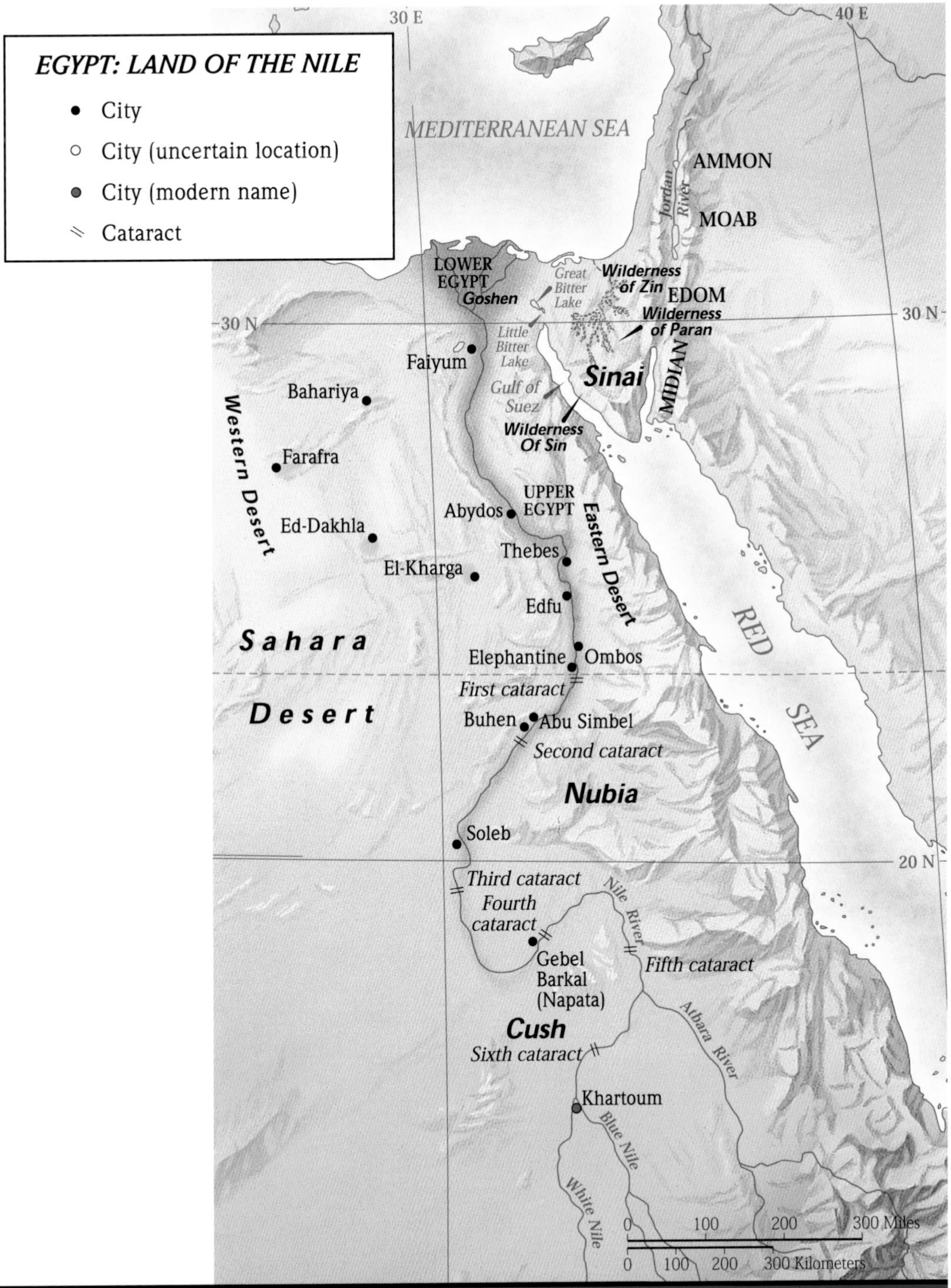

EGYPT: LAND OF THE NILE

- • City
- ○ City (uncertain location)
- ● City (modern name)
- Cataract

30 E
40 E
MEDITERRANEAN SEA
AMMON
Jordan River
MOAB
LOWER EGYPT
Goshen
Great Bitter Lake
Wilderness of Zin
EDOM
Wilderness of Paran
30 N
Little Bitter Lake
Faiyum
Sinai
MIDIAN
Gulf of Suez
Bahariya
Wilderness Of Sin
Western Desert
Farafra
UPPER EGYPT
Abydos
Ed-Dakhla
Thebes
Eastern Desert
El-Kharga
Edfu
RED SEA
Sahara Desert
Elephantine
Ombos
First cataract
Buhen
Abu Simbel
Second cataract
Nubia
Soleb
20 N
Third cataract
Nile River
Fourth cataract
Gebel Barkal (Napata)
Fifth cataract
Cush
Atbara River
Sixth cataract
Khartoum
Blue Nile
White Nile
0 100 200 300 Miles
0 100 200 300 Kilometers

Elder Religious and political leader in the Old Testament. Refers to both Jewish leaders and church leaders in the New Testament.
Ruth 4:1-9; Acts 11:30

Eli (EE ligh) The priest at Shiloh who was in charge of the tabernacle. He met Hannah as she prayed for a child. When her child Samuel was still young, she took him to live with Eli at the tabernacle. **1 Samuel 1:9-28**

Samuel went to Eli and said, "Here I am; you called me." 1 Samuel 3:1-10

Elijah (ih LIGH juh) Prophet from Tishbe in the Northern Kingdom. Elijah is best known for raising a widow's son from the dead, meeting with the prophets of Baal at Mt. Carmel, and making the long journey to Mt. Horeb. Elijah was taken into heaven in a chariot of fire and a whirlwind.
1 Kings 17:17-24; 18:20-39; 19:1-18; 2 Kings 2:11-12

The summit of Mount Carmel where Elijah's altar to God and the altar of the priests of Baal were built

Elisha (ih LIGH shuh) God chose Elisha to take Elijah's place as a prophet. Through Elisha God multiplied the oil of a poor widow. A Shunamite woman and her husband made Elisha a room in the family's house. Later Elisha raised their son from the dead. When Naaman, commander of the Syrian army, came to Israel seeking to be healed of a severe skin disease, Elisha told him to dip seven times in the Jordan River. Naaman reluctantly obeyed and was healed. **1 Kings 19:19-21; 2 Kings 4:1-7; 4:8-36; 5:1-19**

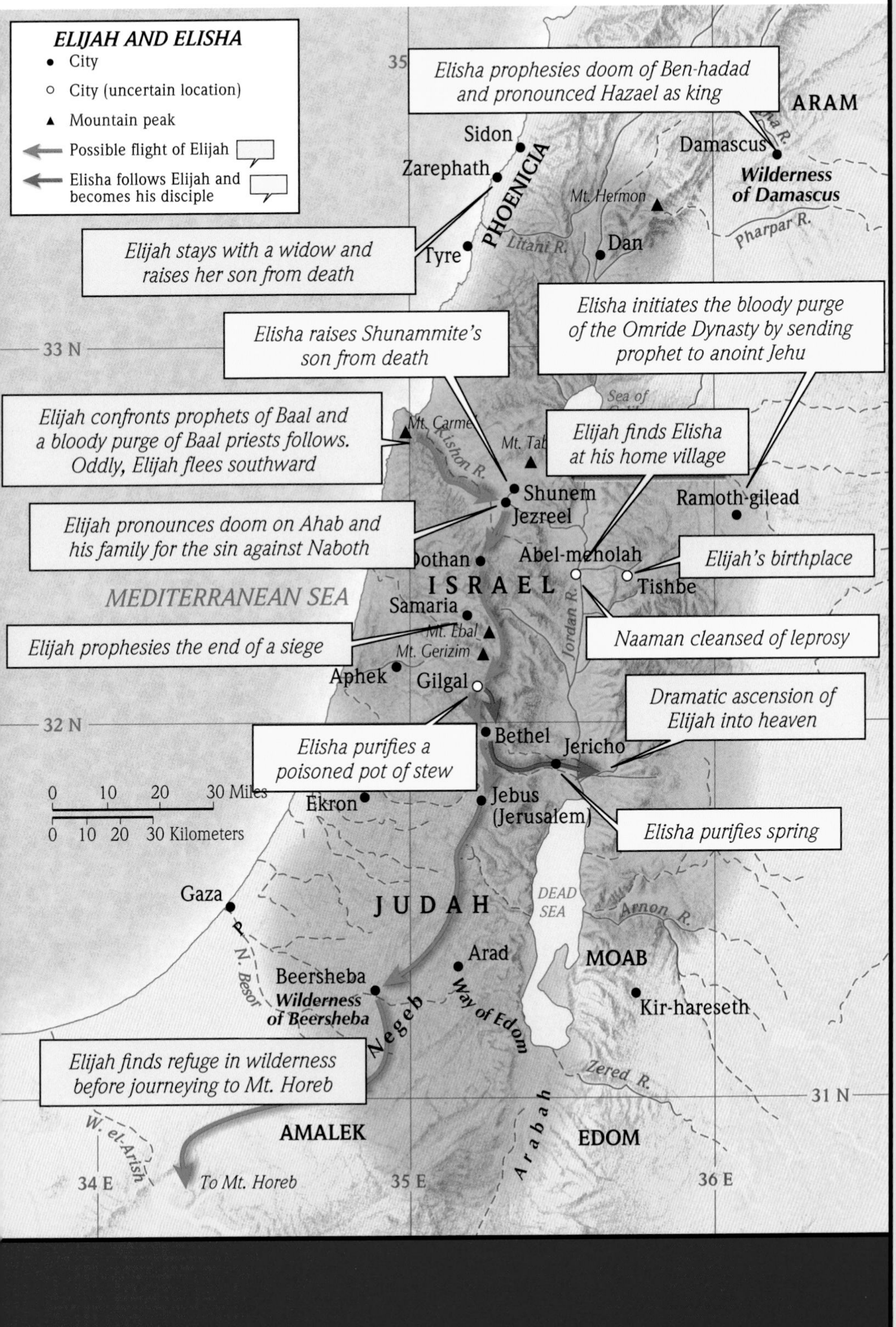

Elkanah (el KAY nuh) Husband of Hannah and father of Samuel. **1 Samuel 1:1-2**

Emmaus (eh MAY uhs) Village about seven miles from Jerusalem and the home of Cleopas and another disciple. As they traveled home after Jesus' crucifixion and burial in Jerusalem, they were joined by a man who told them what the Scriptures said about Jesus. Later they recognized the man as Jesus. **Luke 24:13-35**

Emmaus. According to the Sinai manuscript, Emmaus is thought to be the site of the house of Cleopas.

Engaged, Espoused (KJV) In New Testament times, a Jewish engagement was a binding agreement that could only be broken by divorce. Mary and Joseph were engaged to be married when Mary found that she was going to be the mother of Jesus. **Matthew 1:18-25; Luke 1:26-27**

Emperor Word the New Testament uses to refer to a Caesar of Rome. **Acts 25:21,25,26; 1 Peter 2:13,17**

Trajan was probably the Roman emperor (A.D. 98-117) when John, the last of the twelve apostles, died.

Endurance To keep doing something even when a person is tired and wants to give up. **Hebrews 12:1-2**

Enemy Someone who dislikes another person, wants to harm him, or tries to bully him. Jesus told people to love their enemies. **Luke 6:27-36**

Enoch (EE nuhk)
Man of God who had a close relationship with God. He did not die but was taken to heaven by God.
Genesis 5:21-24

Ephesians
(ih FEE shuhnz) Fifth book of Paul's Letters in the New Testament. Paul may have written to the church at Ephesus while he was in prison in Rome in A.D. 61-62. Paul wrote the letter to share his doctrine of the church. **Ephesians 1:1**

Ephesus (EF uh suhs) Large city located in Asia Minor and a center for politics, religion, and business. While Paul was preaching there, men who made false gods out of silver started a riot because they were afraid that Paul's preaching would put an end to their business. **Acts 19:1-41**

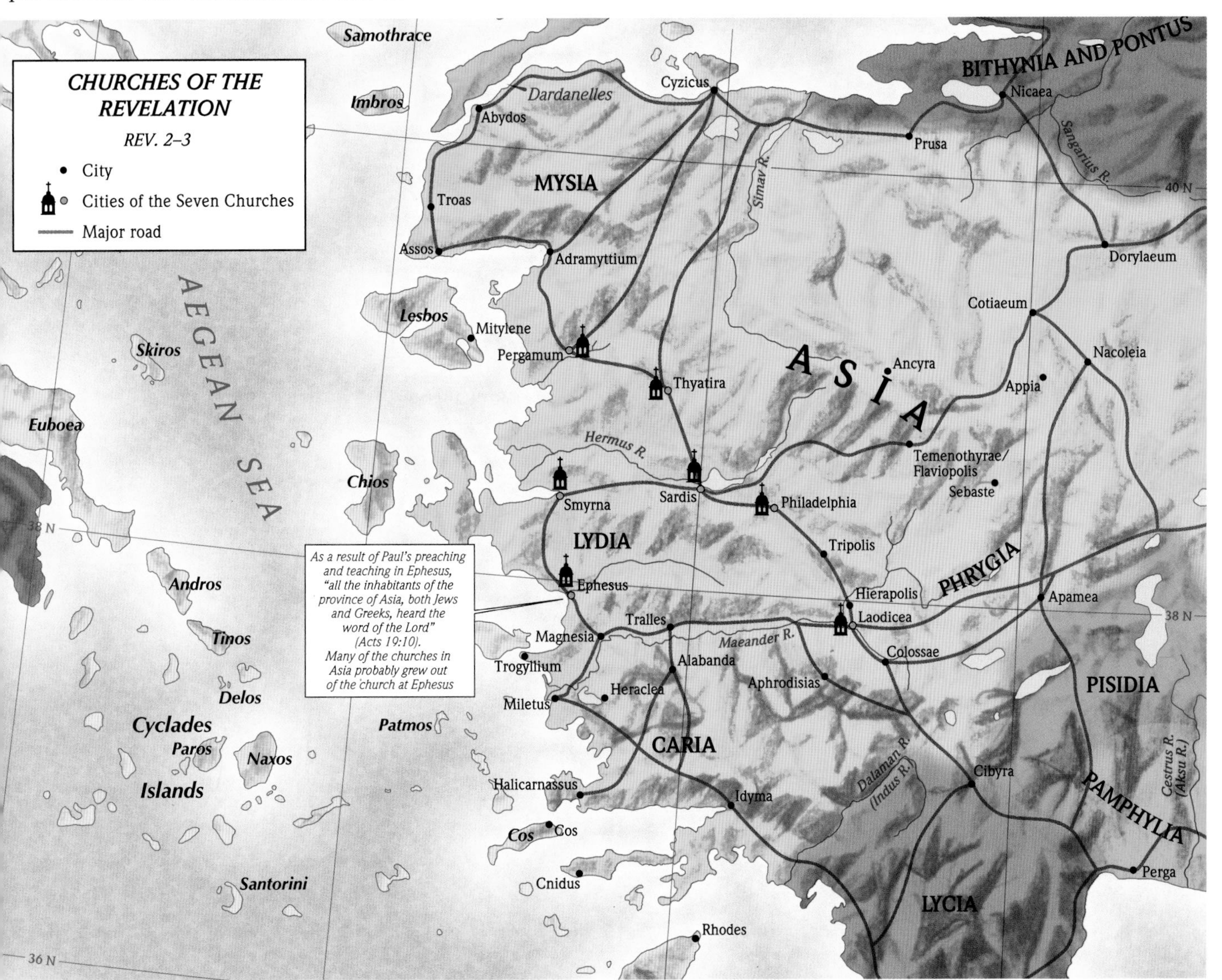

Ephesus: Fourth largest city in the Roman Empire

Ephod (EE fahd) An apron-like piece of clothing worn by priests. On each shoulder was a black stone on which the names six of the twelve tribes of Israel were written. The ephod tied around the waist. **Exodus 28:6-14**

Ephraim (EE fra ihm) Younger son of Joseph by Asenath, daughter of a priest in Egypt. Adopted by his grandfather Jacob. He was the ancestor of the tribe of Ephraim, one the the twelve tribes of Israel. **Genesis 41:50-52; 48:5**

Esau (EE saw) Son of Isaac and Rebekah and elder twin brother of Jacob. He sold his birthright to Jacob, who also tricked him out of his father's blessing. He became the father of the nation of Edom. **Genesis 25:19-26; 25:27-34; 27:1-40**

Esther (ESS tuhr) 1. Hadassah, a Jewish woman whose name was changed to Esther. Later she became the queen of Persia. She and her uncle Mordecai helped save the lives of all the Jewish people in the Persian empire. 2. The last book in the Old Testament division of History. Esther is the only book in the Bible that does not use the name of God. God's work is clear in all the ways Esther and Mordecai worked to save their people. The Jewish festival of Purim is based on the events in the Book of Esther. **Esther 2:7; 9:26-28**

Onyx scepter from about 600 B.C. (Esther 5:2).

Eternal life, Everlasting life (KJV) Living with God in heaven forever. Jesus talked with Nicodemus about eternal life. Jesus said that everyone who believes in Him "will not perish but have eternal life." **John 3:16**

Evangelism Telling people the good news that Jesus wants to be their Savior and Lord. Paul and Barnabas evangelized in many towns. Philip was called an evangelist. **Acts 14:21; 21:8**

Ethiopia/Ethiopian (EE thih OH pih uh\EE thih OH pih uhn) 1. Area south of Egypt, but not the same place as the country of Ethiopia today. 2. An Ethiopian who loved God and had visited Jerusalem was returning home when God sent Philip to tell him about Jesus. The man was an official in the court of the queen of Ethiopia. He believed in Jesus and was baptized. **Acts 8:26-40**

Eunuch (YOO nuhk) A man who because of surgery was not able to have children. Often served in the royal courts. **Acts 8:26-40**

Eve (EEV) First woman created by God, from whom all other people come. (See *Adam*.) **Genesis 2:22; 3:20**

Exile Event in which the people of a conquered country are taken from their land. The northern tribes of Israel were taken into captivity by the Assyrians (722 B.C.). The southern tribe of Judah was taken into captivity by the Babylonians (605, 598, and 586 B.C.). **2 Kings 17:6; 25:8-12**

Exodus (EK suh duhs) 1. Israel's escape from slavery in Egypt and journey toward the promised land under Moses. The Bible tells that the exodus was the work of God. He brought plagues on Egypt, allowed the Israelites to cross the Red Sea on dry land, brought them across the Jordan River, and led them to Jericho in the promised land. 2. The second book in the division of Law of the Old Testament. The book, written by Moses, tells about the exodus and the tabernacle.
Exodus 3–14; Joshua 2–4; Joshua 6; Exodus 25–40

Moses leads the Israelites across the Red Sea on dry ground. Exodus 14:15-31

Ezekiel (ih ZEE kih uhl) 1. Prophet taken into captivity by the Babylonians with others from Judah. 2. The fourth book in the division of Major Prophets of the Old Testament. The book is a series of messages from God through Ezekiel to the people of Judah in exile.
Ezekiel 1:1-3; 8:1; 20:1-2

A reproduction of the prophet Ezekiel, originally painted by Michaelangelo between 1508 and 1512 for the ceiling of the Sistine Chapel in Rome.

Ezra (EZ ruh) 1. Priest and scribe in exile in Persia. King Cyrus sent Ezra and a large group of Israelites back to Jerusalem. Ezra's mission was to study the law of the LORD, obey it, and teach it in Israel. 2. Tenth book in the division of History of the Old Testament. This book tells the story of the exiles' returning to Jerusalem and beginning to rebuild the temple.
Ezra 1:1-4; 3:10-11; 7:8-10

Ff

Aa Bb Cc Dd Ee Ff Gg Hh Ii Jj Kk Ll Mm Nn Oo Pp Qq Rr Ss Tt Uu Vv Ww Xx Yy Zz

Faith One of the nine qualities seen in the fruit of the Spirit. Faith is belief that what God has told a person about Himself and people in the Bible is true. Such belief makes a difference in attitudes, thoughts, words, and actions toward God, other people, and a person's own self. Faith pleases God. Failure to trust God through faith is a sin. **Psalm 56:11; 62:8; Galatians 5:22; Hebrews 11:1-6; James 1:22-25; 2:14-26**

Faithful Trustworthy or dependable. God is known for His faithfulness or trustworthiness. People who trust God and do what He commands are known as faithful people. **Psalm 33:22; 2 Thessalonians 3:3**

False Not true or real. Paul warned the church at Corinth to beware of false apostles and false teaching. **2 Corinthians 11:13**

Family Group of persons related to one another by marriage, blood, or adoption. God created families when He created Adam and Eve. **Genesis 2:7, 20-24**

Famine Shortage of food, usually caused by drought. The Bible tells of many droughts. Naomi and her husband and sons moved to Moab because of a famine in Judah. **Ruth 1:1**

Lack of rain is one of the causes of famine.

Fasting Not eating food for an extended period of time in order to pray and discover God's will. **Acts 13:2-3**

Father/father 1. One name for God is Father. In the New Testament, Jesus called God "Father" and taught His disciples to pray to God as Father. 2. The male parent in a family. **Genesis 29:12; Luke 2:49; Matthew 6:9**

Felix (FEE liks) Governor of Judea at the time Paul the apostle visited Jerusalem. Paul defended himself before Felix and was held under guard for two years. **Acts 24:10-27**

Fellowship Describes the close relationship that Christians should have with one another and with God. **Acts 2:42; 1 John 1:3**

Festival/Feast Jewish celebration that helped the people remember God's great acts. The Passover helped people remember the death of Egypt's firstborn sons and animals, the tenth of God's plagues. The Festival of Weeks celebrated harvest time. **Exodus 12:1-28; 34:22**

JEWISH FESTIVALS AND FEASTS

FESTIVAL/FEAST	SEASON	DESCRIPTION	REFERENCE
Passover	Spring	Celebrates the final plague on Egypt when the firstborn of the Egyptians died and the Israelites were spared because of the blood smeared on their doorposts. Jesus celebrated Passover with His disciples.	Exodus 12:1-28; Leviticus 23:5; Luke 22:7-8
Feast of Unleavened Bread	Spring	Follows Passover and celebrates the Israelite's deliverance from Egypt.	Leviticus 23:6-8
Pentecost Feast of Weeks Day of Firstfruits	Summer	Harvest celebration. The term "weeks" was used of the seven weeks from the barley harvest to the wheat harvest. In the New Testament the Holy Spirit came upon the disciples at Pentecost at the festive time when Jews from different countries were in Jerusalem to celebrate this annual feast.	Numbers 28:26-31; Acts 2:1-4
Day of Atonement Yom Kippur	Fall	A day of fasting, repentance, and focusing on God. The only day in the year when the high priest entered the holy of holies in the temple.	Leviticus 16:1-34
Feast of Tabernacles Feast of Booths	Fall	Celebrates the fall harvest of crops and celebrates the booths ("tabernacles" or temporary dwellings) in which the Israelites lived after their exodus from Egypt. The dedication of Solomon's temple took place at this feast.	Leviticus 23:33-44; 1 Kings 8:1-11
Feast of Trumpets Rosh Hashanah	Fall	Day of blowing of the trumpets on the first day of the seventh month of the Jewish religious calendar. Rosh Hashanah takes place 10 days before the Day of Atonement.	Leviticus 23:24-27
Feast of Purim	Spring	Celebrates the deliverance of the Jewish people in the days of Esther.	Esther 9
Feast of Dedication Hanukkah	Winter	Celebrates the rededication of the Temple in 164 B.C. Jesus celebrated the Feast of Dedication in Jerusalem.	John 10:22-23

Festus (FESS tuhs) Governor of Judea from about A.D. 58-62. He followed Antonius Felix (A.D. 52-58). Paul the apostle asked to be tried before Caesar and Festus granted that request. **Acts 25:1-12**

Paul before Festus

Field Land that is not fenced and could be used for pasture, crops, or hunting. Jesus told parables about planting seed in a field and about buying a field. **Matthew 13:31-32,44**

Fig tree Fruit tree from which Adam and Eve used leaves to make clothing. **Genesis 3:7**

Fish/fishing/fishermen
1. Fish are animals living in the water and breathing through gills. 2. Fishing is the job of catching food to provide for a family or to sell. In New Testament times, men caught fish on the sea of Galilee and sold them.
3. Fishermen used nets and worked from boats to catch fish. Jesus asked fishermen Peter, Andrew, James, and John to follow Him as His disciples. **Matthew 4:18-22**

Sea of Galilee in Capernaum.

Flock Sheep or goats under the care of a shepherd. Shepherds who were caring for their flock at night were the first visitors to see the Baby Jesus. **Luke 2:8**

Shepherd leading his sheep

Firstborn First son born to a husband and wife. Was required to be dedicated to God. The birthright of a firstborn included a double portion of the estate and leadership of the family. Esau was the firstborn of Isaac and Rebekah, but he sold his birthright to his twin, Jacob, for a bowl of stew. **Genesis 25:27-34**

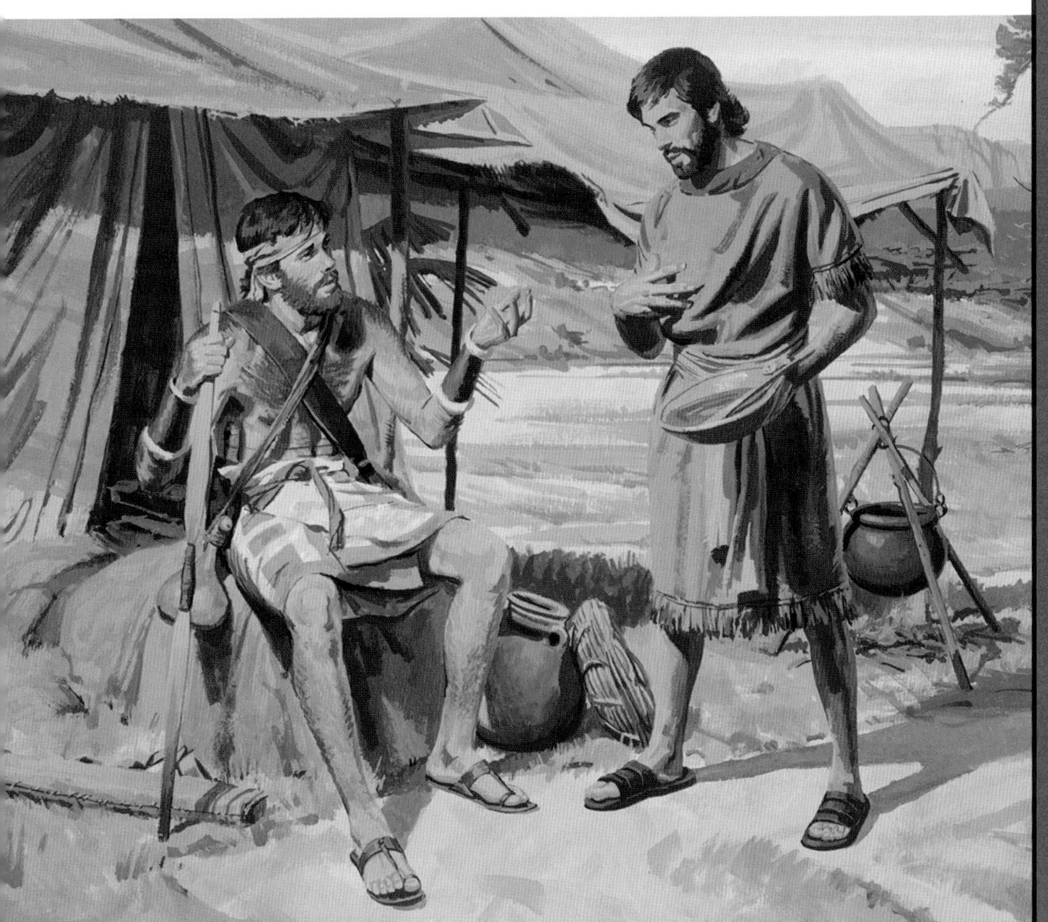

Aa Bb Cc Dd Ee Ff Gg Hh Ii Jj Kk Ll Mm Nn Oo Pp Qq Rr Ss Tt Uu Vv Ww Xx Yy Zz

Flood Large amounts of water covering the land. Genesis tells the story of the flood that covered the whole earth and of how God provided for Noah, Noah's family, and selected animals. **Genesis 6–9**

Fortified Having walls built around a city as a defense against enemy armies. Jericho was a fortified city when Joshua led the Israelites to march around it seven days. **Joshua 6:1-21**

This trench cut into the ruins of Old Testament Jericho shows how strongly fortified the city was.

Frankincense Ingredient used in making the perfume for the most holy place in the tabernacle. It comes from trees in the balsam family. Was one of the gifts presented to the child Jesus by the wise men (See *Myrrh*.) **Matthew 2:11**

Follow To go with someone; to become a disciple of a teacher. Jesus' disciples followed Him and learned from Him for three years. **Matthew 9:9**

Food (See *Foods in Bible Times* chart, p. 63-64.)

Ford Shallow place in a stream or river that a person or group can cross by foot. **Genesis 32:22**

Jacob and his family crossed the ford of the Jabbok River as he went to meet his brother Esau.

Foreigner Person living or traveling in a country other than his own. **Luke 17:11-19**

Forgive To refuse to punish someone who has hurt you or sinned against you. Jesus taught Peter to forgive people. Jesus forgave the people who crucified Him. God's forgiveness of sin comes at a great cost-Jesus' death on the cross. **Matthew 18:21-34; Luke 23:32-34; Hebrews 9:22.**

Fruit of the Spirit Result of the work of the Holy Spirit in a Christian's life: love, joy, peace, patience, kindness, goodness, faith, gentleness, and self-control. **Galatians 5:22-23**

Furnace Large, ovenlike structure made of brick or stone and used to heat materials such as metal and clay to high temperatures. The three friends of Daniel were thrown into a fiery furnace because they refused to worship a gold statue. **Daniel 3:8-30**

FOODS IN BIBLE TIMES

Bread Basic food of most people in Bible times. Bread was made by grinding wheat or barley on a millstone and cooking it in a clay oven or on a griddle or pan. Bread was used as an offering to God.
Leviticus 2:4-10; John 6:9

Cheese Dairy product that was part of Bible times meals. David took cheese to his brothers who were serving in Saul's army.
1 Samuel 17:17-19

Dates Fruit of the date palm, highly valued by desert travelers who ate them fresh, dried them, or made them into cakes. David gave everyone a date cake when he brought the Ark of the Covenant into Jerusalem. **2 Samuel 6:17-19**

Fig Grows on fig trees. Figs could be eaten fresh in the summer when they were ripe, or stored for use in cakes. Adam and Eve used leaves from the plant to make clothing. Jesus cursed a fig tree because it was without fruit. **Genesis 3:7; Mark 11:13-14,20-21**

Fish Animals living in water and breathing through gills. Fish were a favorite food in Bible times. The most famous Old Testament fish was the great fish of the book of Job. In the New Testament, four of Jesus' apostles were fishermen: Peter and Andrew, James and John. Fish provided food for the common people. Jesus ate fish with the disciples in Jerusalem and by the Sea of Galilee. The primary method of preparing fish was broiling.
Job 1:17; Matthew 4:18-22; 14:17; Luke 24:42; John 21:13

Fruit In Bible times people ate apples, figs, grapes, olives, and pomegranates.
Matthew 21:34

FOODS IN BIBLE TIMES

Goat's milk Milk produced by a goat and used for drinking. One of the truths from Proverbs tells about taking care of the flocks and having plenty of goat's milk. **Proverbs 27:27**

Honey Produced by bees and used as sweet food. The Old Testament refers to wild honey in honeycombs and a syrup made from honey, grapes, and dates. In the New Testament, honey was mentioned as a food for people who lived in the wilderness. John the Baptist ate honey when he preached in the wilderness. **2 Chronicles 31:5; 2 Kings 18:32; Matthew 3:4**

Lamb Young sheep. Roasted for meat. A lamb without blemish was roasted for the Passover meal. **Exodus 12:21**

Leeks Grass like herb. Egyptian food eaten by the Hebrews in captivity. **Numbers 11:5**

OlivesGrow on trees with gray-green leaves and cream- colored flowers. Fruit ripens near the end of summer. Unripe fruit is green, and ripe fruit is black. Olives were used for food and also used to make oil. Olive oil was used to light the lampstand in the tabernacle. **Exodus 27:20-21**

Pomegranates Fruit about the size of a tennis ball. Grows on a bush, is full of seeds, and is sweet to eat. God told Moses to decorate the hem of the priest's robe with pomegranates made of yarn. They were engraved on the columns of Solomon's temple. **Exodus 28:33; Deuteronomy 8:8; 1 Kings 7:18**

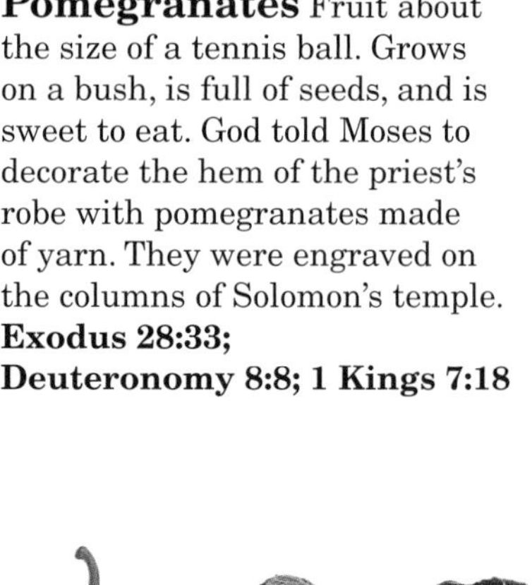

Vegetables In Bible times people ate onions, leeks, lentils, garlic, cucumbers, and melons. Daniel and his friends at vegetables and water instead of the king's food. **Daniel 1:8-16**

Gg

Gabriel

(GAY brih el) Angel, or heavenly messenger, who brought messages from God to people. He announced the births of John the Baptist and Jesus. **Luke 1:8-20; 26-38**

The angel Gabriel appears to Mary.

Gad (GAD) Seventh son of Jacob by Leah's maid Zilpah. Ancestor of the tribe of Gad, one the twelve tribes of Israel. **Genesis 30:9-11**

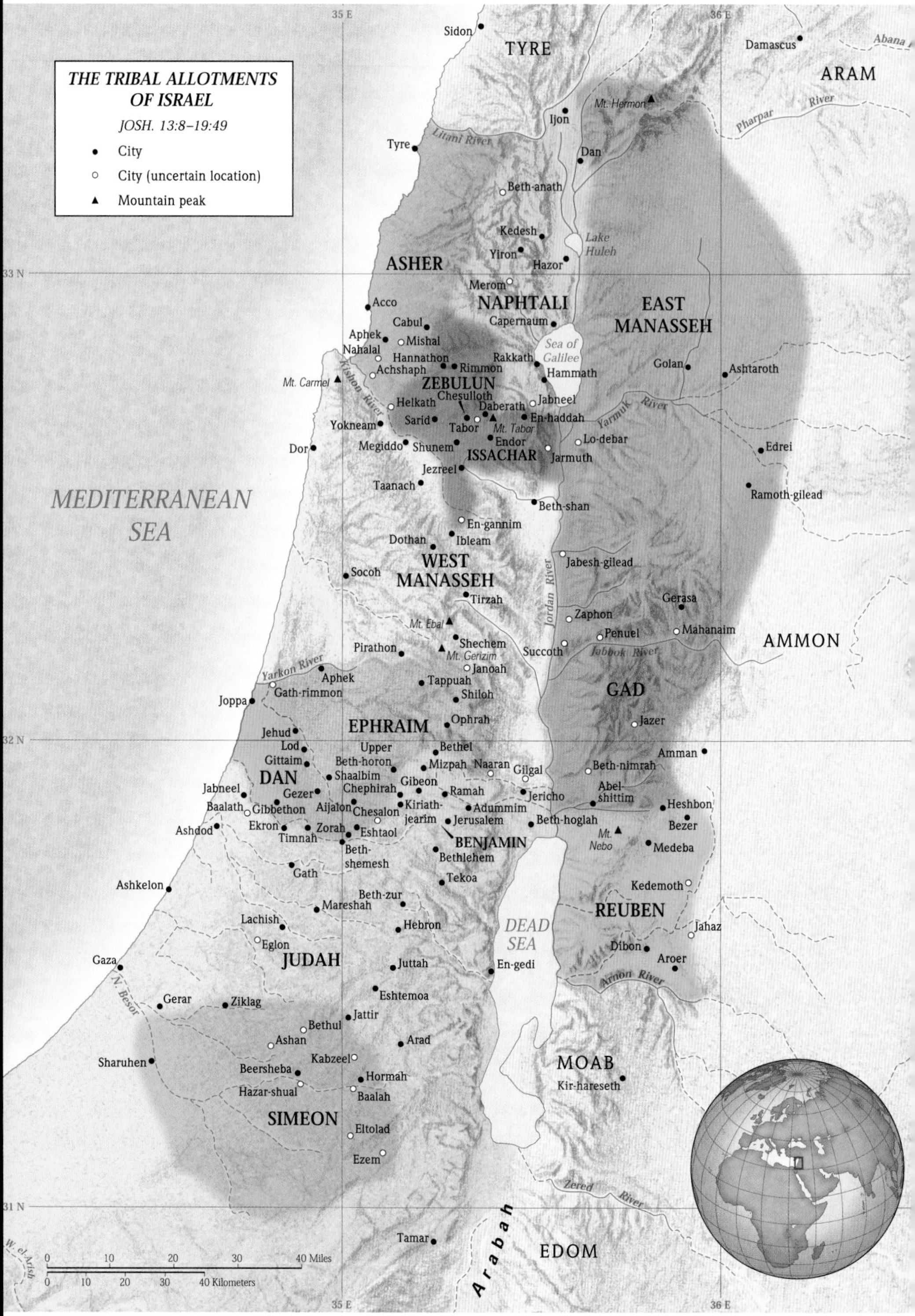

THE TRIBAL ALLOTMENTS OF ISRAEL
JOSH. 13:8–19:49

- • City
- ○ City (uncertain location)
- ▲ Mountain peak

Tribal territory of Gad.

Galatia (guh LAY shuh) Paul visited Galatia, a Roman province, on his second and third missionary journeys. This area is now known as Turkey. **Acts 18:23**

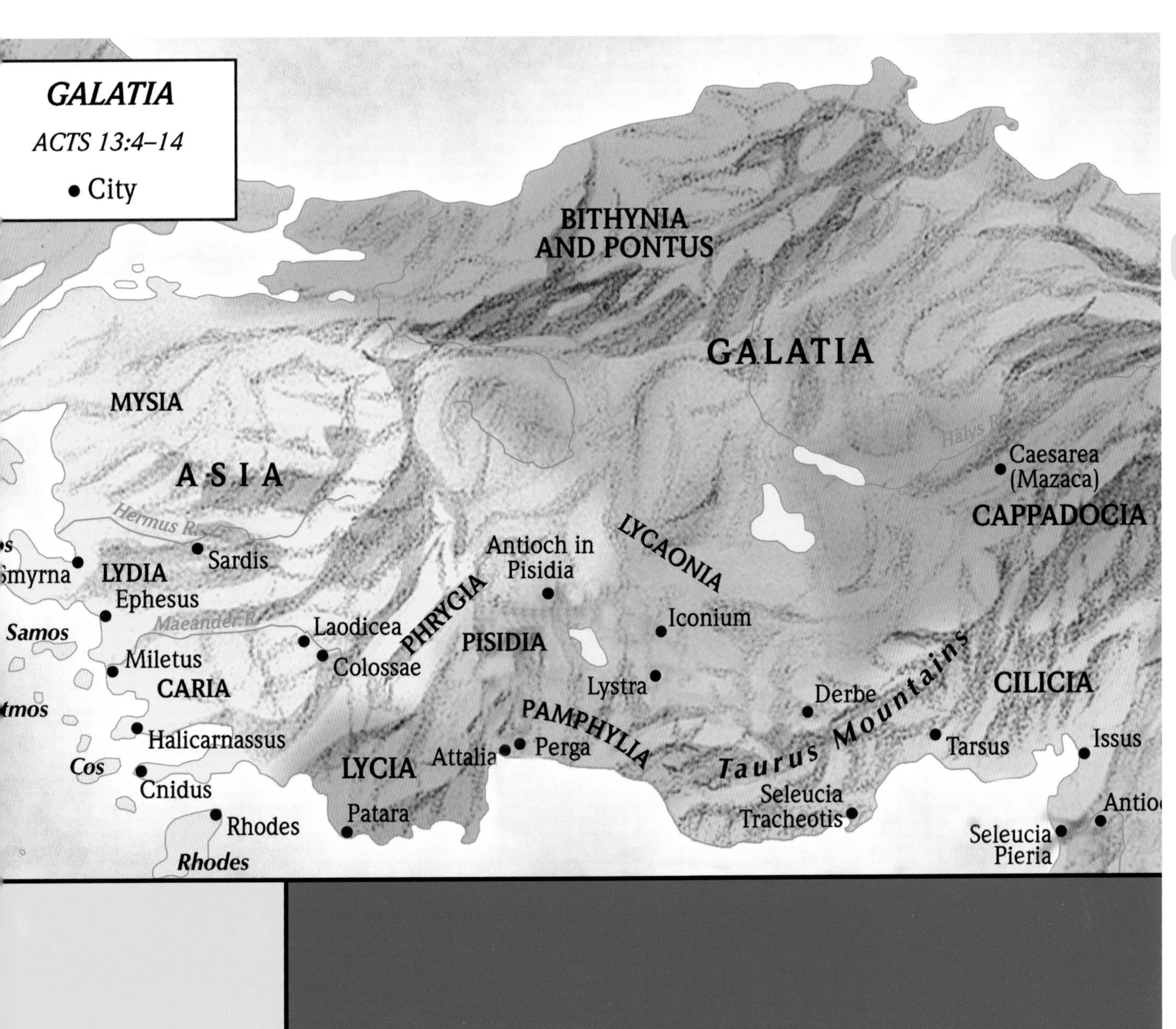

Galatians

(guh LAY shuhnz) Fourth book in Paul's Letters of the New Testament. Paul wrote to the Christians in Galatia encouraging them to turn from false teachings, reminding them that they are saved by their faith in Jesus and not by their ability to keep the law, and encouraging them to live by the Holy Spirit.
Galatians 1:6; 3:11; Galatians 5:22-25

Galilee

Galilee (GAL ih lee) Northern part of Palestine, west of the Sea of Galilee. In Jesus' time, Herod Antipas was the governor. Jesus spent much of His earthly ministry in Galilee and worked many miracles in the area. **Matthew 3:13; 4:23; Luke 2:39-40**

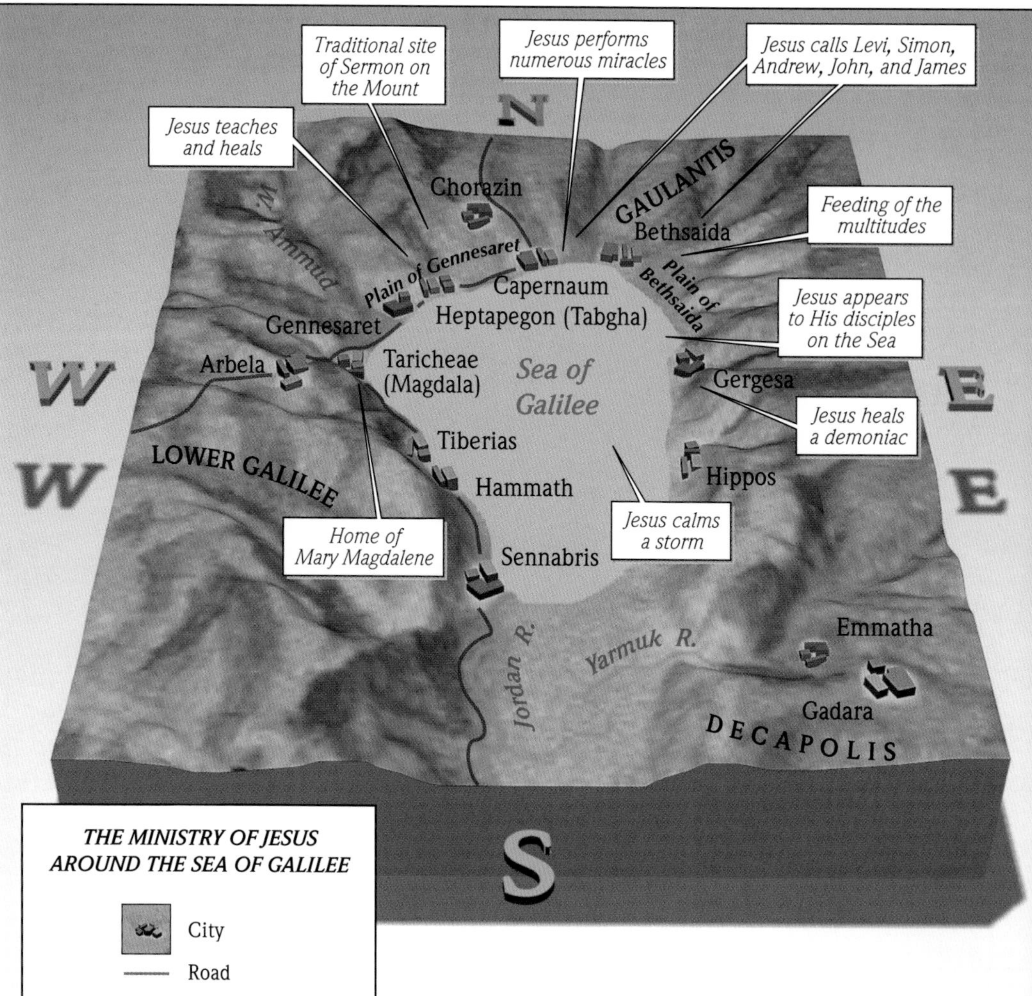

Galilee, Sea of

Galilee, Sea of Freshwater lake in hills of northern Palestine subject to sudden and violet storms. The lake is called Chinnereth in the Old Testament and Sea of Galilee, Sea of Tiberias, or Sea of Gennesaret in the New Testament. **Matthew 15:29**

The view of the Sea of Galilee from the mountains of Galilee

Gamaliel

Gamaliel (guh MAY lih uhl) Pharisee who was a member of the Sanhedrin and one of Paul's teachers. **Acts 5:34-42; Acts 22:3**

Garden Enclosed plot of ground on which flowers, vegetables, herbs, or fruit and nut trees are grown. God planted a garden in Eden. Jesus prayed in the garden of Gethsemane on the night He was arrested.
Genesis 2:8; Mark 14:32

Garrison 1. Group of soldiers stationed for the defense of a country.
2. The place where soldiers are stationed.
2 Samuel 8:5-6

Gate Door or wall that sets a boundary between that which is inside and that which is outside. In Bible time, gates provided entrance into cities and villages. Closed gates provided protection. The city of Jerusalem had many gates through which people could enter. Jesus healed a man who had been sick for 38 years near the Sheep Gate. The Sheep Gate is also known as the Lion's Gate or Stephen's gate. **John 5:2**

Zion Gate in Jerusalem

Generation
Group of people who were born and lived at about the same time. The length of a generation was different at different times in biblical history.
Exodus 1:6; Numbers 32:13

Genesis
(JEN ih siss) First book of the Bible and first book in the division of Law of the Old Testament. Written by Moses. Genesis 1—11:9 describes the creation of all things by the mighty acts of God and tells how people chose to sin against God. Genesis 11:10—50:26 describes the beginnings of the chosen people of God through Abraham, Isaac, Jacob, and Joseph.
Genesis 1:1; 12:1-3

Gentiles
(JEN tighl) People who are not Jews. God called Paul to preach the gospel to the Gentiles. **Acts 13:46-48**

Gentleness
One of the nine qualities seen in the fruit of the Spirit. Gentle persons are strong and kind at the same time. They consider the needs and feelings of others. **Galatians 5:22-23**

Gennesaret, Sea of (gih NESS uh ret) Also known as Sea of Galilee or Sea of Tiberias. Jesus calmed a storm on this lake, and with Jesus' help, Peter walked on water on this lake.
Luke 5:1

Waves pounding in on a stormy day on Gennesaret. Some of Jesus' miracles revolved around stormy weather on this relatively small lake.

Gethsemane
(geth SEM uh nih) Name means "olive press." Where Jesus went after the last supper; a garden outside the city on the Mount of Olives. **Matthew 26:36**

2,000 year old olive tree in the garden of Gethsemane Jerusalem Israel

Gideon
(GID ih uhn) Judge in Israel for 40 years. He saved the Israelites from the Midianites with 100 men armed with trumpets and torches covered by pitchers. **Judges 7:15-23**

The Harod Spring at Ainharod at the foot of the Gilboa Mountain Range. This is where Gideon determined which soldiers would go to battle against the Midianites.

Gilgal
(GIL gal) Place on the eastern side of Jericho where Joshua and the Israelites camped after they crossed the Jordan River. They set up 12 stones they had taken from the river as a reminder of how the Lord had helped them. The 12 stones represented the twelve tribes of Israel. **Joshua 4:19-20**

Joshua watched as a leader from each of the twelve tribes brought up a stone.

Glean
To gather grain or produce left in a field or on a vine or tree by farm workers. Ruth gleaned in a field that belonged to Boaz when she and her mother-in-law needed food. **Ruth 2:17-18**

Woman gathering grain

Glory
A way to describe the importance and shining majesty of God and Jesus. **Exodus 40:34; Luke 9:29-32**

God
(GAHD) Creator and Lord of the universe and Redeemer of His people. God has given people His Word so they may know Him. God is all powerful, all knowing, all loving, and all wise. People believe in different gods, but there is only one true God. God is Trinity (three-in-one): Father, Son, and Holy Spirit. (See *Names of God* chart, p. 125.) **Genesis 1:1; Psalm 119:11,89,105; Isaiah 45:21b; Matthew 28:18-20; John 10:30; 14:9; 14:15-18**

Godliness
Living in ways that please God by making right choices. **1 Timothy 6:11**

Gods
Objects made of wood or stone that people worshiped instead of the one true God. **Exodus 20:3,23**

Gofer wood, Gopher wood (KJV) Material that Noah used to build the ark. **Genesis 6:14**

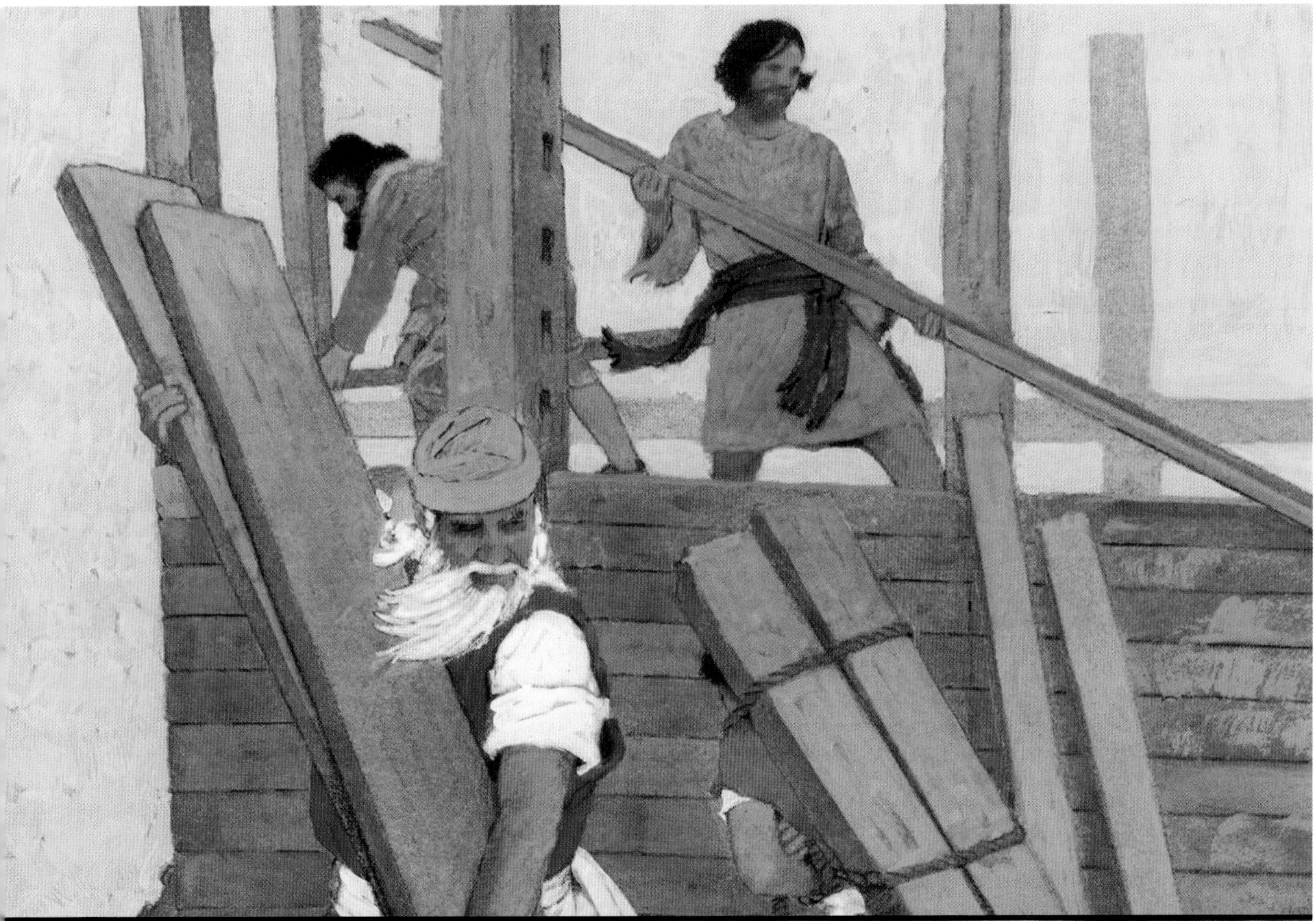

Golden Calf

Young bull created from gold by Aaron for the Hebrew people to worship. God became angry with the people for disobeying Him. **Exodus 32:1-6; Psalm 106:19-20**

Golgotha

(gahl GAHTH uh) Place where Jesus was crucified (See *Calvary; Cross / crucifixion.*) **John 19:17**

Goliath

(guh LIGH uhth) Philistine champion who was 9 feet, 9 inches tall and who challenged Saul's army in the valley of Elah. David used his slingshot and a stone to kill him (See *Champion.*) **1 Samuel 17: 1-52**

Good News

Gospel. The true story of Jesus' coming to earth to be the Savior of the world. (See *Gospel.*) **Mark 1:14**

Goodness

One of the nine qualities of the fruit of the Spirit. To give someone time, attention, or money without expecting that person to give anything back. **Galatians 5:22-23**

Gospel

(GAHS puhl) 1. Good news. The true story of Jesus' coming to earth to be the Savior of the world. Every human being will be judged according to whether they accept or reject this good news. 2. A division of the New Testament that includes Matthew, Mark, Luke, John. These four books tell the good news of God's kingdom established by the life, death, and resurrection of Jesus. **Mark 1:1**

Grace

Undeserved love given to people by God. His grace makes salvation possible through Jesus' death on the cross and resurrection from the dead. **Ephesians 1:7**

Grain

Common grains in Bible times were wheat, barley, and millet. Grains were used to make bread. Joseph stored grain for Egypt in the good years of harvest so there would be grain in the years of drought. **Genesis 41:25-49**

Greece (GREES) Country which is a peninsula between the Aegean Sea and the Adriatic Sea. Paul preached in several Greek cities: Philippi, Thessalonica, Beroea, Athens, and Corinth.
Philippians 1:1; 1 Thessalonians 1:1; Acts 17:10,16; 2 Corinthians 1:1-2

The Parthenon, a temple to the Greek goddess Athena, stands atop the acropolis in Athens.

Greed Strong desire to have more than one needs, such as money, clothes, and houses. **Luke 12:15**

Greek 1. Original language of the New Testament. 2. Person who is born in the country of Greece. Timothy's father was a Greek.
John 19:20; Acts 16:1

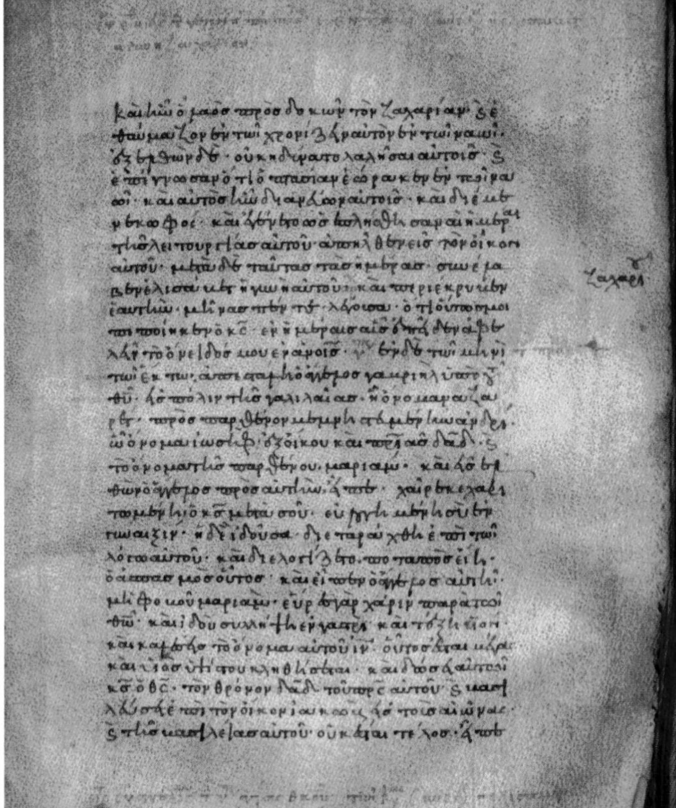

A 10th-11th century Greek manuscript of Luke's Gospel. The passage in the photo is from Luke 1:21-34.

Guard Person assigned to protect or defend a person or thing. When Jesus was buried, Roman soldiers guarded His tomb. **Matthew 27:65-66**

Guardian
Adult who is responsible for a child. Mordecai was the guardian of his cousin Esther. **Esther 2:5-7**

Guest room, Guest chamber (KJV)
Room where travelers could stay. Jesus and His disciples used a guest room for their celebration of Passover on the night Jesus was arrested. **Mark 14:14**

A guest room that is the traditional site of the last supper. This hall in Jerusalem was restored in the fourteenth century.

Guilt Bad feelings people have when they disobey God. **Psalm 38:18**

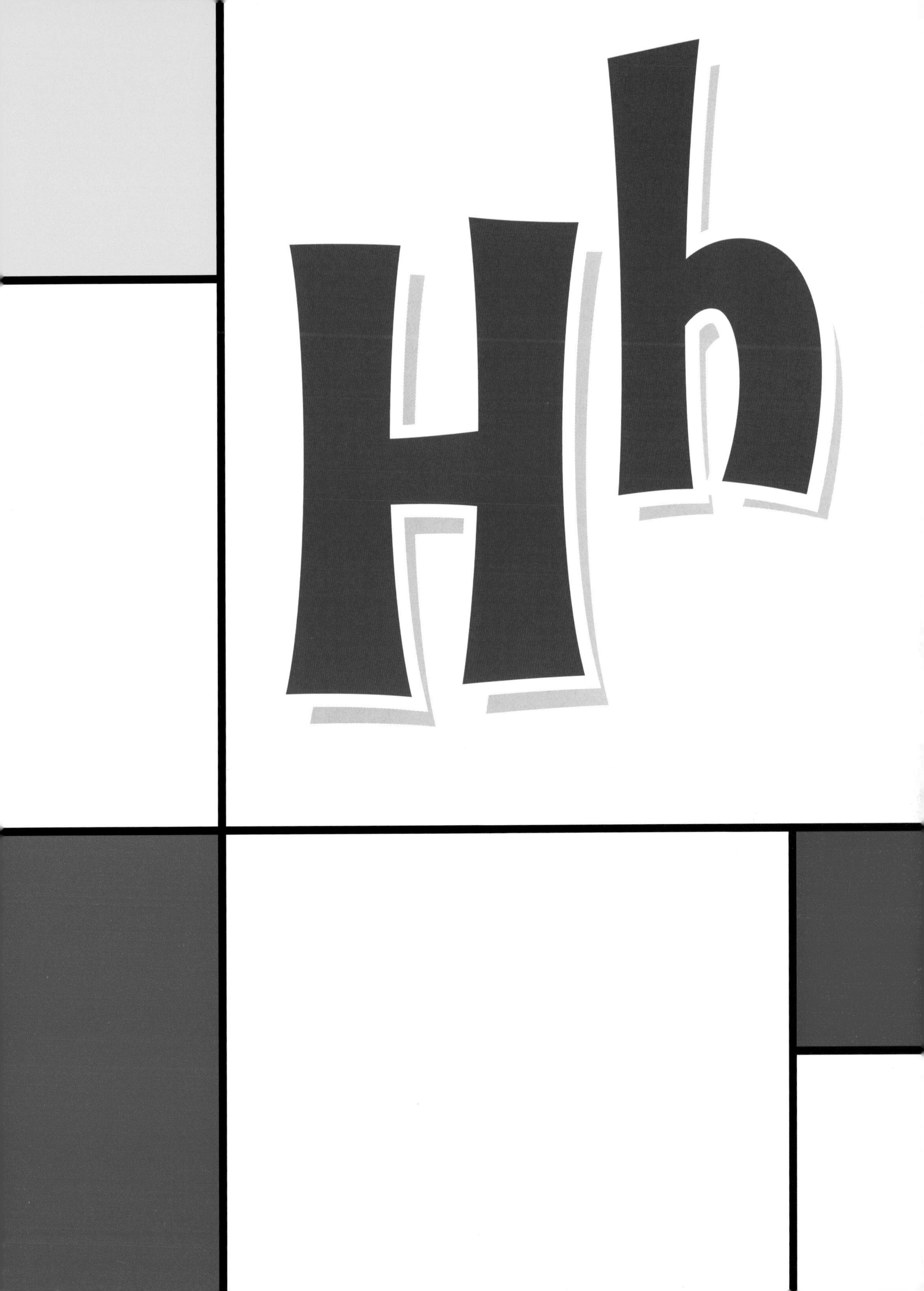
Hb

Habakkuk (huh BAK uhk) 1. Prophet who lived at the same time as Jeremiah and preached around 610 B.C. He may have been a priest of the tribe of Levi. 2. Eighth book in the division of Minor Prophets of the Old Testament. The book reports a dialogue between Habakkuk and God and closes with Habakkuk's prayer to God. Habakkuk expressed great confidence in God even when times were extremely difficult. **Habakkuk 1:1-2, 5; 3:17-19**

Hades, (HAY deez) **Hell** (KJV) Greek word for the place of the dead. In the Old Testament, this concept usually refers to the grave where the dead are buried. In the New Testament, Hades refers to a place of suffering for the wicked. (See *Hell*.) **Matthew 16:18; Luke 16:23**

Haggai (HAG igh) 1. Prophet in Israel after the people returned from exile. He encouraged the Israelites to rebuild the temple in Jerusalem. His first message was in 520 B.C. The people responded to Haggai's messages and the temple was completed March 12, 515 B.C. 2. Tenth book in the division of Minor Prophets of the Old Testament. **Haggai 1:2-5; 13-14; Ezra 6:14-15**

Hail (HAYL) Chunks of ice that fall from the sky like rain. The seventh plague God sent on the Eyptians after Pharoah refused to let the Hebrews leave Egypt. **Exodus 9:13-35**

Hallelujah, (ha luh LOO yuh) **Alleluia** (KJV) (ah luh LOO yuh) Shout of praise that means "Praise Yahweh!" Used in the Old Testament and in the Book of Revelation to give praise to God. **Psalm 106:1; Revelation 19:1**

Haman (HAY muhn) Prime minister under the Persian king Ahasuerus. He hated the Jews and put together a plan to have them all killed. He built a gallows on which to hang Mordecai the Jew because Mordecai would not bow to him. Esther, Mordecai's cousin, helped the king to know about Haman's plans. Haman was hanged on the gallows he had built for Mordecai. **Esther 3:1-11; 7:10**

Hannah (HAN uh) One of the wives of Elkanah and the mother of Samuel. She prayed, asking God to give her a son. Later she took Samuel to the tabernacle to serve with Eli the priest. **1 Samuel 1:2,20**

Hanukkah
(HAH nuh kuh) Eight-day Jewish festival that celebrates the cleansing and rededication of the temple in 164 B.C. One candle is lit each day for eight days. Also known as the Feast of Dedication. Takes place in December. Jesus was in Jerusalem once for this feast.
John 10:22-23

Heal
To make someone well. During Jesus' time on earth, He healed people of many diseases. He healed the blind, the lame, those without hearing, a woman with a crooked back, a man with a paralyzed hand, and many others.
Matthew 9:27; Mark 3:1-6; 7:31-37; Luke 13:10-13

Jesus heals a blind man.

Harvest
Time for gathering crops, such as wheat, grapes, olives, barley, flax, vegetables, and fruits. Also, a time of important religious festivals. Ruth gathered barley in the field of Boaz. (See *Seasons*.) **Ruth 1:22**

Aa Bb Cc Dd Ee Ff Gg Hh Ii Jj Kk Ll Mm Nn Oo Pp Qq Rr Ss Tt Uu Vv Ww Xx Yy Zz

Heart

1. Physical organ that works to send blood to all parts of the body. 2. In the Bible, the heart is the part of the person that makes choices, believes in God, and allows God to work through him.

Psalm 28:7; Proverbs 3:5; Matthew 22:37-38

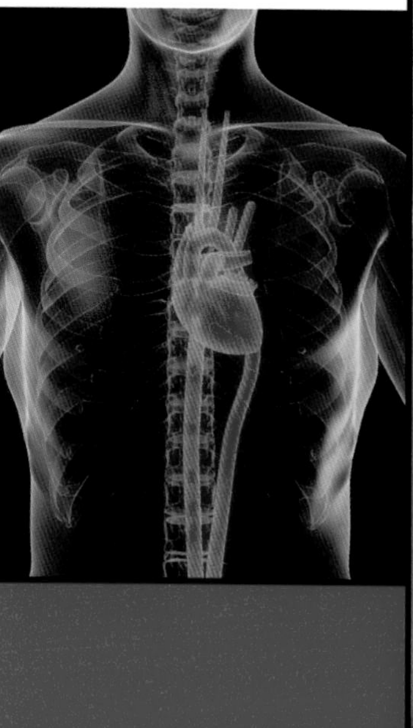

Heaven

1. Part of God's creation above the earth, including air and space. 2. Serves as a home for God and His heavenly creatures. People who accept Jesus as their Savior will live forever with Him in heaven.

Genesis 1:1; Psalm 11:4; John 14:2-3

Heavenly host

Military forces made up of God's angels, sometimes including the sun, moon, and stars, and occasionally Israel. The heavenly host appeared to the shepherds after Jesus' birth.

Luke 2:13

Hebrew (HEE broo) 1. A descendant of Eber. The first time the word is used in the Bible it describes Abram as a Hebrew. After the Babylonian exile in 586 B.C., the term *Jew* was used instead of *Hebrew*. 2. The language in which almost all of the Old Testament was written. **Genesis 11:14-27; 14:13; Exodus 7:16; Esther 3:1-4**

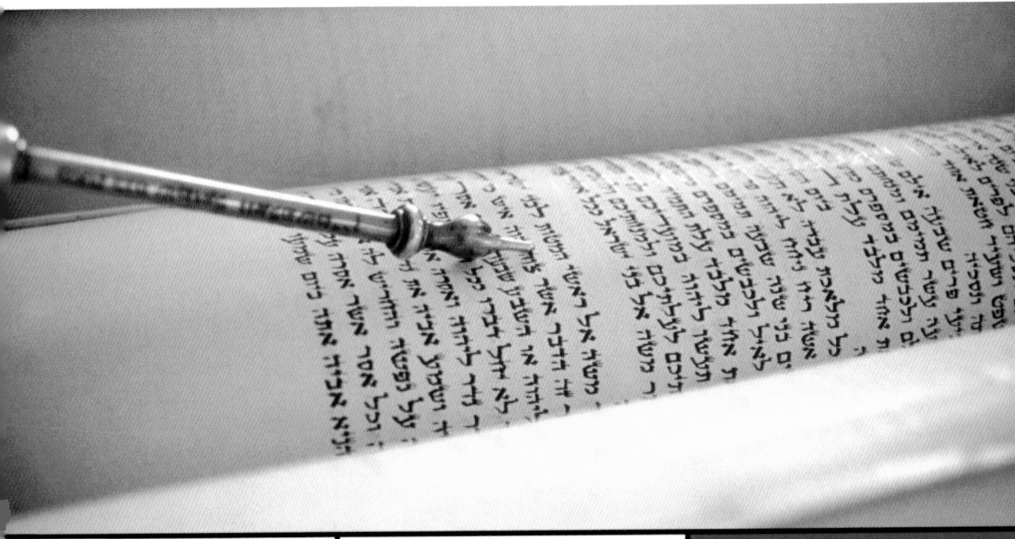

Hebrews
First book in the division of General Letters of the New Testament. The writer wanted people to know that the God of the Old Testament had spoken recently through Jesus, His Son. Hebrews strongly declares the superiority of God's Son over angels, the law, and the covenant God made through Moses. **Hebrews 1:1-4**

Hell
Place where people who reject Jesus go when they die. **Matthew 10:28**

Helmet
Covering made of leather or metal to protect the head during battle. Saul and Goliath wore helmets. During the time of King Uzziah the entire army of Judah wore helmets. Helmets had different designs which helped commanders to recognize one unit from another. This also enabled soldiers to be able determine who was a friend and who was an enemy. Paul used the helmet as a picture of spiritual protection. **1 Samuel 17:5, 38; 2 Chronicles 26:14; Ephesians 6:17; 1 Thessalonians 5:8**

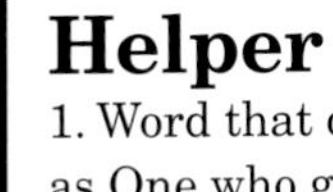

Helper
1. Word that describes God as One who gives assistance and encouragement. The Holy Spirit is described as a Counselor which means Helper. 2. Person who gives assistance to another. **Genesis 2:20; Psalm 46:1; John 14:16-18; 15:26; 16:7**

Herbs
(URBZ or HURBZ) Plants used to add flavor to food. During Passover, the people of Israel eat bitter herbs to remind them of their time of slavery in Egypt. **Exodus 12:8**

Seder plate. One of the items on the Seder plate is bitter herbs call maror. This may be root of horse radish or prepared horseradish. This part of the meal reminds the participants of the bitterness of slavery in Egypt.

Herd (HURD) Group of animals (sheep, cattle, and goats) kept by people to use for food and labor. **Matthew 8:30**

Herod (HEHR uhd) Name given to the family that was ruling Palestine during the first century. Herod the Great was the ruler of Judea when Jesus was born. **Matthew 2:1**

Herodians (hih ROH dih uhnz) Members of a Jewish group that supported Herod Antipas, ruler of Galilee during the time of Jesus' ministry on earth. They were opposed to Jesus. **Matthew 22:15-22; Mark 3:6**

Heresy (HEHR ih see) Opinion or teaching that is not true according to the Bible. **Colossians 2:4**

Hezekiah (HEZ ih kigh uh) King of Judah who fortified the city of Jerusalem and organized an army. He constructed a tunnel through solid rock from the spring of Gihon to the Siloam pool to provide water for the city in time of war. Hezekiah believed in and obeyed God. **2 Kings 18:1-5**

Hezekiah's Tunnel

High priest Priest in charge of the tabernacle or temple worship. Moses' brother, Aaron, was the first high priest. Caiaphas was the high priest when Jesus was crucified. **Exodus 40:12-14; John 18:12-14,19-24**

Hilkiah (hil KIGH uh) High priest who helped Josiah when he wanted to repair the temple. Hilkiah found the book of the Law in the temple. **2 Kings 22:3-13**

Hilkiah shows King Josiah the book of the Law.

Hittites (HIT tightz) One of the groups of people who lived in Canaan. Originally, they lived in a place that is present-day Turkey. They came to Canaan about 1200 B.C. Uriah the Hittite was a soldier in David's army and husband to Bathsheba. **2 Samuel 11:3**

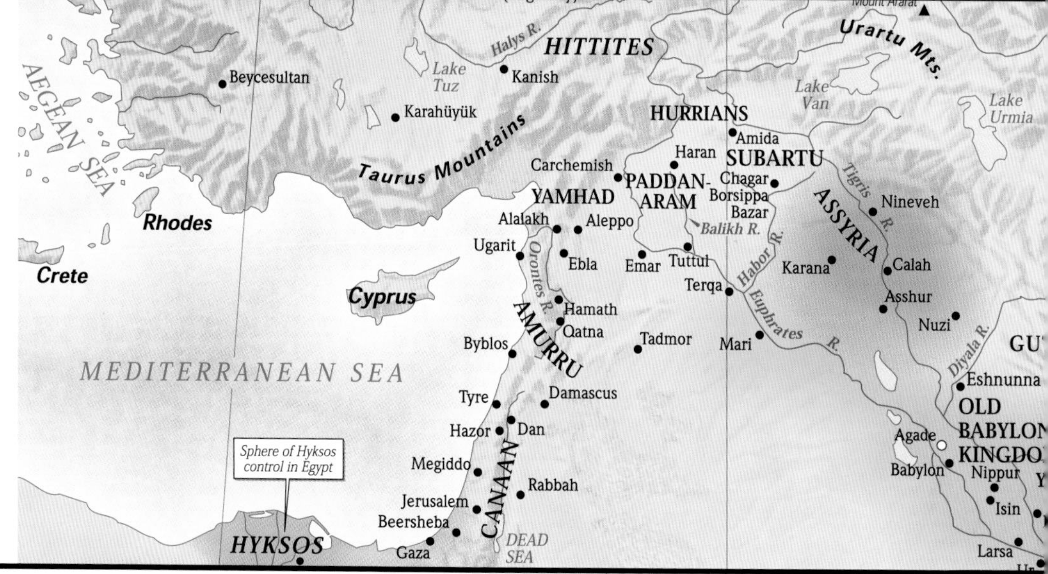

Holy Means "to be separate" and describes God's character as totally unique and separate from what He has created. God's holiness also describes His perfect goodness, purity, and righteousness. God is separated from people because they are sinful and He is holy. Jesus' death on the cross made possible a relationship between God and man. Hannah praised God as holy after the birth of Samuel. Jesus referred to God as holy when He taught His disciples how to pray.
1 Samuel 2:2; Luke 11:2

Holy Spirit, Holy Ghost (KJV) The Holy Spirit is the Spirit of God who helps people understand and accept God's plan of salvation. The Holy Spirit is the third Person of the Trinity—Father, Son, and Holy Spirit. Through the Holy Spirit, God acts to reveal His will, helps Christians tell others about Jesus, and helps them know how to live in ways that please God. The Holy Spirit comes to live within those who trust Jesus as Savior and Lord.
John 14:25-26

Homage (AH mij) To show special honor and respect. Samuel knelt in homage before King Saul. Bowing is another way people paid homage in Bible times. Joseph brothers bowed before him. **Genesis 50:15-21; 1 Samuel 24:8**

Holy of Holies Inner part of the tabernacle or temple. Separated from the other parts of the tabernacle or temple by a thick curtain, the holy of holies contained the Ark of the Covenant. In the tabernacle and in Solomon's temple, God's presence dwelled above the cherubim on the ark. **Exodus 25:10-32; 26:33-34**

Cut-away view of Solomon's temple at Jerusalem showing the porch, the holy place, and the holy of holies where the two giant cherubim and the Ark of the Covenant were placed.

Honor
(AH nuhr) To show respect to God and to people.
Exodus 20:12; Psalm 105:3

Horeb (HOH reb) Another name for Mount Sinai where God spoke to Moses through the burning bush and where God gave the Ten Commandments to Moses and the people of Israel. **Exodus 3:1-12; 19:18–20:17**

Hosanna (hoh ZAN nuh) Means "save now." The people joyfully shouted "Hosanna" to Jesus when He entered Jerusalem five days before He was crucified. **Matthew 21:14-16; Mark 11:8-10**

Hosea (hoh ZAY uh) 1. Prophet from the Northern Kingdom of Israel. God used the prophet's marriage as a symbol of His relationship with the kingdom of Israel. 2. First book of the division of Minor Prophets in the Old Testament. The book tells of God's love for the sinful people of Israel. **Hosea 1:1-2**

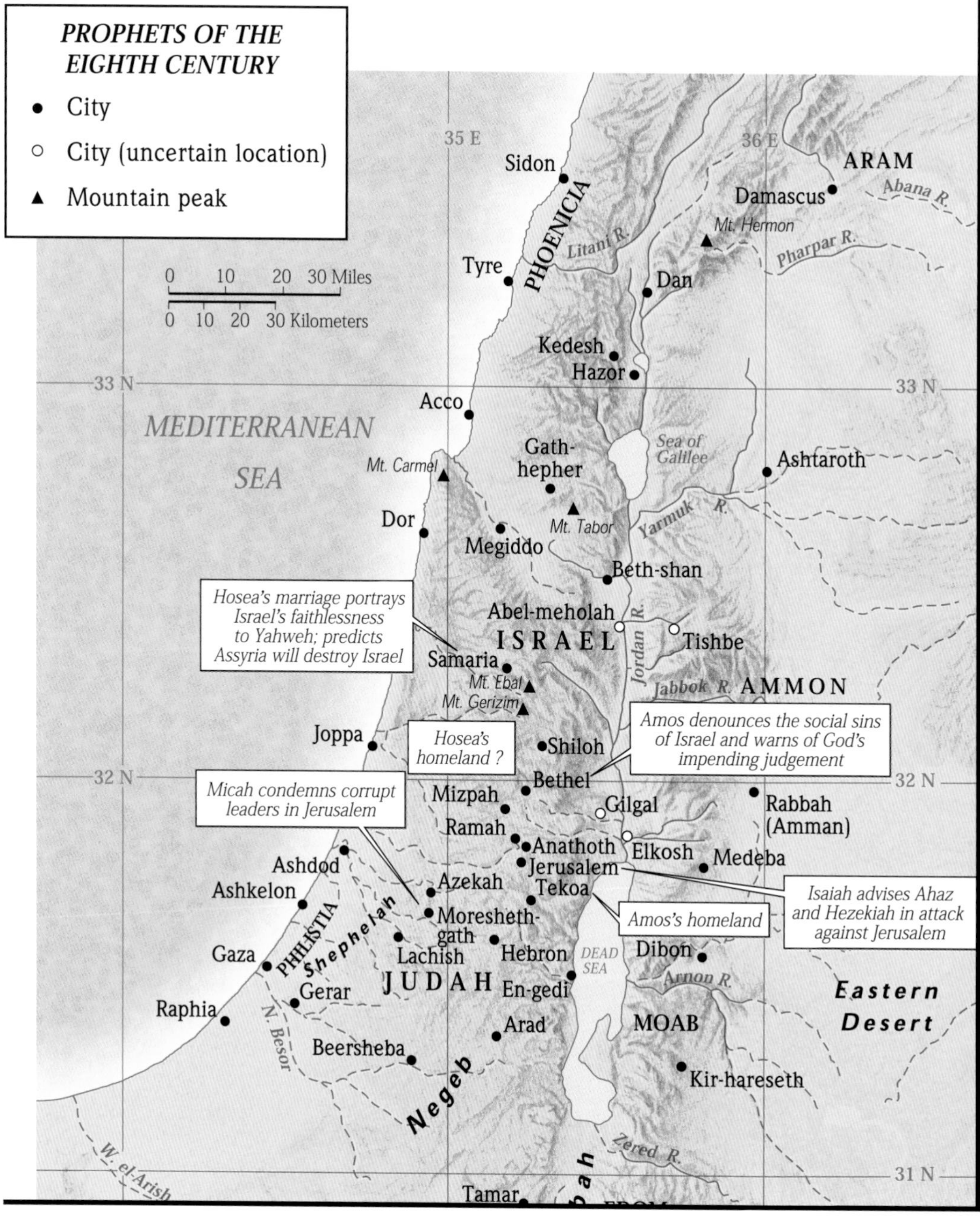

PROPHETS OF THE EIGHTH CENTURY

- ● City
- ○ City (uncertain location)
- ▲ Mountain peak

Hosea's marriage portrays Israel's faithlessness to Yahweh; predicts Assyria will destroy Israel

Hosea's homeland ?

Micah condemns corrupt leaders in Jerusalem

Amos denounces the social sins of Israel and warns of God's impending judgement

Amos's homeland

Isaiah advises Ahaz and Hezekiah in attack against Jerusalem

Hospitality (hahs pih TA lih tee) To entertain or receive a stranger or visitor into one's home as an honored guest and to provide the guest with food, shelter, and protection. **Romans 12:13**

Humility (hyoo MIH lih tee) Attitude of submission to God and gentleness toward other people. Because everyone is important to God, the humble person is willing to help other people and to make them feel important. **Philippians 2:3**

Husband A man who is married to a woman. Joseph was the husband of Mary. **Matthew 1:19**

Hymn Song of praise to God. **Ephesians 5:19**

Hypocrisy (hih PAH krih see) People who say they love God but whose words do not match their actions. **Matthew 23:28**

Hyssop (HISS uhp) Small, bushy plant. Stalks of hyssop have small white flowers in bunches. Used as a "brush" to wipe the door posts of Israelite homes with the blood of the Passover lambs. A branch of hyssop held the sponge used to offer vinegar to Jesus at His crucifixion. **Exodus 12:22; John 19:29**

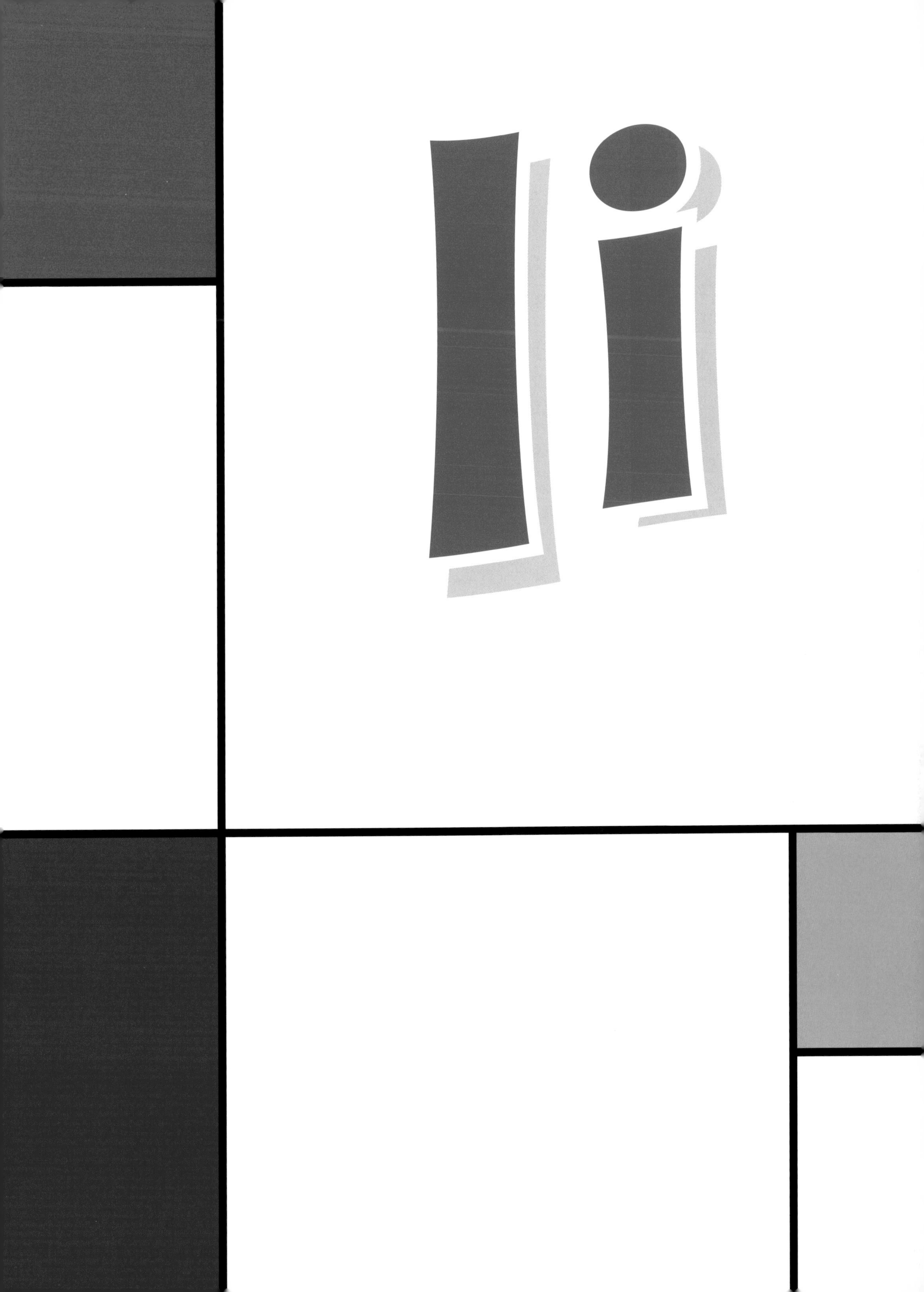

Iconium
(igh KOH nih uhm) City of Asia Minor that Barnabas and Paul visited during their first missionary journey. Paul endured sufferings and persecution at Iconium. **Acts 13:51; 2 Timothy 3:11**

Idol
(IGH duhl) Object that people worshiped instead of the one true God. Some idols were in the shapes of people, animals, or other beings. Other words in the Bible to describe idols are "image" and "statue." **Exodus 20:4-6; 32:1-8; Daniel 3:1-7**

Idolaters,
(igh DAHL eh tuhrz)
Heathen (KJV)
People who worshiped idols. **Matthew 6:7**

Idolatry
(igh DAHL eh tree) The worship of idols. **1 Corinthians 10:14**

Immanuel
(ih MAN yoo el) Means "God with us." Name of the son that Isaiah said would be born during Isaiah's lifetime. Later, Jesus was the complete fulfillment of Isaiah's prophecy. *Immanuel* is another name for Jesus. (See *Names of Jesus* chart on p. 125.) **Isaiah 7:14; Matthew 1:22-23**

Incarnation
(IN kahr NAY shuhn) Refers to God's revealing Himself as a human. Jesus, God's Son, was born in Bethlehem and lived on earth for over 30 years. Only Jesus has ever been fully God and fully man at the same time. **John 1:1-18**

Incense
(IN sens) Smoke produced by the burning of sweet-smelling spices along with the offering of sacrifices. Incense used in worship had to be prepared carefully according to strict guidelines. Zechariah was burning incense in the temple when he was visited by the angel Gabriel. **Exodus 25:6; 37:29; Exodus 30:7-8,34-35; Luke 1:8-20**

Inheritance
(in HER ih tuhns) To receive property or money as a free gift from one's father. God gave the Israelites the promised land as an inheritance. In one of Jesus' parables, the younger son asked for and received his part of the inheritance from his father. **Joshua 1:1-6; Luke 15:11-32**

Inn
Stopping place for travelers. A first century inn had a walled-in area with a well. A larger inn might have had small rooms surrounding the courtyard. People and animals stayed together. Jesus was born in a stable because the inn was full. The good Samaritan took the hurt man to an inn. **Luke 2:7; 10:30-35**

One of the traditional sites of The Inn of the Good Samaritan near Jericho. The large shed with a courtyard in the back is built on a ancient foundation.

Innkeeper
Host or hostess at an inn. The innkeeper in the story of the good Samaritan provided food and medical care. **Luke 10:30-35**

Insect
(See *Insects of the Bible* on p. 87-88.)

Inspired
Word that describes how the Bible differs from all other writings. Although the Bible has many writers, God is the Author of the 66 books that make up the Bible. He chose each of the human writers and guided their writing with the result that these writings are true and can be fully trusted. **2 Timothy 3:16; 2 Peter 1:20-21**

Intercession
(IN tuhr SEH shuhn) To pray to God for other people. Moses interceded for the Israelites, asking God to forgive them for making and worshiping a golden calf. Paul told Timothy to intercede for everyone. **Exodus 32:11-14; 1 Timothy 2:1**

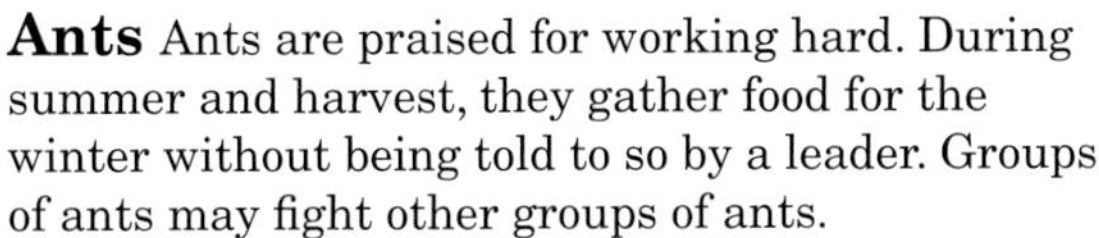

Ants Ants are praised for working hard. During summer and harvest, they gather food for the winter without being told to so by a leader. Groups of ants may fight other groups of ants. **Proverbs 6:6-8; 30:24-25**

Bees Armies are described as swarming bees. Samson's riddle mentions bees making honey. **Deuteronomy 1:44; Judges 14:5-9; Psalm 118:12**

Fleas Small, wingless insects that bite and feed on people and animals. David compared himself to a flea. **1 Samuel 24:12-14; 26:20**

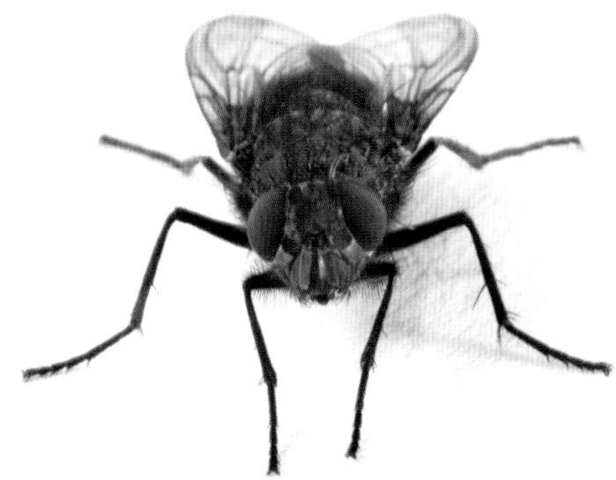

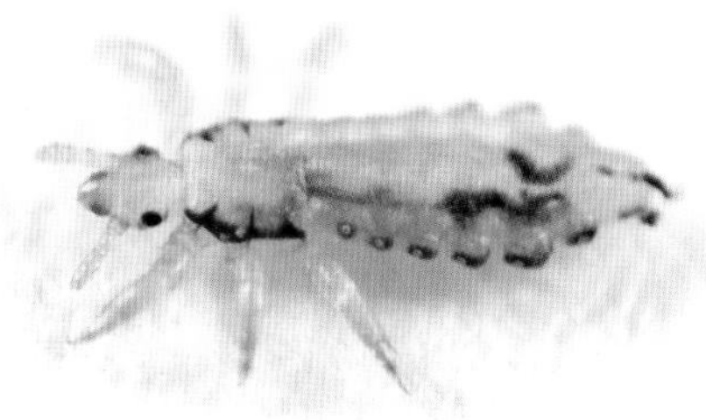

Flies Flying insects that are pests to people. God sent Egypt a plague of insects that are some translations call "flies." This was the fourth plague. **Exodus 8:21-24**

Gnats, Lice (KJV) Tiny insects that fly and may leave bites that sting and burn. Sometimes a million gnats may fly in a swarm.The third plague God sent the Egyptians. **Exodus 8:16-18**

INSECTS OF THE BIBLE

Grasshoppers Can fly 15 miles per hour and may be found at sea 1,200 miles from land. May be eaten by people. **Leviticus 11:22**

Locusts Similar to the grasshopper. As the swarm of locusts moves across the land, it devours all the plants. The eighth plague God sent the Egyptians to eat plants that survived the plague of hail He had sent. The Bible gives people permission to eat locusts. John the Baptist ate locusts. **Exodus 10:4-5; Leviticus 11:22; Proverbs 30:27; Matthew 3:4**

Moths Born as caterpillars, they later become moths. Moths fly at night and may destroy things, such as clothes and some crops. **Matthew 6:19-20**

Wasps/Hornets Stinging insects that God used to drive Israel's enemies out of Cannan. **Exodus 23:28**

Worms There are different kinds of worms in the Bible. Some worms produce a scarlet (dark red) dye. Herod died from worms. **Exodus 25:4; Acts 12:23**

Isaac

(IGH zik) Means "laughter." One of the patriarchs of Israel, Isaac was the only son of Abraham and Sarah. Abraham was 100 years old and Sarah was 90 when Isaac was born. Isaac and his wife Rebekah had twin sons, Esau and Jacob. **Genesis 21:1-5; 25:20-26; Exodus 3:6**

Ishmael

(ISH may el) Means "God hears." Son of Abraham by Hagar, Sarah's slave. **Genesis 16:11**

Abraham and Sarah hold their infant son Isaac.

Israel

(IZ ray el) 1. Means "God strives," "God rules," "God heals," or "he strives against God." God gave Jacob this new name. 2. Name of the Northern Kingdom after Jeroboam led the northern tribes to separate from the southern tribes and form a separate kingdom. **Genesis 32:28; 1 Kings 12**

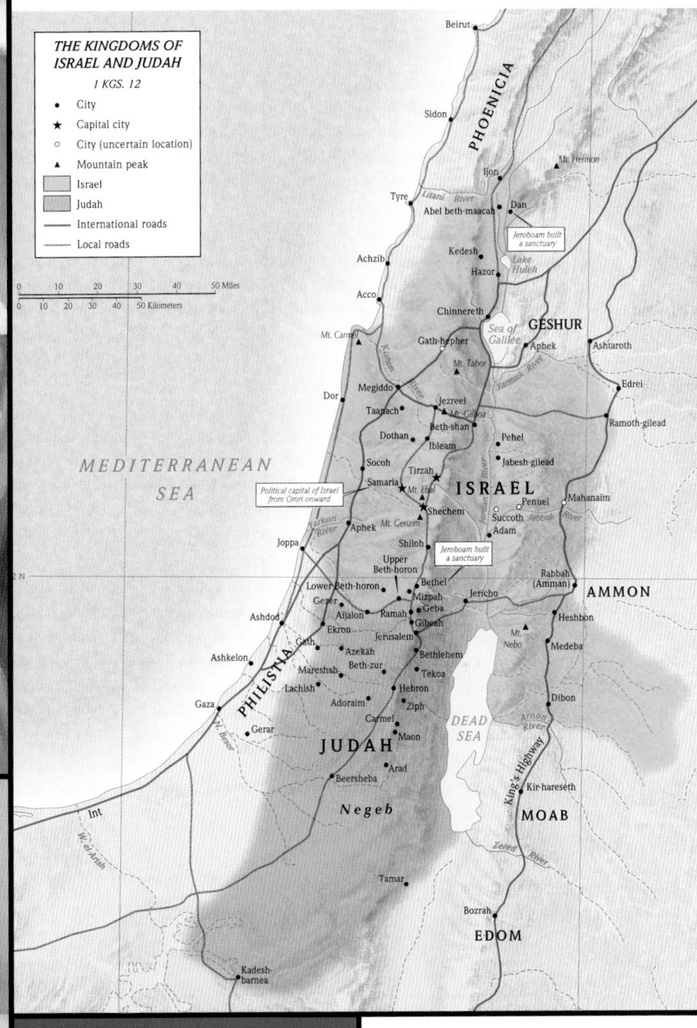

Isaiah

(igh ZAY uh) 1. Means "Yahweh saves." Isaiah was a prophet to the Southern Kingdom of Judah. 2. First book of the division of Major Prophets of the Old Testament. Includes prophecy about the Messiah. After publicly reading from the book of Isaiah, Jesus told His hearers that He was the One those Scriptures referred to. **Isaiah 9:6-7; 61:1-2; Luke 4:16-21**

Jesus read the Scripture in the synagogue.

Israelites

(IZ ray uh ightz) People who were citizens of Israel, even when in exile. **Exodus 3:9**

Issachar

(ISS uh KAHR) Ninth son of Jacob by his wife Leah. He was the ancestor of the tribe of Issachar, one of the twelve tribes of Israel. **Genesis 30:18**

Italy

(IT uh lih) Boot-shaped peninsula between Greece and Spain. Extends from the Alps on the north to the Mediterranean Sea on the south. Tentmakers and future church leaders Aquila and Priscilla met Paul after they moved to Corinth from Italy. Paul was shipwrecked on his way to Italy as a prisoner. **Acts 18:2; 27:1-44**

Ivory

(IGHV ree) Means "tooth," because it comes from elephant tusks. Ivory was used for decoration on thrones, beds, houses, and the decks of ships. Boxes, gaming boards, figurines, spoons, and combs were sometimes were made of ivory. **1 Kings 10:18**

Ivory comb from ancient Egypt

Jj

Jabin

(JAY bin) Means "he understands." Leader of northern groups of kings who attacked Joshua at the waters of Merom. **Joshua 11:1-8**

Jacob (JAY kuhb)

Means "he grasps the heel" or "he cheats." Isaac and Rebekah's younger twin son. Cheated his twin brother Esau out of his birthright and his father's blessing. Father of the twelve ancestors of the twelve tribes of Israel. God changed his name to "Israel."
Genesis 25:24-26; 27:36; Genesis 32:28; 46:8-27; Exodus 1:1-5

Rebekah and Jacob plot to cheat Esau of his blessing.

Jacob's Well

Place in Samaria where Jesus stopped to rest as He traveled from Judea to Galilee. There He met and talked with a Samaritan woman and helped her know He is God's Son.
John 4:3-8

Traditional site of Jacob's well in the city of Sychar

Jailer

One who manages a jail and keeps prisoners from escaping. In Philippi, Paul and Silas were placed in a Roman jail. After an earthquake opened the doors of the jail, the jailer asked Paul what he needed to do to be saved. **Acts 16:25-34**

Paul told the Philippian jailer, "Believe on the Lord Jesus, and you will be saved—you and your household." **Acts 16:31**

James

(JAYMZ) 1. James, the son of Zebedee and brother of John, was one of Jesus' twelve apostles. Jesus called James and John "sons of thunder."

2. James, the son of Alphaeus, was also one of Jesus' twelve apostles.

3. James, the half brother of Jesus, at first did not believe in Jesus as God's Son. Later he did believe. After Jesus' resurrection and ascension, James became a church leader in Jerusalem.

4. Second book in the General Letters division of the New Testament. Written by James, the half brother of Jesus, the letter explains how God wants Christians to live. **Matthew 4:21-22; 10:3; 13:55; James 1:22-25**

Jeremiah

(JER ih MIGH uh) 1. A prophet in Judah during the reign of many kings from about 627 to 586 B.C. God called him to be a prophet when he was a young man and told him that even before he was born, God had a plan for his life. He preached about the coming judgment of God on the nation because the people had disobeyed God. God told him to take a scroll and write all the words He commanded. Jeremiah dictated the words to Baruch, who wrote them on a scroll. Later the king cut the scroll in pieces and put them in the fire. Jeremiah dictated a second scroll to replace the one that was burned. His enemies had him thrown into a cistern and later locked up in the courtyard of the guards.

2. The second book in the Major Prophets division of the Old Testament, written by the prophet Jeremiah. He called on the people of Judah to turn away from their idol worship and other sins. When Jerusalem was destroyed by the Babylonians in 586 B.C., Jeremiah moved to Mizpah. Later, he was deported to Egypt against his will. **Jeremiah 1:1-10; 36:1-32; 52:28**

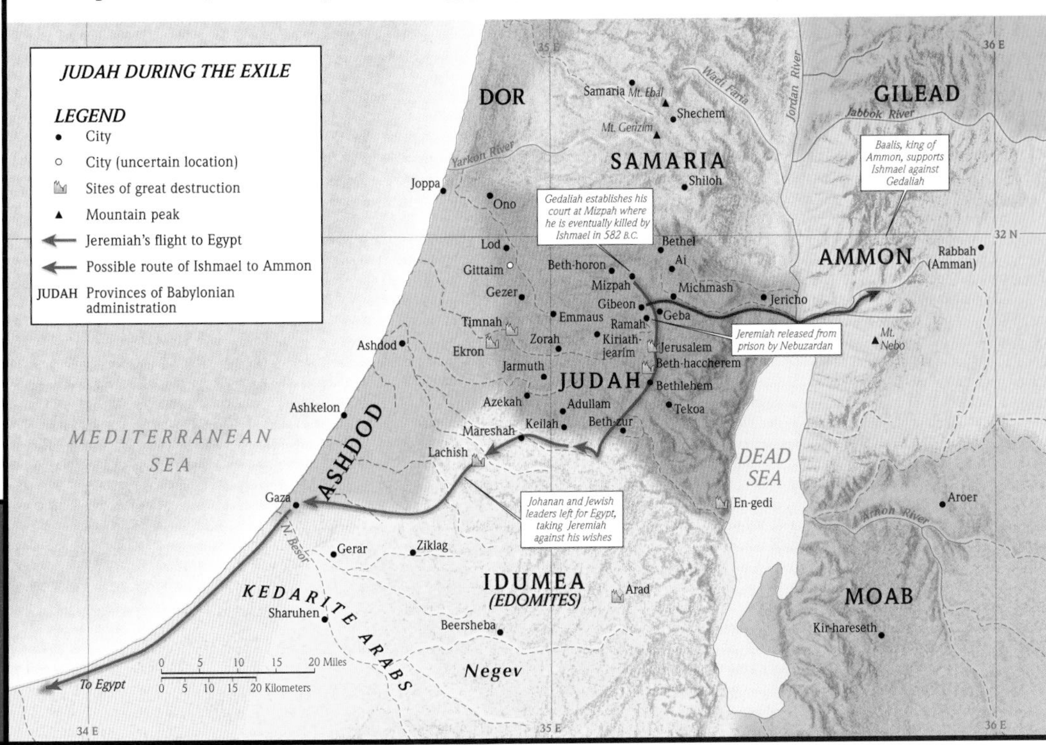

Jealous

1. Since God is the one true God and demands complete obedience, He is sometimes referred to as a jealous God. God requires that people worship only Him and no other gods.

2. To want something that someone else has. Joseph's brothers were jealous of him. **Genesis 37:11; Exodus 20:5**

Jehovah

(KJV) (jeh HOH vuh) English word for *Yahweh*, the Hebrew name for God. **Genesis 22:14**

Jericho

(JER ih koh) One of the oldest cities in the world (9000 B.C.) and known as the "city of palms." The combination of rich soil, abundant spring water, and constant sunshine made Jericho an attractive place for settlement. When God was ready for the people of Israel to enter Canaan, He told Joshua to lead his army around the city once a day for six days. On the seventh day they were to march around the city seven times. When they obeyed God, the walls of Jericho would fall. Joshua and the people obeyed, and Jericho was the first city conquered by Israel in the promised land. Herod the Great built New Testament Jericho a mile and a half south of the location of the ancient city. Jericho was the home of Zacchaeus, the tax collector whose life was changed by Jesus. **Joshua 6:1-21; Luke 19:1-10**

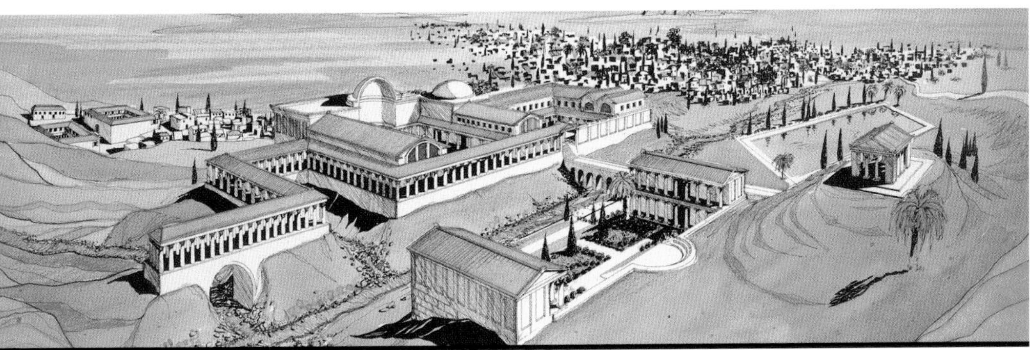

Jerusalem (jih ROO suh lem) City set high on a plateau in the hills of Judah, considered sacred by Judaism, Christianity, and Islam. Besides the name "Jerusalem," the city is also called "the City of David" and "Zion." David brought the ark of the covenant into Jerusalem and made the city the capital of Israel. Jerusalem came to be known as "the city of our God," "the city of the great King."

Under Solomon, the temple was constructed in Jerusalem. Since the people abandoned God, He eventually abandoned His chosen city to the Babylonians in 586 B.C. About 70 years later, the Persian king Cyrus allowed many exiles to return and rebuild the city and the temple. Jerusalem was important in Jesus' life. It was there that Joseph and Mary presented Him to the Lord when He was 8 days old. When He was 12 years old, He went to Jerusalem with His parents. There He talked with the teachers of the Law and amazed them with His understanding. As an adult, Jesus taught many times in Jerusalem. It was there that He was crucified and raised from death. The church began in Jerusalem only a few weeks after Jesus' resurrection. It was there that the Holy Spirit came on His followers, giving them the wisdom and power to take His message to the nations. **2 Samuel 5:6-7; Jeremiah 52:12-13; Luke 2:41-50; Acts 2:1-13**

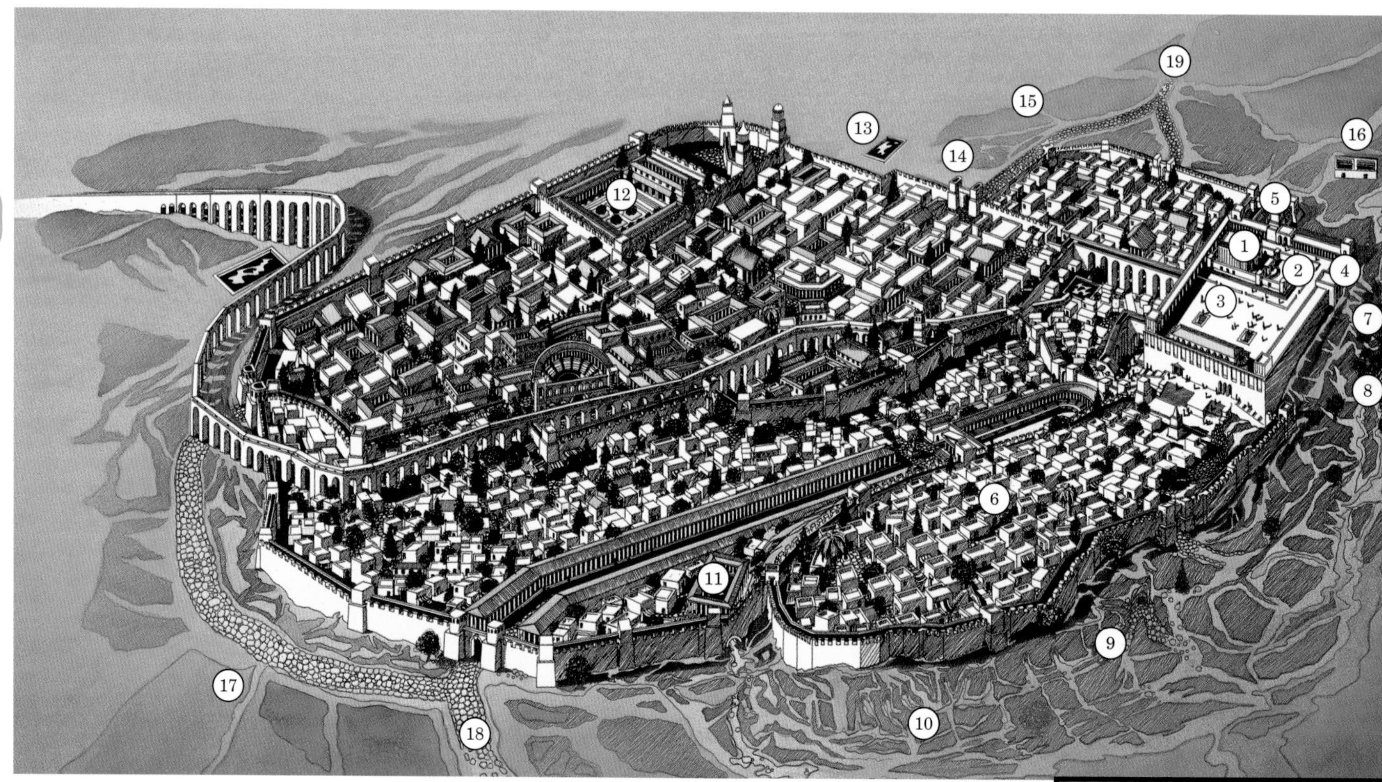

1. The temple (Herod's temple)
2. Women's court
3. Court of the Gentiles
4. Eastern Gate (Golden Gate)
5. Antonia Fortress
6. City of David
7. Garden of Gethsemane
8. Mount of Olives
9. Kidron Valley
10. Gihon Spring
11. Pool of Siloam
12. Herod's Palace
13. Sheep Pool
14. Traditional Golgotha
15. Traditional tomb of Jesus
16. Pool of Bethesda
17. Hinnon Valley
18. Road to the Dead Sea
19. Road to Samaria

Jesse (JESS ih) Father of David the king. He lived in Bethlehem and was the son of Obed and the grandson of Boaz and Ruth. Isaiah listed Jesse as an ancestor of Jesus. **Ruth 4:21-22; 1 Samuel 16:1; Isaiah 11:1**

Jesus Christ Jesus' proper name comes from the Hebrew "Joshua," meaning "Yahweh saves" or "salvation is from Yahweh." Christ is the Greek term for "anointed." (See *Messiah.*)

Jesus was fully human and fully God at the same time. He was not part human and part God. Though really human, Jesus differed from all other people in two ways. First, He was born to a virgin; He had no human father. (See *Virgin.*) Second, unlike any other person, Jesus was without sin.

Jesus was also fully God. He is the second person of the Trinity: Father, Son, and Holy Spirit. Jesus performed actions that people cannot do. He forgave sins. He had complete power over nature as when He calmed the storm on the Sea of Galilee, twice fed groups of thousands by multiplying a few loaves of bread and fishes, and walked on water. He healed all kinds of diseases—physical, mental, emotional, and spiritual. He raised the dead to life.

Even though Jesus was fully God and fully man, He gave Himself as a sacrifice for sin by dying on a Roman cross. On the third day, God the Father raised Jesus from death by the power of the Holy Spirit.

Jesus' purpose was to seek and to save the lost. He came to bring eternal and meaningful life to those who were dying both physically and spiritually.

Jesus was a master teacher. Even those who did not follow Him admitted, "No man ever spoke like this." At the close of His Sermon on the Mount, the multitudes were amazed at how He taught.

Jesus spent His three years of public ministry preparing twelve men to continue His purpose of telling people how to have eternal life. Following His resurrection, He ascended to God the Father. About seven weeks after His ascension, Jesus sent the Holy Spirit to His followers in Jerusalem. Through His Spirit within His followers, the church, Jesus has continued to carry out the purposes for which He came 2,000 years ago.

At some time in the future, Jesus, who ascended to the Father, will return to complete God's purposes in creating and redeeming His people, taking them to live with Him forever.

Matthew 1:18-25; 7:28-29; John 3:16; 7:46; 8:46; Act 1:1-11

Jethro (JETH roh) Priest of Midian and the father-in-law of Moses. He helped Moses see the need of including other men as judges and advisers to the people of Israel.
Exodus 18:1-27

Jew (JOO) Term used to refer to Israelites after the Babylonian exile. Before the exile the people were called Hebrews. Jesus was a Jew as were the twelve apostles and Paul.
(See *Hebrew.*) **John 4:9**

Jewelry
(JOO uhl rih) Rings, necklaces, and bracelets, usually made of gold, silver, and beautiful stones. As the Hebrews left Egypt, the Egyptians gave them jewelry. Later this jewelry was used to build the tabernacle.
Exodus 3:22; 35:21-22

Jezebel

(JEZ uh bel) Wife of King Ahab of Israel, she introduced the worship of Baal to the Israelites. Jezebel tried to kill all of God's prophets in Israel. She plotted to have Naboth killed when he would not sell King Ahab his land. Jezebel was killed by her own servants when Jehu overthrew Ahab's family. **1 Kings 16:29-33; 18:4; 21:4-10**

Site of Ahab's palace

Joab

(JOH ab) Oldest son of Zeruiah, the sister of David. Military commander during most of David's reign. Loyal to David, Joab successfully led David's armies. Joab killed David's son Absalom when he rebelled against his father. **2 Samuel 2:13; 18:9-15**

Job

(JOHB) 1. Wealthy man who feared God and acted in ways that pleased Him. 2. The book of Job is the first book in the division of Poetry in the Old Testament. The book tells the story of the man Job, whom God allowed the devil to test. The book explores questions about God's power, goodness, and the reality of suffering. **Job 1:1-22**

Jochebed

(JAHK uh bed) Wife of Amram and the mother of Miriam, Aaron, and Moses. When Pharaoh declared that all boy babies should be put to death, Jochebed hid her son Moses. Later she placed him in a basket, put the basket in the reeds by the bank of the Nile river, and left his sister Miriam to watch. Moses' life was saved when Pharaoh's daughter took him from the basket and made him her son. She asked Jochebed to take care of Moses while he was still a baby. **Exodus 2:1-10; 6:20**

Joel

(JOH el) 1. Prophet whose preaching ministry produced the book of Joel. 2. Second book in the division of Minor Prophets of the Old Testament. Written to the people of Judah, calling them to repent, and warning them about God's judgment. He foretold the coming of the Holy Spirit on all believers. **Joel 1:1; 2:28-29**

John

(JAHN) 1. John the Baptist was the son of Zechariah and Elizabeth. He told people about the coming of the Messiah, Jesus. John lived in the wilderness, ate locusts and wild honey, and wore camel's hair and a leather belt. John baptized Jesus in the Jordan River.

2. One of Jesus' twelve apostles. John was son of a successful fisherman, Zebedee. He and his brother James were called from their family fishing business to follow Jesus as His disciple. James and John were called "sons of thunder." John was at the cross with Jesus' mother and the other women. He is credited with writing five of the New Testament books. According to tradition, John lived to an old age in Ephesus, where he preached love and fought against false teachings. A beautiful church bearing John's name still exists in Ephesus, present day Turkey.

3. The fourth book in the Gospel division of the New Testament. John wrote about Jesus as the Son of God. Probably the most famous verse in the Bible is John 3:16.

4. John wrote three letters: 1,2, and 3 John. They are the fifth, sixth, and seventh books in the General Letters division of the New Testament.

5. Revelation, last book of the Bible and the only book of prophecy in the New Testament, was written while John was exiled on the island of Patmos, off the coast of Asia Minor.
Mark 3:17

"Standing by the cross of Jesus were His mother, His mother's sister, Mary the wife of Clopas, and Mary Magdalene. When Jesus saw His mother and the disciple He loved standing there, He said to His mother, 'Woman, here is your son.' Then He said to the disciple, 'Here is your mother.' And from that hour the disciple took her into his home" (John 19:25-27).

Jonah (JOH nuh) 1. Prophet to Nineveh, capital of the Assyrian Empire. Jonah also preached in the northern kingdom during the time of Jeroboam II. 2. Fifth book in the Minor Prophets division of the Old Testament. This book tells how God used Jonah to show that He loves all people, Gentiles as well as Jews. At first Jonah refused to obey God and preach to the people of Nineveh. Jonah tried to run from God by getting on a boat traveling to Tarshish. After being thrown into the sea, God delivered Jonah from drowning by having him swallowed by a great fish and delivered on dry land. Jonah later preached to the Ninevites but pouted when the people chose to obey God. **2 Kings 14:25 Jonah 1:1-17; 2:10; 3:1-10; 4:1-10**

Reconstructed site of ancient Joppa from where Jonah sailed as he attempted to flee from the Lord.

Jonathan (JAHN uh thuhn) Oldest son of King Saul and best friend of David. Jonathan and David promised each other to be friends for life. Jonathan warned David about his father's plot against David's life. Jonathan was killed by the Philistines in a battle at Mt. Gilboa. In later years, after David became king of Judah, he showed kindness to Jonathan's son, Mephibosheth. **1 Samuel 13:16; 18:1-4; 31:1-2; 2 Samuel 9:1-3**

Mt. Gilboa, the site where Jonathan and King Saul were killed by the Philistines

Joppa (JAHP uh) City on the Mediterranean coast, Joppa is located about 35 miles northwest of Jerusalem. In Joppa, Simon Peter was praying on the flat roof of a house when he saw in a dream what seemed to be "a large sheet being lowered to the earth by its four corners." Through this dream God showed Peter that he needed to tell the Gentiles about Jesus. **Acts 10:9-35**

Jordan River Longest and most important river of Palestine. Lot chose for himself "all the valley of the Jordan." Under the leadership of Joshua, Israel crossed the Jordan "on dry ground." Elisha instructed Naaman, commander of the army for the king of Aram, to wash in the Jordan seven times to heal his skin disease. John the Baptist baptized Jesus at the Jordan River. **Genesis 13:11; Joshua 3:15-17; 2 Kings 5:1-19; Matthew 3:13-17**

Jordan river

Joseph (JOH zif)
1. Son of Jacob by Jacob's favorite wife, Rachel. Joseph was Jacob's favorite son. Joseph had dreams that showed him ruling over his family, which made his brothers jealous of him. His brothers sold Joseph to a caravan of Ishmaelites. Joseph was taken to Egypt, where he later became second in command to the pharaoh. Later his father, Jacob, moved the rest of his family to Egypt.
2. Husband of Mary, mother of Jesus. Took Mary to his family home in Bethlehem and was with her at Jesus' birth. He probably died before Jesus began His public ministry.
3. Joseph of Arimathea was a rich member of the Sanhedrin and a secret disciple of Jesus. After the crucifixion, he requested Jesus' body from Pilate and laid it in his own unused tomb. **Genesis 37; 46:1-47:12; Matthew 1:18-25; 2:1-23; John 19:38-42**

Joseph oversees the filling of the storehouses in Egypt.

Joshua (JAHSH yoo uh) 1. After Moses died, Joshua led the Israelites to take control of the promised land. Joshua was on Mt. Sinai when Moses received the Law. He was also one of the 12 spies Moses sent to investigate Canaan. He and Caleb were the only two who returned with a positive report. 2. First book in the division of History of the Old Testament. The book is named after Joshua. The central character of the book is not Joshua but God, who fights for Israel and drives out the enemies before them. God promised that He would give Israel the land that He had pledged to their fathers. The book of Joshua shows how God fulfilled this promise. **Genesis 15:18-21; Exodus 3:8; 32:17; Numbers 14:28-30, 38**

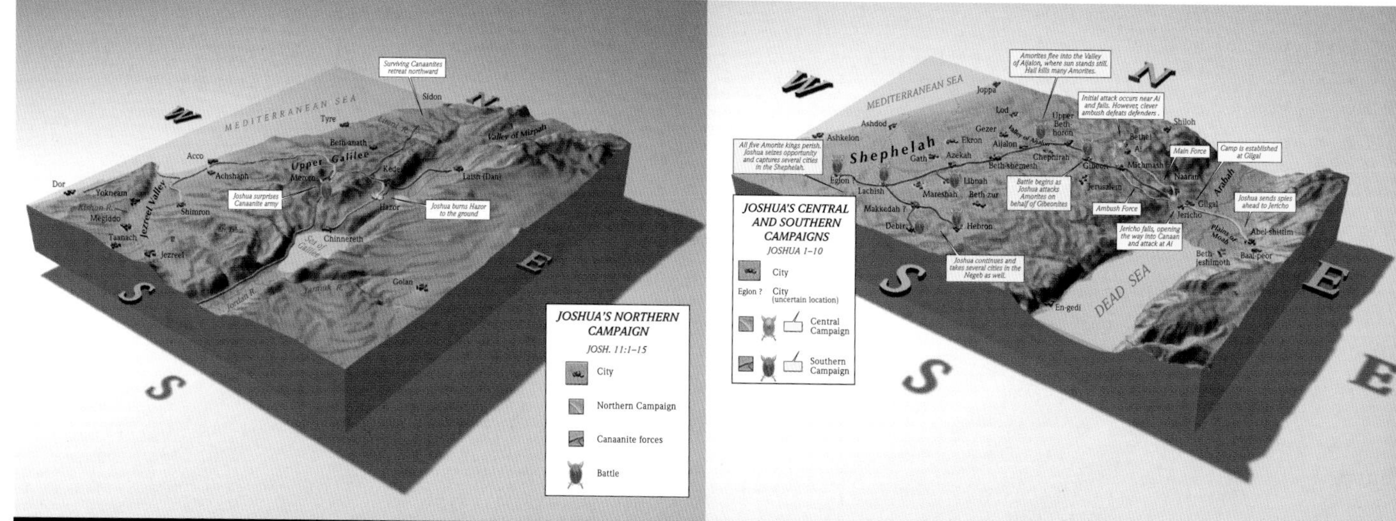

Judah (JOO duh) 1. Fourth son of Jacob by his wife Leah. He was the ancestor of the tribe of Judah, through which Jesus came. 2. Tribe of Judah that occupied the territory west of the Dead Sea which included the city of Jerusalem. 3. When Israel was divided following the death of Solomon, the Southern Kingdom was named Judah, and the Northern Kingdom was named Israel. **Genesis 29:35; Joshua 15:2-4; 1 Kings 12:17**

Josiah

(joh SIGH uh) Became king of Judah at the age of 8. Josiah led the people back to God and had the altars to idols torn down. When he was 26, the "book of the Law" was discovered while repairs were being made on the temple. When he heard the message of the book, Josiah tore his clothes, a sign of repentance, and humbled himself before God. Josiah read the book to the people of Judah, who also repented of their sins (See *Hilkiah.*)
2 Kings 22:1–23:3

Joy One of the nine qualities seen in the fruit of the Spirit. Joy is delight that comes from knowing and serving God. When a person knows and believes in Jesus, he can be happy, even when bad things happen. **Galatians 5:22-23**

Judas (JOO duhs)

1. Half brother of Jesus.
2. Apostle of Jesus, also called Thaddaeus.
Mark 3:18; 6:3

Judas Iscariot

(iss KAR ih aht) Apostle of Jesus who betrayed Jesus for 30 pieces of silver. Judas Iscariot was the only apostle from Judea. He acted as treasurer for the disciples but was known to steal the money for himself. **Matthew 26:47-50; 27:3-5; John 12:4-6; 13:21-30; John 18:1-5**

Jude (JOOD)

1. Half-brother of Jesus and brother of James, a leader of the Jerusalem church.
2. Eighth book in the General Letters division of the New Testament. This letter of only 25 verses addresses the problem of false teachings in the early church. Jude called on believers to stand firm in the faith. **Mark 6:3; Jude 1**

Judea

(joo DEE uh) Place-name meaning "Jewish." A land area that changed with different leaders but always included Jerusalem and the surrounding area. The area was known as Judah until the Babylonian exile; it was then called Judea.
Matthew 2:1

Judges

(JUH jihz) Second book in the History division of the Old Testament. Judges describes the work of the different leaders God gave the Israelites between Joshua's death and Samuel's anointing Saul, Israel's first king. When the people sinned, God punished them by sending a foreign nation to oppress them. The people would repent and cry out for help. God would then send a judge, or military leader, to overthrow the enemy and deliver His people. The best-known judges are Deborah, Gideon, and Samson.
Judges 4:1–8:35; 13:1–16:31

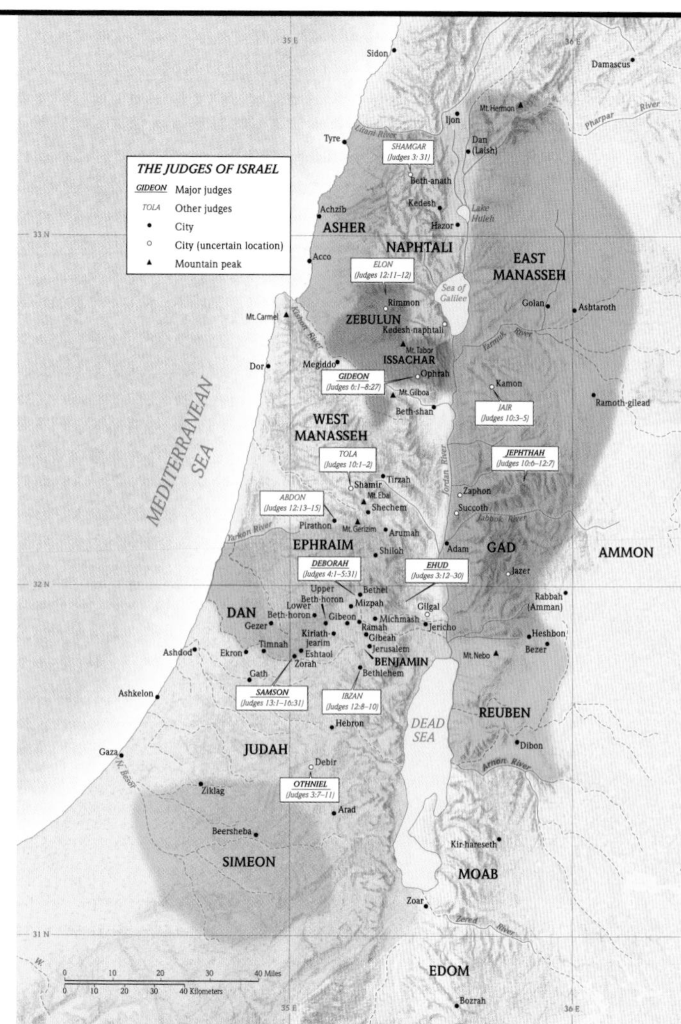

Judgment

1. One of God's roles is "Judge of all the earth." God evaluates each person and punishes sins or gives rewards. Although all humans have sinned, Jesus' death and resurrection make possible the forgiveness of sins, escape from God's punishment, and a loving relationship with God.

2. When a person wrongly evaluates another person's attitudes and actions without first realizing his own faults and weaknesses. Often the result is that the person making the judgment decides he or she is better than someone else. Jesus taught that this is wrong.
Exodus 6:6;
Matthew 7:1-5;
John 3:17-19; 5:24

Justify/ Justification

Act of God based on Jesus' death on the cross that makes possible a friendly relationship between people and God.
Romans 5:1,15-16

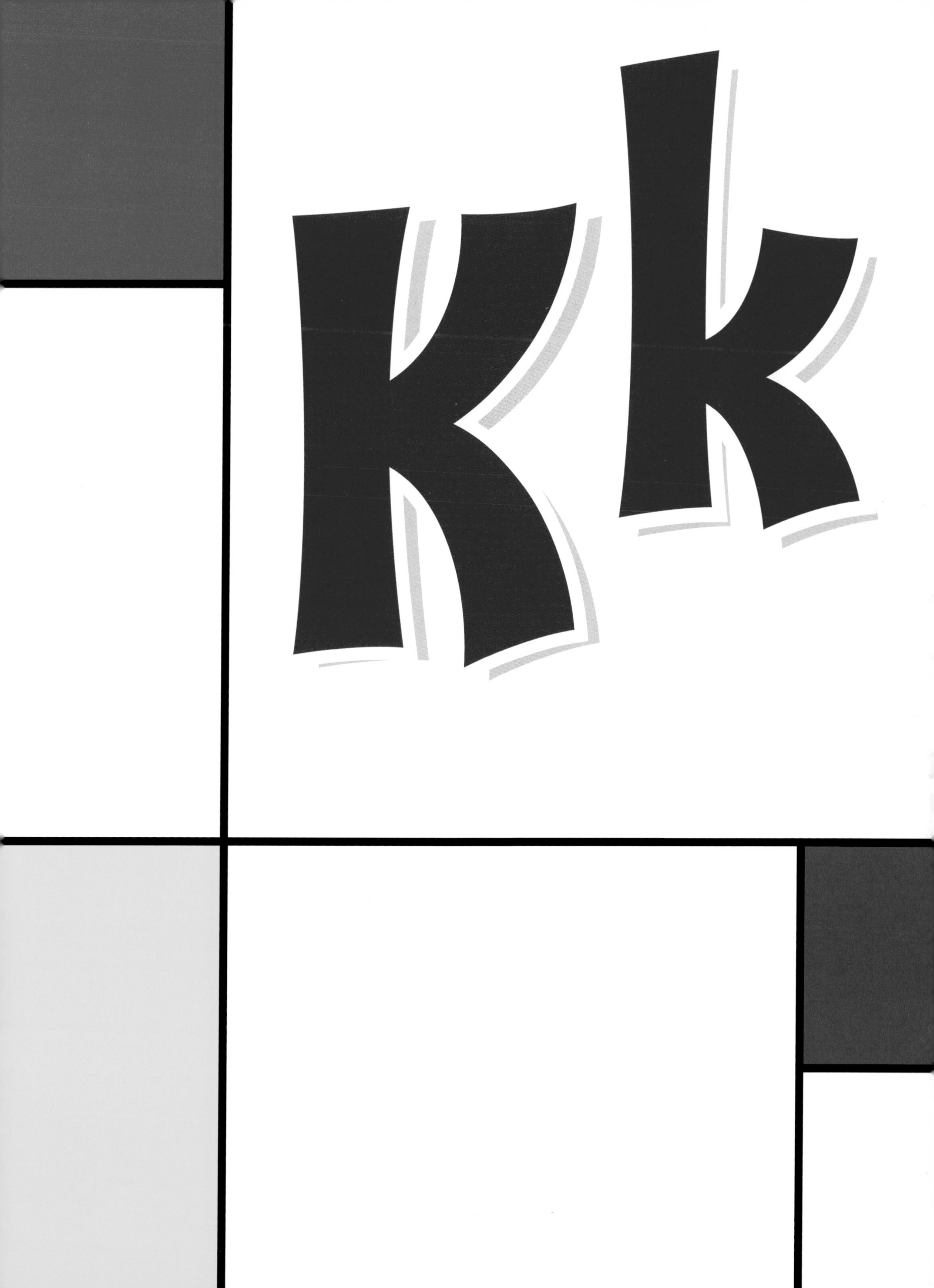
Kk

Kadesh-Barnea

Kadesh-Barnea (KAY desh bahr NEE uh) Where the Israelites stayed for most of the 38 years after leaving Mount Sinai and before entering the promised land. Moses sent out the 12 spies into Canaan from Kadesh-barnea. **Numbers 13:3-21,26**

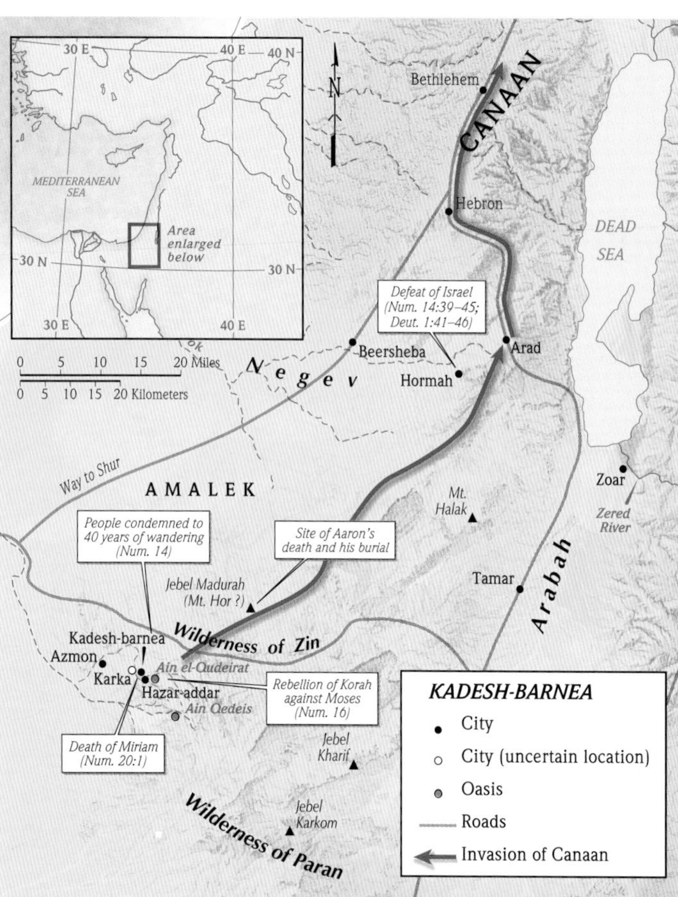

Kidron Valley

Kidron Valley (KID ruhn) Deep ravine beside Jerusalem separating the temple mount and the city of David on the west from the Mount of Olives on the east. After the Last Supper Jesus went through the Kidron Valley on His way to the Mount of Olives. **John 18:1**

Kindness

Kindness One of the nine qualities seen in the fruit of the Spirit. People demonstrate kindness by treating others as they want to be treated. **Galatians 5:22-23**

King

King Male leader of a country or nation with total control over the nation and its people. Samuel anointed Saul as the first king of Israel. When Saul disobeyed God, Samuel anointed David as the next king. Approximately 15 years later, at the age of 30, David became king of Judah. Seven years later, he had united the twelve tribes and was king over all Israel (1003 B.C.). At his death, his son Solomon became king (970 B.C.). **1 Samuel 10:1,24-25; 1 Samuel 16:1-13; 1 Kings 1:32-40**

Kingdom

Kingdom Country or nation ruled by a king. **1 Samuel 24:20**

Kingdom of God

Kingdom of God God rules with all power over all His works as King. He wants people to follow His rule because they love and trust Him. Jesus preached many times about the Kingdom of God. **Matthew 6:10**

Kings

Kings 1. First Kings is the sixth book in the division of History of the Old Testament. This book tells the history of Israel from King Solomon's reign through the division of Israel into two kingdoms. 2. Second Kings is the seventh book in the division of History of the Old Testament. This book tells the history of the divided kingdoms. Israel, the northern kingdom, was conquered by the nation of Assyria. Judah, the southern kingdom, was conquered by Babylon, and many of the people were taken away in exile. **1 Kings 4:1; 2 Kings 22:1-2**

Kinsman

Kinsman Male relative who had responsibilities for his family members. When a married man died, his brother married the man's widow so that she could have male children to keep the family name and inheritance. The living kinsman was known as his dead brother's kinsman redeemer. **Ruth 3:9-12**

Knead

Knead (NEED) When a person uses her hands to make bread by mixing flour, water, and oil. The mixture is allowed to stand in the bowl until it is ready to cook. **Exodus 12:34**

Kneel

Kneel (NEEL) To bend both knees in a position of prayer. Daniel knelt to pray to God three times a day. Paul said that at the name of Jesus all people would kneel before Him. **Daniel 6:10; Mark 1:40-42; Philippians 2:10**

Knowledge

Knowledge (NAH lij) The Bible tells about God's knowledge. God knows all things. He knows people's thoughts, including their secrets. He knows past, present, and future events. The Bible also speaks about human knowledge. Knowledge of God is the greatest knowledge a person can have. In the Old Testament the Israelites knew God through His actions for His people and His inspired Word. In the New Testament people knew God through His Son, Jesus, and the inspired writings of what is now called the Old Testament **Psalm 44:1,21; 139:1-18; Jeremiah 29:11; John 17:3**

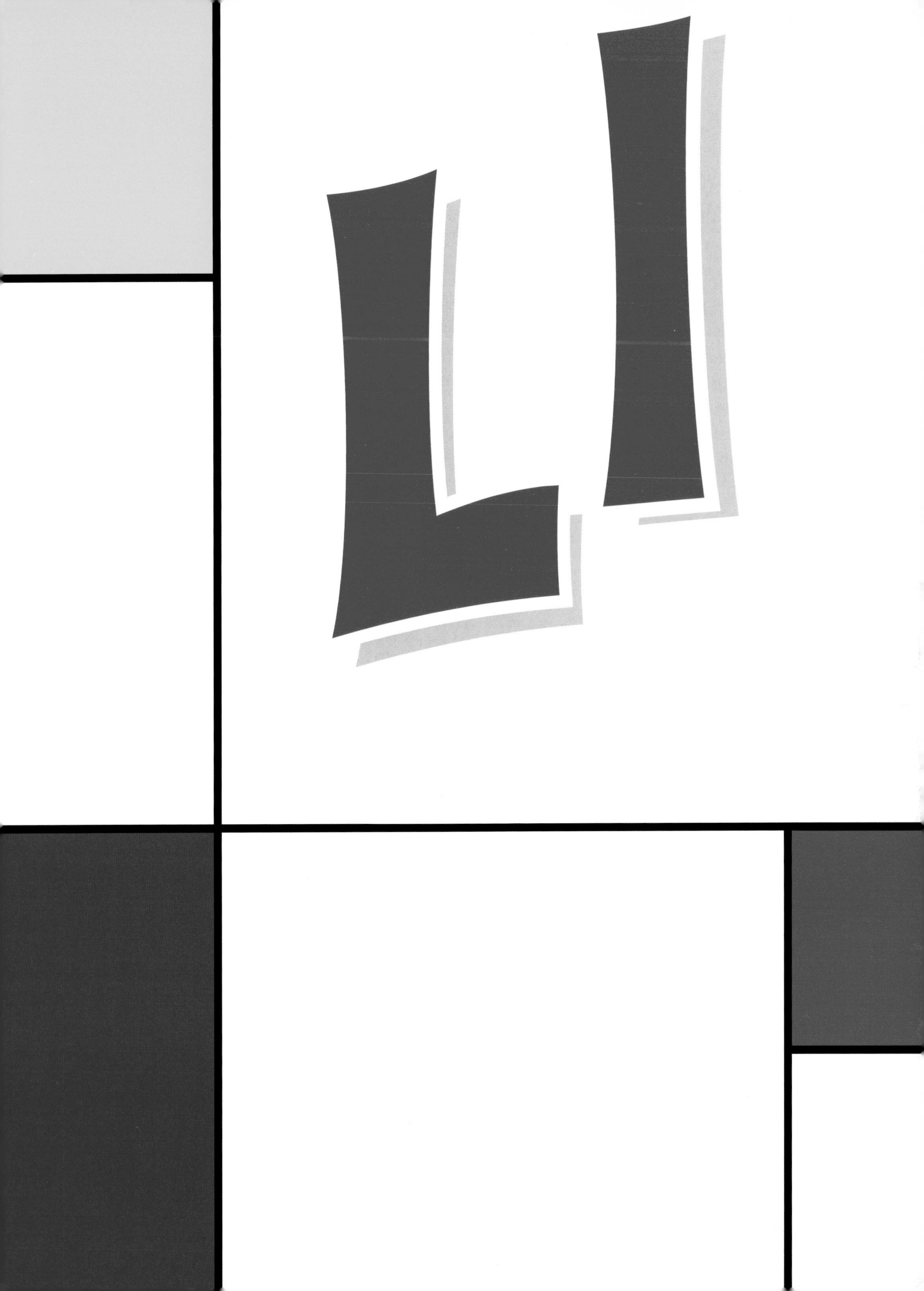

Laban (LAY buhn) Rebekah's brother; father of Leah and Rachel. Laban agreed to give his daughter Rachel as payment for Jacob's seven years of labor. But Laban tricked Jacob into marrying his older daughter, Leah. Jacob married Rachel and worked seven more years.
Genesis 24:29; 29:15-30

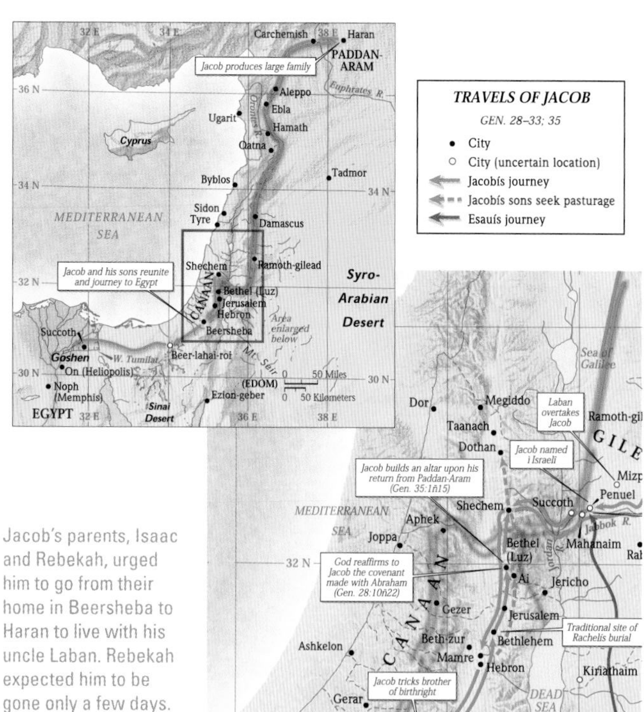

Jacob's parents, Isaac and Rebekah, urged him to go from their home in Beersheba to Haran to live with his uncle Laban. Rebekah expected him to be gone only a few days. He was actually gone 20 years.

Laban argues with his son-in-law, Jacob.

Lamb of God

Name given to Jesus by John the Baptist. The name comes from the lambs that were used in the temple sacrifice. A lamb was sacrificed during the annual Passover as well as in the daily sacrifices of Israel. Jesus fulfilled the promise made by the prophet Isaiah that God would provide a sacrifice who would make salvation possible for all peoples.
Exodus 12:1-38; John 1:29

John the Baptist tells his disciples that Jesus is the Lamb of God who takes away the sin of the world.

Lame

Physical condition in which walking is difficult or impossible. Jesus healed people who were lame. God helped Peter and John heal a lame man at the temple in Jerusalem.
Matthew 15:29-31; Acts 3:1-10

Four men bring a friend to Jesus. **Mark 2:1-12**

Lament (luh MENT) Mourning (KJV)

To cry and be sad because of something really bad that has happened.
Psalm 30:11

Lamentations

(LA men TAY shuhnz)
Third book in the Major Prophets division of the Old Testament. Jeremiah the prophet wrote about the sadness of the people of Judah over the destruction of Jerusalem and the temple in 587 B.C.
Lamentations 5:1

Lamp Open, bowl-like pottery with a pinched spout and a wick. Lamps burned olive oil to make light. A woman and her husband built a room for Elisha with a bed, a table, a chair, and a lamp.
2 Kings 4:8-10

Ancient lamp

Last Supper Passover meal Jesus shared with His disciples before the crucifixion. This 1500-year-old Hebrew tradition was a yearly reminder to God's people of how He had delivered them from slavery in Egypt. As Jesus and His disciples participated in this meal, Jesus took two familiar parts of the Passover meal, unleavened bread and the cup, and used them as reminders. The bread is a reminder of Jesus' broken body. The cup is a reminder of His blood given for the forgiveness of sin. Jesus commanded His disciples to continue to eat this meal to help people remember His death until He returns. (See *Lord's Supper*.)
Mark 14:12-26

Jesus shares Passover with His disciples the day before His crucifixion.

Laver (LAY vuhr)
Molten sea (KJV)
Large basin or bowl used by the priests to wash their hands and feet before they served in the tabernacle or temple. Solomon's temple had a huge laver that was called the reservoir; and it also had ten smaller basins.
Exodus 40:30-31;
1 Kings 7:23-40;
2 Chronicles 4:2-5

Laodicea
(lay AHD ih SEE uh) City in southwest Asia Minor near the city of Colossae. In the Book of Colossians, Paul asked the Christians in Colossae to share his letter to them with the Christians in Laodicea. He then told the Colossians to read a letter he had sent to the Laodiceans. Laodicea was a wealthy city known for making cloth, producing black wool, and banking.
Colossians 2:1;
Revelation 3:14-22

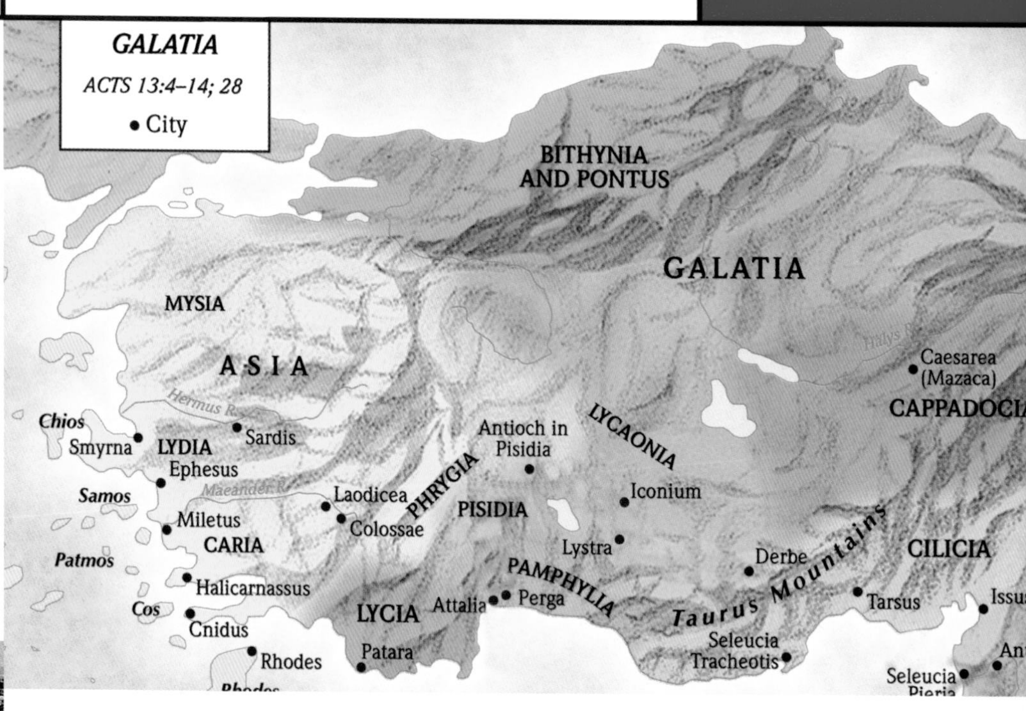

Above: Laodicea is located on an ancient highway that ran from Ephesus to Syria. The major weakness of Laodicea was lack of water. This need was met by bringing water six miles north from Denizli through a system of stone pipes.
Left: Archaeological remains of an early church located at Laodicea in Turkey.

Law/laws Commandments, customs, judgments, and rules found in the books of Law (Genesis, Exodus, Leviticus, Numbers, and Deuteronomy). These commandments and rules told the people of Israel how God wanted them to live. The best known of the laws are the Ten Commandments, which God gave to Moses on Mt. Sinai. God did not say obedience to the laws was the way to be saved. However, God wanted people to obey His laws because they loved Him. (See *Ten Commandments*.) **Exodus 20; Deuteronomy 4:8**

Many consider Jebel Musa to be the site of Mount Sinai where the Lord gave the Law to Moses.

Lazarus (LAZ uh ruhs) Means "one whom God helps." Lazarus of Bethany was a personal friend of Jesus and the brother of Mary and Martha. Jesus raised Lazarus from the dead after Lazarus had been in the tomb for four days. Lazarus was at the Passover celebration in Bethany six days later. **John 11:1-49; 12:9-11**

The traditional site of the tomb of Lazarus in Bethany

Leah (LEE uh) Older daughter of Laban, and Jacob's first wife. Jacob had asked to marry Rachel but was tricked by her father, Laban, into marrying Leah. Leah had six sons with Jacob (Reuben, Simeon, Levi, Judah, Issachar, Zebulun) and a daughter (Dinah). Her handmaid, Zilpah, had two sons with Jacob (Gad, Asher). Jesus is a descendant of Leah. **Genesis 29:16; 29:31-35; Genesis 30:10-12,17-20**

Leaven (LEV uhn) Yeast or another ingredient used to make bread rise. Bread without leaven was prepared for the Feast of Unleavened Bread that was celebrated during the Passover festival. This unleavened bread was flat and reminded the Israelites of the time God delivered them from slavery in Egypt. The Israelites had to leave Egypt in a hurry and did not have time for bread to rise. **Exodus 12:1-20; Leviticus 23:4-8**

Unleaved bread

Lebanon (LEB uh nuhn) Country at the eastern end of the Mediterranean Sea and the western end of Asia. In the Old Testament, Lebanon was the northern boundary of Israel. Lebanon had many forests, especially the "cedars of Lebanon." These cedars, as well as other trees of Lebanon, were used in building David's palace and Solomon's temple and palace buildings.
Joshua 1:4; 1 Kings 7:2; Isaiah 2:13

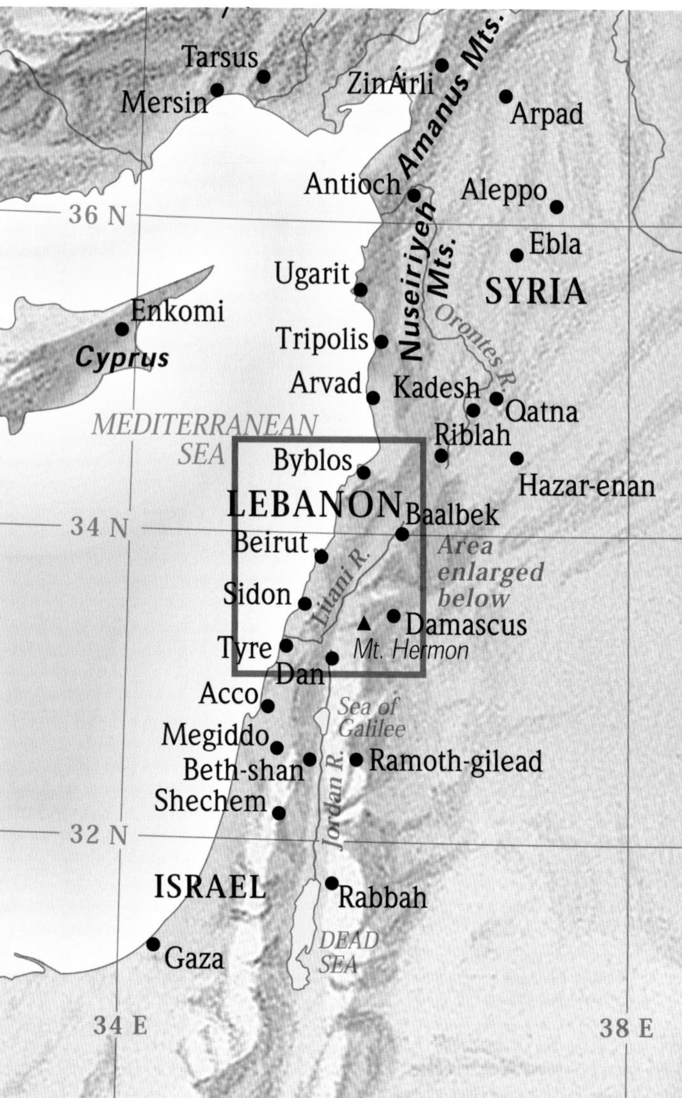

Legion (LEE juhn) Roman military term.
1. Legions were made up of the best soldiers in the army. At different times in Rome's history, the legion numbered between 4,500 and 6,000 soldiers.
2. A large number of demons.
3. The host of angels.
Matthew 26:53; Luke 8:30

Leper (LEP uhr) (KJV) Person with leprosy. Jesus touched and healed lepers. **Mark 1:40-45**

Jesus heals 10 men who were lepers.

Leprosy (LEP ruh see) Describes a variety of skin disorders. For the Hebrews, leprosy was bad because the disease kept people from worshiping God at the temple with other people. Anyone who came in contact with a leper was considered unclean. Lepers could not live near anyone else. Elisha told Naaman to dip in the Jordan River seven times to be healed of leprosy. **Leviticus 13:3; 2 Kings 5:1-19**

Letter, epistle (KJV) A written communication from one person, church, or group to another. Paul wrote letters to encourage and teach people in the churches he started. Some of these letters were written by a scribe while Paul told him what to write. Many other people in the Bible wrote and sent letters.
Romans 16:22; 1 Thessalonians 5:27

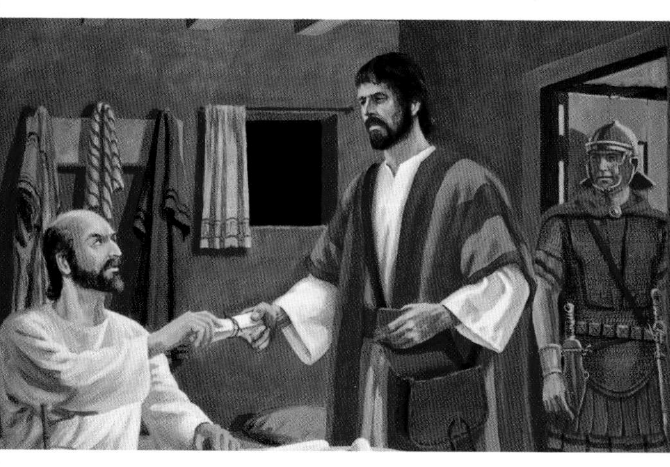
Paul sends Epaphroditus back to Philippi carrying Paul's letter to the Philippians.

Levi (LEE vigh)

Third son of Jacob by his wife Leah. He was the ancestor of the tribe of Levi, one of the twelve tribes of Israel. Levi's descendants became a tribe of priests of which there were three orders: high priest, priests, and Levites. Aaron was Israel's first high priest. **Genesis 29:34; Numbers 1:47-54**

Leviticus

(lih VIT ih kuhs) Third book in the division of Law of the Old Testament. Leviticus continues the history told in the Book of Exodus. Moses wrote this book that contains the ceremonial and religious laws. The Israelite tribe of Levi had the job of making sure the people followed that law. **Leviticus 1:1**

Levites (LEE vightz)

The third of three orders of Israel's priesthood. After the tabernacle was built, the Levites were in charge of moving it and helping in worship at the tent. The Levites helped in worship by preparing grain offerings, taking care of the holy items, and singing praises to God. When Solomon built the temple, the Levites began serving there.

All of Israel's tribes except the tribe of Levi were given land in Canaan. The Levites were given 48 different cities throughout Canaan.

Jesus told a story about a priest and a Levite who refused to stop and help a man who had been beaten and left for dead. **Numbers 1:47-54; 35:1-8; 1 Chronicles 6:31-53; 2 Chronicles 29:27-30; Luke 10:25-37**

Levites and other people sing to God.

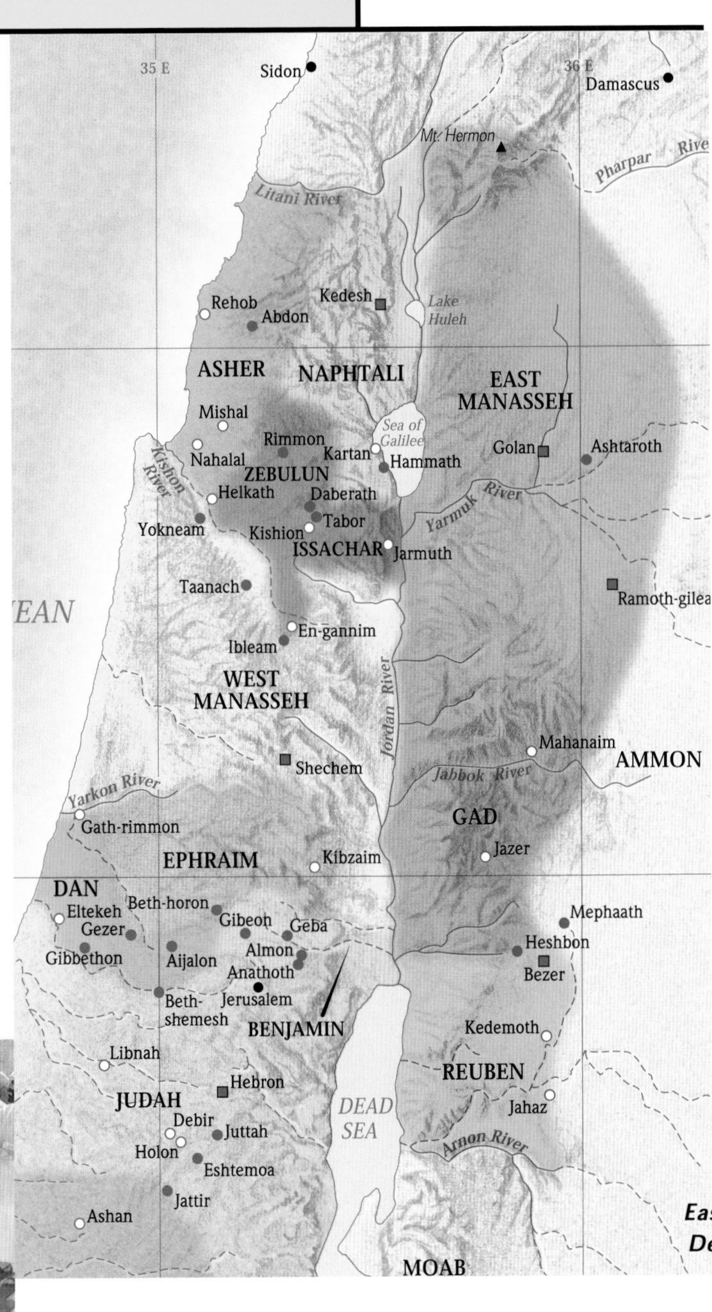

Each of Israel's tribes except the tribe of Levi was given its own territory in the promised land. The Levites were given 48 cities, scattered in each of the twelve tribal territories.

Line, Family lineage (KJV) Descendants of one man. Mary's husband, Joseph, was of the family line of David. **Luke 2:4**

Linen (LIH nin) Most common fabric used in Bible times, spun from the flax plant and bleached before being made into clothing and curtains. The tabernacle curtains and the high priest's garments were of finely woven linen. **Exodus 26:1; 28:6**

Lintel (LIN tuhl) Wooden crossbeam over a doorway. During the last plague, God sent the death angel throughout Egypt. The firstborn sons of the Egyptians and their animals died. God told the people of Israel to avoid the death angel by sprinkling the blood of a lamb on the lintel and the doorposts. **Exodus 12:21-23**

A lintel above a door on an old monastery in Tuscany

Loaves (LOHVZ) Round-shaped bread made from grain and cooked over fire. The most common loaves were paper thin and used to scoop food from a common pot. Other loaves were heavier, like biscuits. Andrew found a young boy with loaves and fish and brought him to Jesus. **Matthew 26:23; John 6:1-13**

Five loaves and two fish

Lois (LOH iss) Mother of Eunice and grandmother of Timothy. **2 Timothy 1:5**

Longsuffering (KJV) Means "patient." **Galatians 5:22**

Lord/Lord Another name for God that means "God is the owner of the earth." It can mean "Master" or "one to whom all things belong." (See *Yahweh*.) **Genesis 12:1-4; Psalm 114:7**

Lord's Day Sunday, the first day of the week. After Jesus' resurrection on Sunday, Christians began to worship on Sunday. **Revelation 1:10**

Lord's Supper Special time to help Christians remember Jesus' death. The bread and the cup remind Christians that Jesus died for their sins. Jesus took the first Lord's Supper with His disciples. (See *Last Supper*.) **Luke 22:14-23**

A Christian receiving the Lord's Supper.

Lost Someone who does not know Jesus as his or her Savior and Lord is lost. When Jesus went to Zacchaeus's house, He told people that He came to seek and to save those who are lost. **Luke 19:9-10**

Lot (LAHT) Nephew of Abraham. When Abraham left Haran for Canaan, Lot and his household went with him. Abraham and Lot settled in Canaan. Abraham and Lot had so many herds and flocks that there was not enough grass and water for all of them. Abraham suggested that they separate, and he allowed Lot to take his choice of the land. Lot chose the well-watered Jordan Valley. **Genesis 11:27; 12:5; Genesis 13:1-12**

Love One of the nine qualities of the fruit of the Spirit. The New Testament uses different Greek words for love. The most important love is the love God has for people. God wants Christians to love one another with that same kind of love. **John 3:16; 1 Corinthians 13; Galatians 5:22**

Luke (LOOK) 1. Author of the third book of Gospels and the book of Acts in the New Testament. He traveled with Paul. Paul identified Luke as a Gentile doctor. 2. The third book in the division of the Gospels of the New Testament. Written for the Greeks, the book tells of Jesus' humanity and His death on the cross. **Luke 1:1; Acts 1:1; 2 Timothy 4:11; Colossians 4:14**

Lydia (LID ih uh) First person to become a Christian at Philippi. She sold purple cloth. Lydia invited Paul and his friends to stay in her home. **Acts 16:11-15**

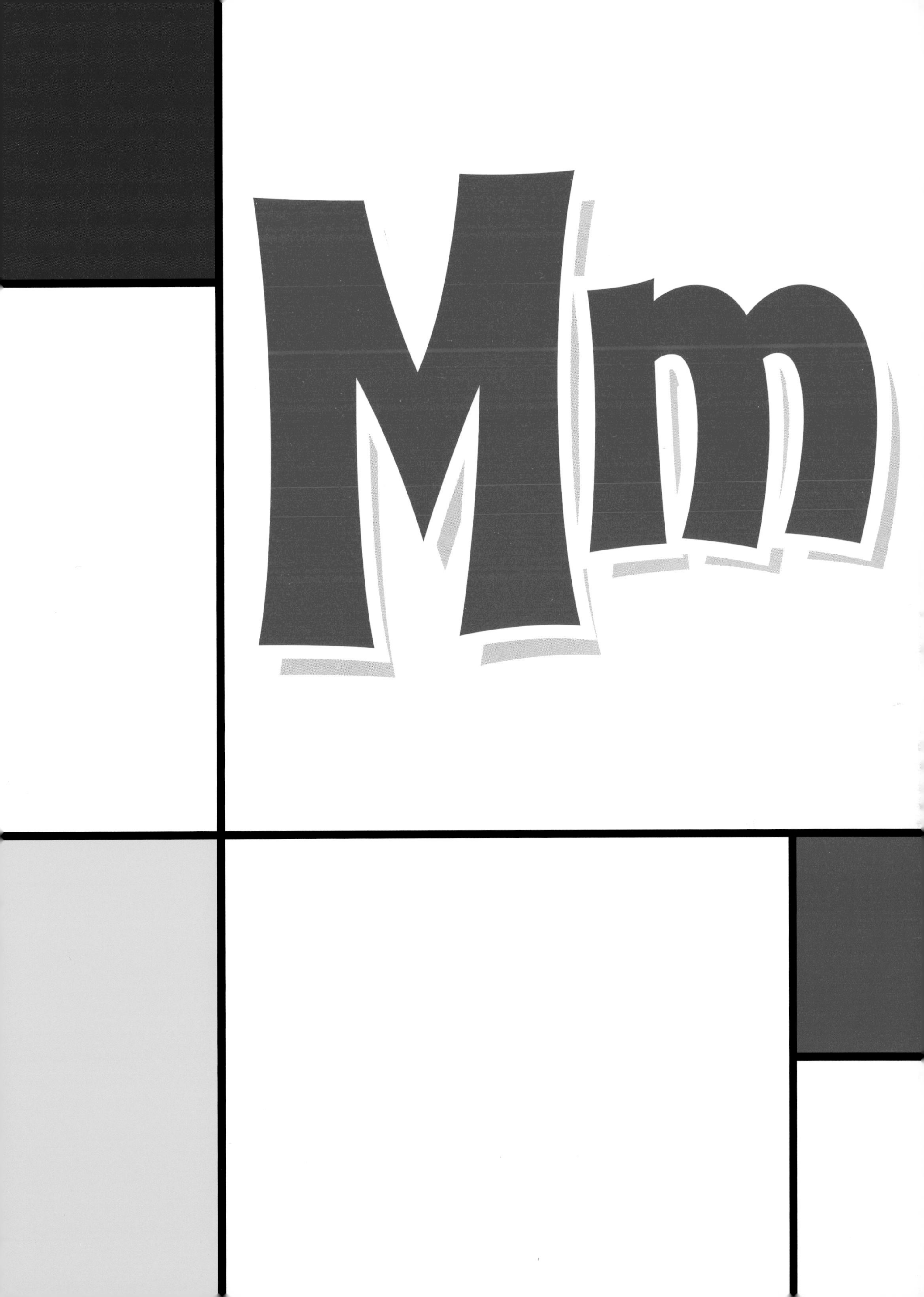
Mm

Magi (MAY jigh) Wise men, priests, and astrologers. Their study of the stars led them to Palestine to find and worship Jesus, the newborn King. They may have been from Babylon, Persia, or the Arabian Desert. The Bible does not say how many magi worshiped Jesus, although they brought Him three gifts—gold, frankincense, and myrrh. Jesus may have been about two years old when the magi found Him (See *Wise Men.*) **Matthew 2:1-12**

The wise men visit Jesus and present gifts to Him.

Magistrate (MAJ ih STRAYT) Government official. In the Old Testament, a magistrate may have been a judge. In the New Testament, a magistrate was a military commander or government official of a city. Magistrates were responsible for putting Paul and Silas in prison in Philippi. Later they apologized to Paul and Silas. **Ezra 7:25; Acts 16:16-40**

Malice (MAL us) Intent or desire to hurt someone. God commands Christians to get rid of malice in their lives. **Colossians 3:8**

Malachi (MAL uh kigh) Means "my messenger." 1. Prophet who preached to the Jews after the Jewish captives had returned from the exile and resettled their homeland. 2. Last book in the division of Minor Prophets and last book of the Old Testament. The book encouraged the Jews to change their wrong attitudes about God and worship by trusting God. The people needed to give tithes and offerings to God and to honor one another. **Malachi 3:10**

Malta (MAWL tuh)
Melita (MEL ih tuh) (KJV) Island in the Mediterranean Sea, located 50 miles southwest of Sicily. After being shipwrecked, Paul, other prisoners, and soldiers swam or floated on broken pieces of the ship to Malta. The people of the island were kind to Paul and the other survivors. While building a fire, a snake bit Paul, but he was not hurt.
Acts 27:39–28:10

Manna (MAN uh) Food that God gave the Israelites after they escaped from Egypt. The small round grains or flakes appeared with the dew around the Israelites' camp each morning except for the Sabbath. The people ground and baked them into cakes or boiled them. God provided manna for 40 years. Following God's instructions, a jar of manna was placed in the ark of the covenant to remind the Israelites of how God took care of them.
Exodus 16:13-36; Hebrews 9:3-4

The Israelites pick up manna in the desert

Manger (MAYN juhr) Feeding trough used for cows, sheep, goats, and other livestock. Probably made of stone. The place where Jesus was laid after His birth.
Luke 2:7,12,16

A stone manger from Megiddo that dates to the time when Solomon was king of Israel. This is like the manger in which Jesus was laid at His birth.

Mark (MAHRK) Second and shortest book in the Gospel division of the New Testament. Written for Gentile Christians, the book explains Jewish customs to people not familiar with Jewish life. Mark began the book with Jesus' ministry as an adult. He wrote more about the actions of Jesus than about what Jesus said.
Mark 1:1-15

Mark, John John Mark, as Luke calls him in Acts, was the son of Mary, in whose house the church was meeting when an angel freed Peter from prison. He was Barnabas' cousin and a companion of Barnabas and Paul on their first missionary journey. Later when Barnabas wanted to take John Mark on another missionary trip, Paul refused to let John Mark go with them. Barnabas took John Mark and went to Cyprus. Paul left on another trip with Silas. Later, Paul and Mark became friends again. John Mark is the author of the Gospel of Mark.
Acts 12:11-12; 13:5,13; 15:36-40; Colossians 4:10; 2 Timothy 4:11

A street by the marketplace in Perga, the city from which John Mark left Paul and Barnabas on their first missionary journey. He returned to Jerusalem.

Marketplace/Market (KJV)
Narrow streets and many buildings in towns and villages left little room for a public marketplace. Shops were built into homes or clustered in the gate area. Merchants had booths just inside the city gate or sold things outside the gate area in an open space or square. This area also served as a place for troops to gather, for public meetings and victory celebrations, and for displaying of captives. In the marketplace in Athens, Paul told people about Jesus.
Acts 17:17

Marriage (MA rihj)
When a man and a woman tell God and each other that they promise to love each other more than they love any other man or woman for as long as they live. The first marriage was between Adam and Eve.
Genesis 2:18-25; Matthew 19:4-6

Rings are reminders of the promises a man and woman make to each other when they get married.

Mars Hill (MAHRZ) Also known as the Areopagus. Hill overlooking the city of Athens where the philosophers of the city gathered to talk about their ideas. Paul talked with some of the men of Athens on Mars Hill and taught them about Jesus. **Acts 17:19-34**

Mars Hill in Athens, a place where Greeks gathered for discussion and debate

Martha

(MAHR thuh) Means "lady of the house." Martha followed and believed in Jesus, lived in Bethany, and was Mary and Lazarus's sister. She welcomed Jesus as a guest in her home and became frustrated when she served Jesus while her sister Mary listened to Him.
Luke 10:38-42; John 12:2

View of the ancient village of Bethany, home of Mary, Martha, and their brother Lazarus

Martyr

(MAHR tuhr) Means "witness." Someone who suffered or died because of his message about God's truth. Stephen was the first Christian martyr.
1 Kings 19:2;
Acts 7:54-60; 22:19-20

Mary (MAY rih) The New Testament mentions seven different Marys. 1. Mary, Jesus' mother, was a young virgin who lived in Nazareth. Her relative Elizabeth was the mother of John the Baptist. Mary was engaged to and later married Joseph (Luke 1:26-38).

2. Mary Magdalene, from Magdala in Galilee, was one of the women who followed and supported Jesus. According to the Gospel of John, she was the first person to see Jesus after His resurrection (Luke 8:2).

3. Mary of Bethany was the sister of Martha and Lazarus. She anointed the feet of Jesus with expensive perfume (Luke 10:38-42).

4. Mary, the mother of James the Younger, Joses, and Salome, was present at Jesus' death and burial. She discovered the empty tomb following Jesus' resurrection (Mark 15:40-41).

5. Mary, wife of Clopas (John 19:25). She may have been the same Mary as Mary, the mother of James the Younger, Joses, and Salome. She was present at Jesus' death.

6. Mary, mother of John Mark, lived in the house where many of Jesus' disciples met and prayed when Peter was in prison (Acts 12:12-16).

7. Mary from Rome was a believer whom Paul greeted in his letter to the Christians in Rome (Romans 16:6).

An angel appears to Mary Magdalene and another Mary at the tomb of Jesus. The angel tells the women not to be afraid. Jesus is no longer in the tomb. He has been resurrected.

Mason Builder who uses brick or stone.
1 Chronicles 22:2-4,14-16

Masonry done under the direction of King Herod. Herod completed many building projects when he was king of the Jews

Mast (KJV) A long pole on a ship that supports a sail.
Isaiah 33:23

Fishing boats on the Nile River

Master 1. Someone in charge of a household or in charge of servants or slaves. 2. Another name for "teacher." Jesus was sometimes referred to as "Master."
Genesis 39:1-2; Luke 17:12-13

Matthew (MATH yoo) Means "the gift of Yahweh." 1. Matthew was a tax collector who became one of Jesus' twelve apostles. Also known as Levi. 2. The first book of the New Testament and the first book in the Gospel division. Matthew wrote to the Jews, telling them that Jesus was the Messiah promised in the Old Testament. In his genealogy of Jesus, Matthew shows that two of Jesus' earthly ancestors were Abraham and King David, who were important in Jewish history. The book includes Jesus' Sermon on the Mount and His Great Commission.
Matthew 1:2,6; 5:1–7:29; 9:9-13; 10:3; 28:18-20; Luke 5:27

Matthias (muh THIGH uhs) After Judas Iscariot betrayed Jesus and Jesus returned to heaven, a group of followers of Jesus prayed and chose Matthias to take Judas' place as one of the twelve apostles of Jesus. **Acts 1:23-26**

Measure (See *Table of Weights and Measures in the Bible*, p. 117.)

TABLE OF WEIGHTS & MEASURES IN THE BIBLE

Biblical Unit	Language	Biblical Measure	U.S. Equivalent	Metric Equivalent	Various Translations
WEIGHTS					
Gerah	Hebrew	1/20 shekel	1/50 ounce	.6 gram	gerah; oboli
Bekah	Hebrew	1/2 shekel or 10 gerahs	1/5 ounce	5.7 grams	bekah; half a shekel; quarter ounce; fifty cents
Pim	Hebrew	2⁄3 shekel	1⁄3 ounce	7.6 grams	2/3 of a shekel; quarter
Shekel	Hebrew	2 bekahs	2⁄5 ounce	11.5 grams	shekel; piece; dollar; fifty dollars
Litra (pound)	Greco-Roman	30 shekels	12 ounces	.4 kilogram	pound; pounds
Mina	Hebrew/Greek	50 shekels	1 1⁄4 pounds	.6 kilogram	mina; pound
Talent	Hebrew/Greek	3,000 shekels or 60 minas	75 pounds/ 88 pounds	34 kilograms/ 40 kilograms	talent/talents; 100 pounds
LENGTH					
Handbreadth	Hebrew	1⁄6 cubit or 1⁄3 span	3 inches	8 centimeters	handbreadth; three inches; four inches
Span	Hebrew	1⁄2 cubit or 3 handbreadths	9 inches	23 centimeters	span
Cubit/Pechys	Hebrew/Greek	2 spans	18 inches	.5 meter	cubit/cubits; yard; half a yard; foot
Fathom	Greco-Roman	4 cubits	2 yards	2 meters	fathom; six feet
Kalamos	Greco-Roman	6 cubits	3 yards	3 meters	rod; reed; measuring rod
Stadion	Greco-Roman	1⁄8 milion or 400 cubits	1⁄8 mile	185 meters	miles; furlongs; race
Milion	Greco-Roman	8 stadia	1,620 yards	1.5 kilometers	mile
DRY MEASURE (To measure amounts of dry things such as grain)					
Xestes	Greco-Roman	1/2 cab	1 1/6 pints	.5 liter	pots; pitchers; kettles; copper pots; copper bowls; vessels of bronze
Cab	Hebrew	1/18 ephah	1 quart	1 liter	cab; kab
Choinix	Greco-Roman	1/18 ephah	1 quart	1 liter	measure; quart
Omer	Hebrew	1/10 ephah	2 quarts	2 liters	omer; tenth of a deal; tenth of an ephah; six pints
Seah/Saton	Hebrew/Greek	1/3 ephah	7 quarts	7.3 liters	measures; pecks; large amounts
Modios	Greco-Roman	4 omers	1 peck or 1/4 bushel	9 liters	bushel; bowl; peck
Ephah [Bath]	Hebrew	10 omers	3/5 bushel	22 liters	bushel; peck; deal; part; measure; six pints; seven pints
Lethek	Hebrew	5 ephahs	3 bushels	110 liters	half homer; half sack
Kor [Homer]/ Koros	Hebrew/Greek	10 ephahs	6 bushels or 200 quarts / 14.9 bushels or 500 quarts	220 liters/525 liters	cor; homer; sack; measures; bushels/sacks; measures
LIQUID MEASURE (To measure amounts of liquids such as oil or water)					
Log	Hebrew	1/72 bath	1/3 quart	.3 liter	log; pint; cotulus
Xestes	Greco-Roman	1/8 hin	11/6 pints	.5 liter	pots; pitchers; kettles; copper bowls; vessels of bronze
Hin	Hebrew	1/6 bath	1 gallon or 4 quarts	4 liters	hin; pints
Bath/Batos	Hebrew/Greek	1 ephah	6 gallons	22 liters	gallon(s); barrels; liquid measures
Metretes	Greco-Roman	10 hins	10 gallons	39 liters	firkins; gallons

Mediterranean Sea

(MED ih tuh RAY nih uhn) Most of the important nations of ancient times were either on the shores of the Mediterranean Sea or operated in its 2,200 miles of water. The nations were Israel, Syria, Greece, Rome, Egypt, Philistia, and Phoenicia. The Mediterranean Sea served as the western border for the land of Canaan and the territory of Judah. Paul made three missionary journeys across the Mediterranean. Under Roman arrest, Paul made his final voyage across the Mediterranean Sea and shipwrecked. **Numbers 34:6; Joshua 15:12; Acts 27**

Mediterranean Sea at Caesarea Maritima, the port city Herod the Great built to honor Augustus Caesar

Meekness

One of the nine qualities seen in the fruit of the Spirit. A person with this quality is humble and gentle and usually shows patience in suffering, along with faith in God. In the New Testament Jesus is the best example of meekness. **Matthew 5:5; 11:29; Galatians 5:23**

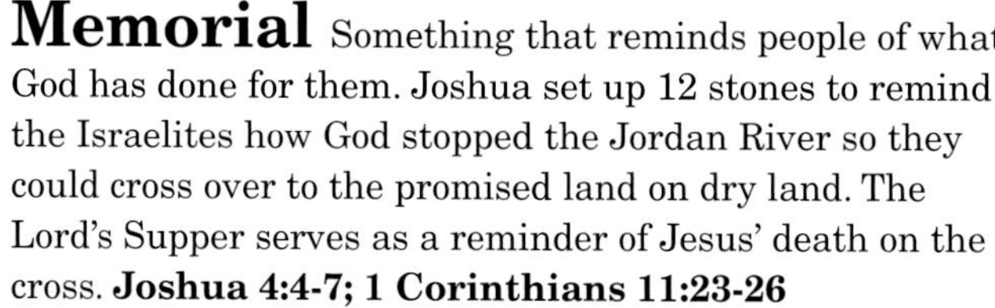

Memorial

Something that reminds people of what God has done for them. Joshua set up 12 stones to remind the Israelites how God stopped the Jordan River so they could cross over to the promised land on dry land. The Lord's Supper serves as a reminder of Jesus' death on the cross. **Joshua 4:4-7; 1 Corinthians 11:23-26**

Standing stones at Gezer dating to about 1500 B.C. The Lord told Joshua to set up 12 stones on the west bank of the Jordan River. These stones reminded the people that "the LORD's hand is mighty" (**Joshua 4:24**).

MENE, MENE, TEKEL, PARSIN

(MEE-nih, MEE-nih, TEK-el, PAHR-sin)

Mene Mene Tekel Upharsin

(KJV) Words written by the fingers of a man's hand on the palace wall of King Belshazzar of Babylon. The words were interpreted by the prophet Daniel. He told the king that it meant "numbered, weighed, and divided," or that the king and his kingdom had been weighed in the balance and found wanting. The kingdom would be divided and given to his enemies, the Medes and Persians. The kingdom was overthrown that very night. **Daniel 5:1-30**

Merchant Someone who buys and sells things. Merchants of Tyre sold fish and other merchandise. Some merchants became rich. **1 Kings 10:15; Nehemiah 13:15-20; Matthew 13:45**

Trajan's Market in Rome, a second century A.D. "shopping center" where merchants sold their goods

Mercy One of God's attributes and a characteristic God expects Christians to have. People experience God's mercy when He forgives them. People show mercy when they forgive others. God shows mercy by His actions, such as freeing the Israelites from Egypt and giving them food when they were in the wilderness. God does not show mercy to people because they deserve it. Mercy is always the gift of God.
Exodus 16:31-35; 1 Samuel 10:17-18; Matthew 5:7

Mercy seat
Means "to wipe out" or "cover over." Slab of pure gold measuring about 45 inches by 27 inches that sat on top of the ark of the covenant. It was the base for the golden cherubim and symbolized the throne from which God ruled Israel. On the Day of Atonement, the high priest sprinkled the blood of a sacrificial lamb on the mercy seat as a plea for forgiveness for the sins of the nation.
Exodus 25:17-22; Leviticus 16:2,15; Numbers 7:89

A model of the ark of the covenant

Meshach (MEE shak) One of the three Hebrew young men who were taken from Jerusalem along with Daniel to serve in King Nebuchadnezzar's court. God delivered them from the fiery furnace. **Daniel 1:1-7; 3:1-30**

Mesopotamia (MESS uh puh TAY mih uh) Area between the Tigris and Euphrates rivers. The homeland of Abraham. Mesopotamia supplied chariots and cavalry for the Ammonites' war with David. Both the northern kingdom of Israel and the southern kingdom of Judah went into exile in Mesopotamia. **Genesis 11:31–12:4; Genesis 28:6; 2 Kings 24:14-16; 1 Chronicles 19:6**

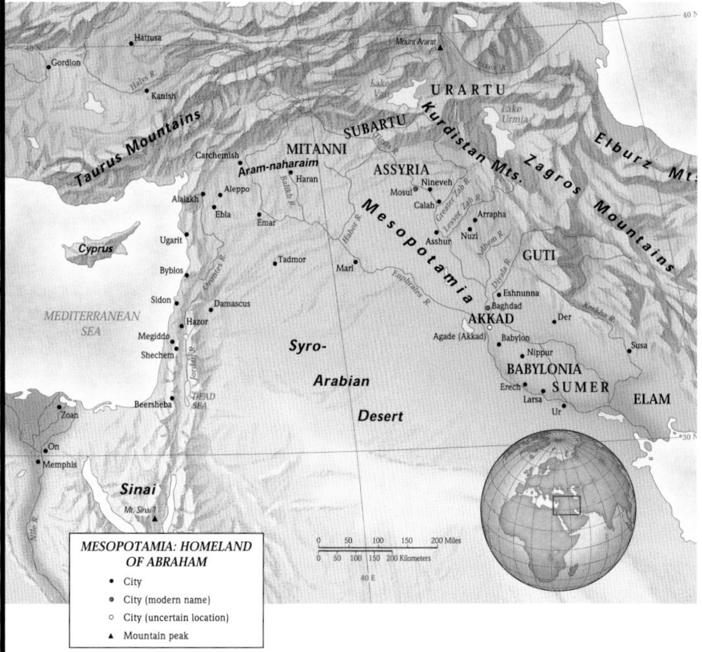

Messenger One sent with a message. Angels were messengers sent from God. Old Testament prophets and priests also were messengers. John the Baptist was a messenger who preached about the coming Messiah.
Isaiah 44:26; Malachi 2:7; Mark 1:2-8

Messiah
(muh SIGH uh) Means "anointed one." Also translated as "Christ." Old Testament prophets told of a coming Messiah who would be Israel's Savior. Although Jesus is the Messiah, many Jews rejected Him because they thought the Messiah would be a warrior-king who would overthrow their enemies. Instead, Jesus died on the cross and was resurrected on the third day to provide eternal life for everyone who believes in Him.
Mark 8:29; Luke 24:46-47

Mezuzah

(muh ZOO zuh) Means "doorpost." The blood of the Passover lamb was to be applied to doorposts. Today the word *mezuzah* refers to small scrolls inscribed with Deuteronomy 6:4-9 and 11:13-21 and placed in containers attached to the doors of Jewish homes. **Exodus 12:7,22-23**

Handmade mezuzah on the door of a Jewish home with commands from the Torah inside

Miracles

(MIHR ih kuhlz) Unusual events that only God can cause to happen. Sometimes referred to as signs or wonders. Jesus performed miracles to show people that He is God's Son. **Mark 6:2**

Mission(s)

(MIH shuhn) Assignment God gives a person He has chosen to tell another group of people the good news of Jesus.

Missionary

(MIH shuh nehr ee) A Christian chosen by God who obeys and goes to tell another group of people the good news about Jesus. **Acts 13:2-3**

Micah

(MIGH kuh) Means "Who is like Yahweh?" 1. Prophet of the eighth century B.C. who preached during the reigns three of Judah's kings: Jotham, Ahaz, and Hezekiah. Even though Micah preached in Judah, some of his messages were directed toward the northern kingdom of Israel. 2. The sixth book in the Minor Prophets division of the Old Testament. Micah condemned the rich for hurting the poor, criticized unjust business practices, preached against the idolatry of the people, and said the destruction of Judah was an act of God's judgment. At the same time, he spoke messages of hope. Micah also preached that the Messiah would be born in Bethlehem. **Micah 1:1; 5:2; Matthew 2:6**

Mite

(KJV) (MIGHT) Smallest and least valuable coin. **Luke 21:2**

A Jewish widow's mite that was minted during the reign of Tiberius Caesar (A.D. 14-37)

Moab

(MOH ab) Narrow strip of land east of the Dead Sea that was known in biblical times as Moab, today is is part of Jordan. There were peaceful times as well as conflicts between the Israelites and Moabites during the time of the Judges. Ruth was from Moab. **Ruth 1:1-5**

The Moabite Stone was first discovered in 1868 by a German missionary. The Bible tells that Mesha, the king of Moab, had to pay tribute to Ahab, kind of Israel (2 Kings 3:4-5). When Ahab died, Mesha rebelled against Israel and quit paying. The Moabite stone is Mesha's expression of thanks to his god, Chemosh, for delivering Moab from Israel. The Moabite Stone is now in the Louvre Museum in Paris.

Money changers

Persons who sold or exchanged foreign money for Jewish money acceptable in temple worship. In the time of Jesus, money changers set up tables in the temple court of the Gentiles to provide this service for worshipers. In anger at this use of the temple, Jesus drove them out of the temple court along with the sellers of sacrificial animals. **Matthew 21:12-13**

Moreh (MOH reh)
1. Abraham's first place to camp in the land of Canaan. Here he built an altar after God had appeared to him and promised the land to Abraham's decendants. Joshua set up a memorial stone under the oak at Moreh as a reminder of the covenant between God and His people. 2. Hill in tribal territory of Issachar where Gideon reduced the number of his troops by testing the way they drank water. **Genesis 12:6-7; Joshua 24:26; Judges 7:1-8**

The hill of Moreh

Mortar
1. Claylike building material, used to stick brick or stone together. 2. Container used to crush grain, herbs, and olives. **Exodus 1:14; Numbers 11:8**

A stone mortar found at Lachish. Mortars were used for grinding grain and other foods.

Moses (MOH ziss)
Means "drawn out of the water." Leader of the Israelites in their exodus from Egyptian slavery and their time spent in the wilderness as they made their way toward the promised land. Moses was born after Pharoah ordered all Hebrew baby boys to be killed. Moses' mother hid him and later placed him in a basket at the edge of the Nile River. Pharaoh's daughter found Moses at the river and adopted him. Moses grew up in Pharoah's palace. As a man, he was forced to run away to the land of Midian when he killed an Egyptian supervisor who was beating a Hebrew slave. Many years later, God spoke to Moses through a burning bush and called him to lead the Israelites out of Egypt. At Mount Sinai, also known as Mt. Horeb, God gave Moses the law that would tell His people how to live. A summary of Moses' significance is stated at the end of Deuteronomy: "No prophet has arisen again in Israel like Moses, whom the Lord knew face to face" (Deuteronomy 34:10-12). **Exodus 2:1-15; 3:1-22; 20:1-21**

Mother-in-law
Mother of a person's husband or wife. Naomi was Ruth's mother-in-law. Jesus healed Peter's mother-in-law. **Ruth 3:1; Matthew 8:14-15**

Mount of Olives
Mountain east of Jerusalem, across the Kidron Valley. Mentioned in both the Old and New Testaments. The garden of Gethsemane, where Jesus was arrested, was at the base of the Mount of Olives. **Matthew 26:36-46; Mark 14:26-42**

The Mount of Olives viewed through one of the arched eastern entryways at the Temple Mount

Mount Sinai
(SIGH nigh) Another name for Mount Horeb where God spoke to Moses through the burning bush and where God gave the Ten Commandments to Moses and the people of Israel. **Exodus 3:1-22; 19:18–20:17**

Hikers near the top of Mount Sinai

Music
Important part of the lives of people in the Bible as well as people today. Music expresses all kinds of human emotions from joy to sadness. In Bible times people sang as they worked—digging wells, harvesting food, and preparing for battle. A variety of musical instruments was used to provide music in everyday life and in worship. (See *Musical Instruments in the Bible* chart, p. 122.)

Myrrh (MUHR)
Part of certain plants that smelled good and was used as an ingredient in anointing oil, applied as perfume, placed in clothes to make them smell better, given as a gift, and used to prepare dead bodies for burial. Was one of the gifts presented to the Jesus by the wise men. **Exodus 30:23; Esther 2:12; Psalm 45:8; Matthew 2:11; John 19:39-40**

Frankincense and myrrh burn as incense in an antique brass bowl. Chunks of frankincense (left) and myrrh (right) are in the foreground.

MUSICAL INSTRUMENTS OF THE BIBLE

Cymbals Used in worship. May be made of bronze. **1 Chronicles 15:19; Psalm 150:5**

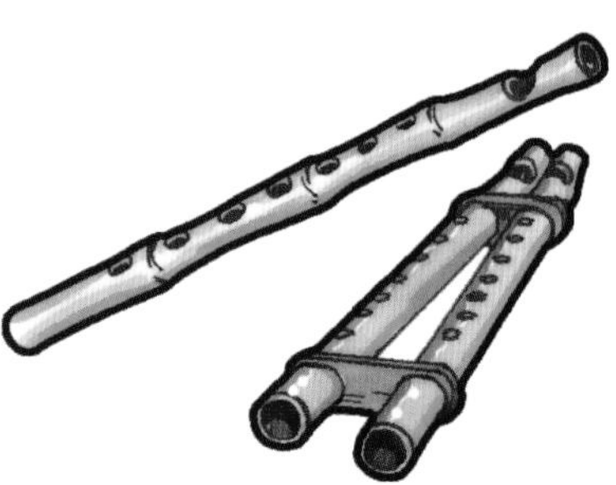

Flute, Pipe (KJV) Played at funerals or feasts. Made of two pipe of reed, metal, or ivory. Used to express joy or sadness. **1 Kings 1:39-40; Matthew 9:23**

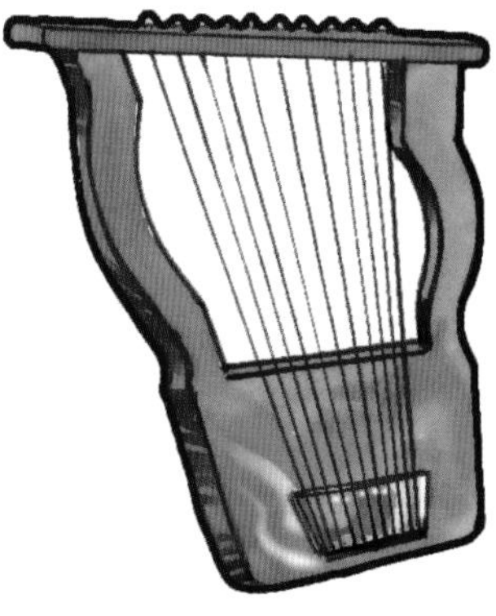

Harp The Egyptians' favorite instrument, made from expensive wood and metal. **1 Kings 10:12**

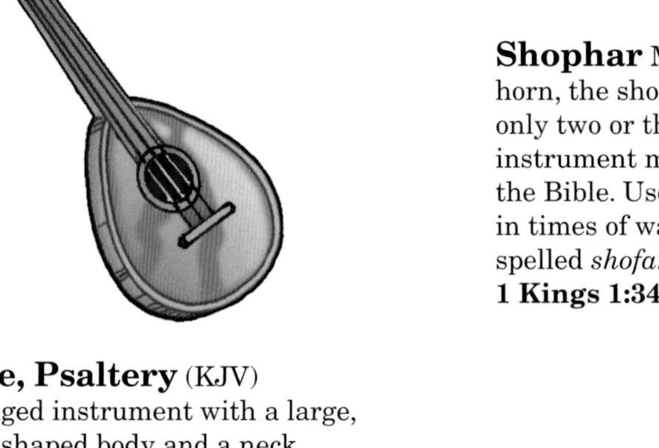

Lute, Psaltery (KJV) Stringed instrument with a large, pear-shaped body and a neck. **Psalms 71:22**

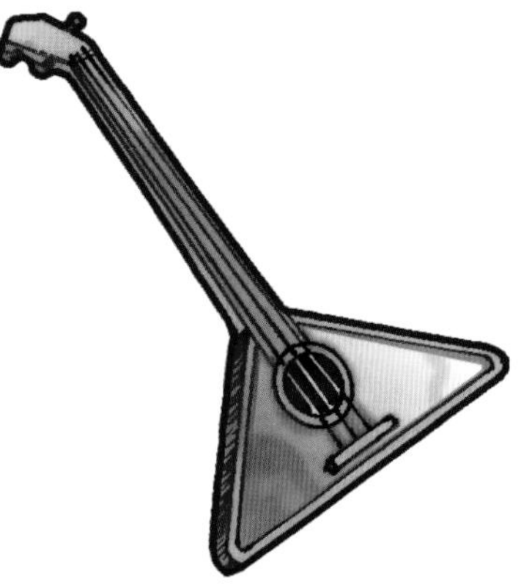

Lyre A stringed instrument used for both worship and other occasions. Was shaped like a rectangle or trapezoid. **2 Samuel 6:5**

Shophar Made from a ram's horn, the shophar could play only two or three notes. The instrument most often named in the Bible. Used to signal events in times of war and peace. Today, spelled *shofar*. **1 Kings 1:34**

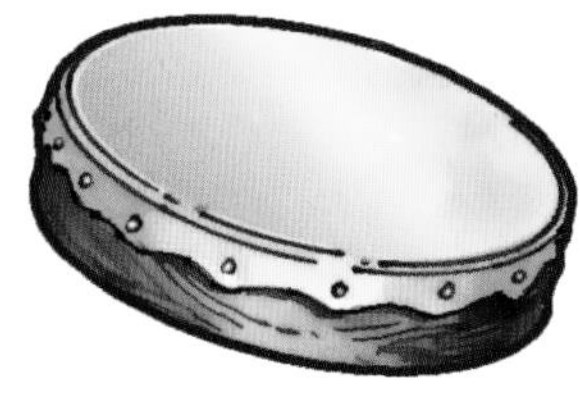

Tambourine, Timbrel (KJV) Often played for happy occasions. May have accompanied dancing. **Exodus 15:20**

Trumpet Made of metal, the end of this straight instrument was flared. Trumpets may have made high, shrill sounds. Priests played trumpets. **Numbers 10:2-10; 2 Chronicles 5:12-13**

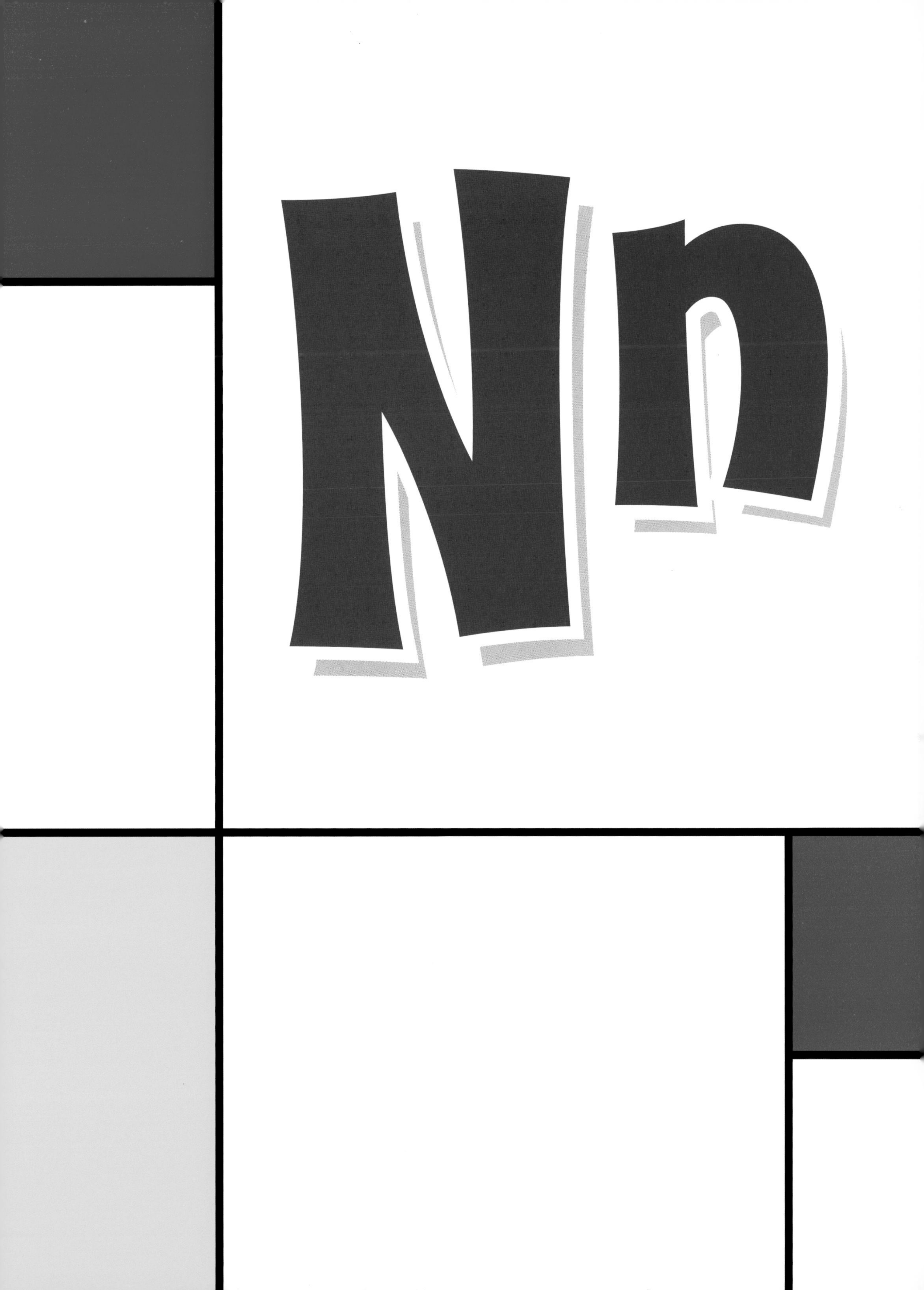
Nn

Naaman

Naaman (NAY uh muhn) Syrian general cured of leprosy when Elisha sent word to him to wash in the Jordan River seven times. **2 Kings 5:1-19**

Naaman is healed of leprosy.

Nahum

(NAY huhm) Name means "comfort, encourage."
1. Old Testament Hebrew prophet who wrote the book of Nahum. 2. Seventh book in the division of Minor Prophets of the Old Testament. The book speaks of God's judgment on Nineveh in order to give comfort to Judah.
Nahum 1:1

Nails

Metal fasteners used in construction and for decoration. The earliest nails were made of bronze. Later larger nails were made of iron. The nails used in the crucifixion of Jesus were likely iron spikes five to seven inches long.
John 20:25

Replica of Roman nails

Naboth

Naboth (NAY bahth) Owner of a vineyard in the Jezreel Valley near the country palace of King Ahab. Ahab wanted the vineyard, but Naboth would not sell it to him because the land was a family inheritance. Jezebel, Ahab's wife, had no regard for Israel's laws. She plotted Naboth's murder on the charge that he had blasphemed God and the king. Naboth's murder brought judgment on Ahab and his family. **Leviticus 25:23; 1 Kings 21:1-24**

Ahab's palace at Samaria

Names of God The names of God help people know who God is and what He does.

NAMES OF GOD

Name	Reference	Meaning	English Name
Elohim	Genesis 1:1	Powerful God	God
Adonai	Genesis 15:2	Lord	Lord God
El Elyon	Genesis 14:19-20	God Most High	God Most High
El Shaddai	Genesis 17:1	Almighty God	God Almighty
Yahweh	Exodus 3:14	Israel's Covenant God	I AM
Jehovah Jireh	Genesis 22:14	The Lord Provides	The Lord Will Provide
Jehovah Rophe	Exodus 15:26	The Lord Heals	The Lord Who Heals You
Jehovah Nissi	Exodus 17:15-16	The Lord Is My Banner	The Lord Is My Banner
Jehovah Mekadesh	Leviticus 20:8	The Lord Who Sanctifies You	The Lord Who Sanctifies You
Jehovah Shalom	Judges 6:24	The Lord Is Peace	The Lord Is Peace
Jehovah Tsidkenu	Jeremiah 23:6	The Lord Is Our Righteousness	The Lord Is Our Righteousness
Jehovah Shammah	Ezekiel 48:35	The Lord Is There	The Lord Is There

NAMES OF JESUS

Name	Reference	Meaning
Jesus	Matthew 1:21	Yahweh Saves
Immanuel	Matthew 1:23	God with us
Son of David	Matthew 9:27	One who brings in the Kingdom
Christ	Matthew 16:16	The Anointed One of God
Son of Man	Matthew 20:28	A divine title of suffering and exaltation
Holy One of God	Mark 1:24	Perfect and sinless
Word	John 1:1	Eternal God who reveals God
Lamb of God	John 1:29	Offered His life as a sacrifice for sins
Savior	John 4:42	One who delivers from sins
Bread of Life	John 6:35	Essential to life
Light of the World	John 9:5	One who brings hope and gives guidance
Good Shepherd	John 10:11	Gives guidance and protection
Son of God	John 20:31	Tells of Jesus' unique and special relationship with God
Lord	Romans 10:9	Sovereign Creator and Redeemer
Lord of Glory	1 Corinthians 2:8	The power of the Living God
Chief Cornerstone	Ephesians 2:20	A Sure Foundation for life
High Priest	Hebrews 3:1	The Perfect Mediator
King of Kings, Lord of Lords	Revelation 19:16	The Sovereign Almighty
Alpha and Omega	Revelation 21:6	The Beginning and Ending of all things

Naphtali (NAF tuh ligh) Son of Jacob and Rachel's maid Bilhah. He was Jacob's sixth son and was the ancestor of the tribe of Naphtali, one of the twelve tribes of Israel. **Genesis 30:5-8**

The tribal allotment of Naphtali

Nard Root used to make expensive fragrance or perfume. A woman in Bethany came to Jesus and poured the fragrance on His head. **Mark 14:3-9**

An alabaster jar. The woman who anointed Jesus broke an alabaster jar that contained expensive nard.

Nathan (NAY thuhn) Prophet in the royal court of King David and in the early years of King Solomon. **2 Samuel 7:1-7; 1 Kings 1:32-40**

Nathan tells King David of God's covenant with him.

Nazareth (NAZ uh reth) Town located in lower Galilee about halfway between the Sea of Galilee and the Mediterranean Sea. Mary and Joseph were from Nazareth and Jesus grew up there. Jesus was rejected by the people of Nazareth and was thrown out of the synagogue there. **Matthew 2:19-23; Luke 4:16-30**

Mount Precipice is a mountain just outside of Nazareth. According to tradition this is where an angry mob attempted to throw Jesus off the cliff.

Nazirite (NAZ uh right) **Nazarite** (KJV) People devoted to God. Two types of Nazirites are found in the Bible. One was for a lifetime. God told the parents before a child was born that he would be a Nazirite. Samson, Samuel, and John the Baptist were lifetime Nazirites. The other was based on a vow by a person for a specific period. Paul took the Nazirite vow for a specific period of time when he was in Corinth. **Judges 13; 1 Samuel 1; Luke 1:15-17; Acts 18:18; 21:22-26**

Nebuchadnezzar (NEB yoo kad NEZ uhr)

King of Babylon 602–562 B.C. Nebuchadnezzar served as a general under his father. His army conquered Judah and took many people to exile in Babylon, including Daniel. **2 Kings 25:8; Daniel 1:1-7**

The Hanging Gardens of Babylon, one of the Seven Wonders of the Ancient World, built by Nebuchadnezzar II

Needle

Small slender tool used in sewing with a hole (called an "eye") at one end through which thread is passed. The needles of New Testament times were similar in size to modern needles with the exception of our smallest needles. Needles were most often made of bronze, although bone and ivory were also used. Jesus said, "It is easier for a camel to go through the eye of a needle than for a rich person to enter the kingdom of God." He meant that a rich person can only be saved by God, who does impossible things. **Matthew 19:23-26**

Negev (NEH gehv)

Dry region in southern Palestine. Abram traveled toward this area and later lived there. After God delivered the Israelites from slavery in Egypt, they wandered in the wilderness for 40 years. Moses sent twelve spies into the Negev to spy out the land. **Genesis 12:9; 20:1; Numbers 13:17,22,29**

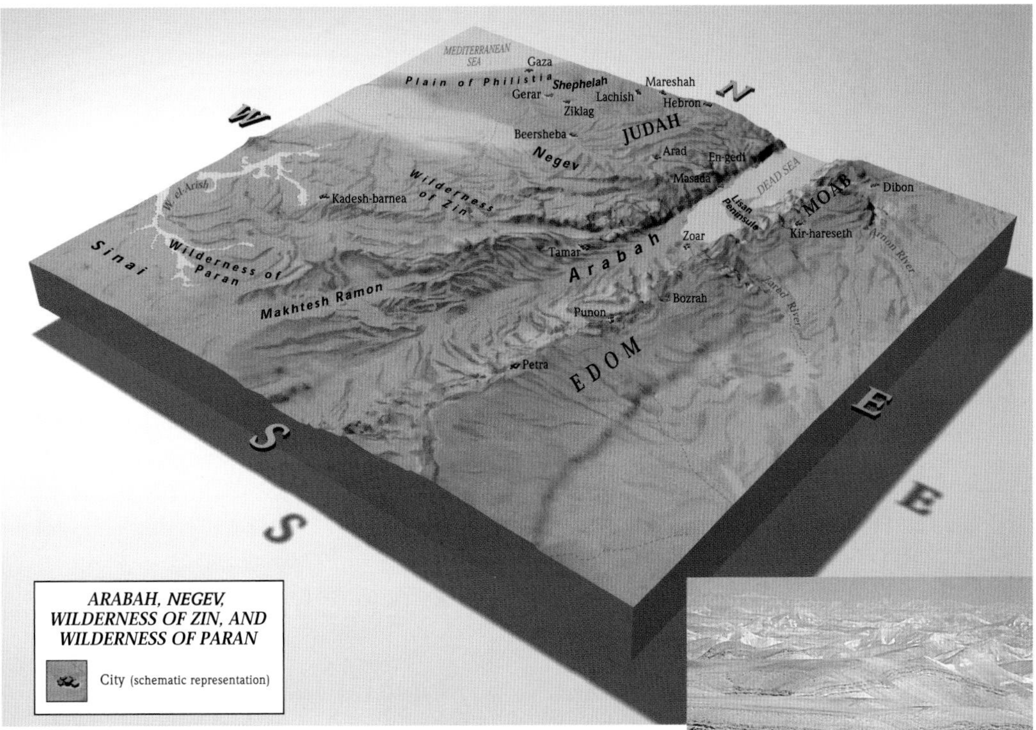

ARABAH, NEGEV, WILDERNESS OF ZIN, AND WILDERNESS OF PARAN

City (schematic representation)

The Negev

Wasteland of the northern Negev in southern Israel

Nehemiah (NEE huh MIGH uh) 1. Nehemiah, the son of Hachaliah, is the main character in the book that bears his name. He lived at the same time as Ezra and Malachi. He was a descendant of Judeans exiled to Babylon. He served as the cupbearer of King Artaxerxes. He received permission to return to Jerusalem, and he led the people to rebuild the wall around the city. 2. Eleventh book in the division of History of the Old Testament. The book tells the history of the Jews after their return from exile and tells how God used Nehemiah to rebuild Jerusalem's city wall. **Nehemiah 1:1; 2:1-8; 6:15-16**

A piece of charred wood from the ruins of Jerusalem when Nehemiah arrived from Persia as the new governor of Judea in 445 B.C.

Nehemiah inspects the walls of Jerusalem.

Neighbor
The Bible does not clearly explain what a neighbor is. However, the Bible does make it clear that people are to love others, even if those other people are different. **Luke 10:25-37**

Nephew Son of a person's brother or sister. Lot was the nephew of Abraham. **Genesis 12:5**

Nero (NEE roh) Became the Roman emperor in A.D. 54 at the age of 13. During his rule, the Great Fire broke out in Rome (A.D. 64). Much of the city was destroyed, including Nero's palace. The story, probably true in part, says that Nero played the fiddle while Rome burned. People knew that he planned to build a much larger palace for himself, and they thought he used the fire to clear off the land. Needing to blame someone for the fire, Nero claimed that the Christians had set the fire. Nero ordered the killing of many Christians.

Nero, Roman emperor from A.D. 54-68

Net Loosely woven mesh of twine or cord used for catching birds, fish, or other animals. **Matthew 4:21-22**

A fisherman repairs his net.

Nicodemus (NIK uh DEE muhs) A Pharisee, "a ruler of the Jews." He was a member of the Sanhedrin, the Jewish ruling group. He helped people understand the Hebrew Scriptures (the Old Testament). Nicodemus talked with Jesus at night and was the first person to hear the words of John 3:16. After Jesus' crucifixion, Joseph of Arimathea took Jesus' body for burial and Nicodemus brought aloes and spices to prepare a king for burial. **John 3:1-16; 19:38-42**

Jesus talks with Nicodemus about being born again.

New Testament Second major section of the Bible with 27 separate books. God inspired at least eight different writers to write the New Testament. The Gospels give four accounts of Jesus' life. Acts is a book of the history of events in the early church. Paul wrote 13 letters to churches and individuals. The division of General Letters contains Hebrews, a letter from James, two letters from Peter, three from John, and one from Jude. The last book of the New Testament is Revelation, a book of prophecy.

DIVISIONS OF THE NEW TESTAMENT

GOSPELS
Matthew
Mark
Luke
John

HISTORY
Acts

PAUL'S LETTERS
Romans
1 Corinthians
2 Corinthians
Galatians
Ephesians
Philippians
Colossians
1 Thessalonians
2 Thessalonians
1 Timothy
2 Timothy
Titus
Philemon

GENERAL LETTERS
Hebrews
James
1 Peter
2 Peter
1 John
2 John
3 John
Jude

PROPHECY
Revelation

Nile River

(NIGHL) Major river in Egypt. The Nile is the basis of Egypt's wealth. It is the only river to flow northwards across the Sahara Desert. As a slave in Egypt, Jochebed hid her son Moses and later put him in a basket and left him in the reeds in the Nile River to be discovered by the Pharoah's daughter. Years later with the first plague on the Egyptians, Moses struck the Nile River with his staff and it turned to blood.
Exodus 2:1-10; 7:14-27

A closeup view of the Nile next to fertile land irrigated by the Nile. Next to the fertile land is desert.

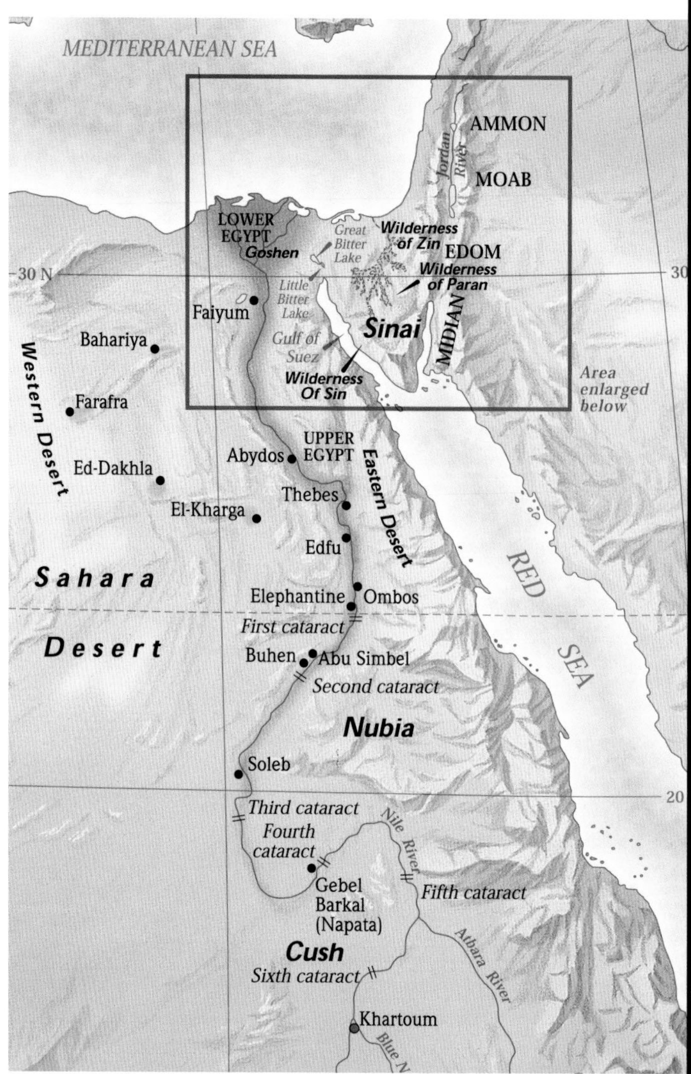

The Nile flows 1675 miles northward to the Mediterranean Sea from sources in both Tanzania and Ethiopia.

Noah (NOH ah)

A good and righteous man, Noah was the father of Shem, Ham, and Japheth who were born when he was 500 years old. God warned Noah that He was going to remove all the people from the earth because of their sin. Noah was a man of faith and obeyed God. God gave Noah instructions to build the ark by which he and his family would survive the coming flood. For at least 100 years, Noah built the ark. Then, God caused the animals to enter it before the rain fell. After 150 days the water began to go down.When the land was dry, Noah, his family, and the animals left the ark. God sent a rainbow to show His promise that He would never destroy the earth again by water.
Genesis 6:9–9:17

Noah and his wife after the flood waters receded

Nineveh

(NIN uh vuh) Greatest of the capitals of the ancient Assyrian Empire from about 800 to 612 B.C. located on the left bank of the Tigris River in northeastern Mesopotamia (Iraq today). It was the enemy city to which God called the prophet Jonah. The book of Jonah calls it "that great city." Nahum, the prophet, said Nineveh would be overthrown, and in 612 B. C. it was.
Jonah 1:2; 4:11; Nahum 3:7

A reconstruction of the Adad Gate that existed in ancient Nineveh. It was named for the Assyrian god Adad. The government of Iraq initiated the reconstruction in the 1960s.

Numbers

(NUHM buhrz) Fourth book in the division of Law in the Old Testament. The book tells of the census or numbering of the people of Israel and the history of their journey after leaving Egypt. Moses wrote this book. **Numbers 1:1-4**

Nurse

To breast-feed a baby. In the Old Testament, children often nursed for as long as three years. **Exodus 2:7-9; 1 Samuel 1:23-24**

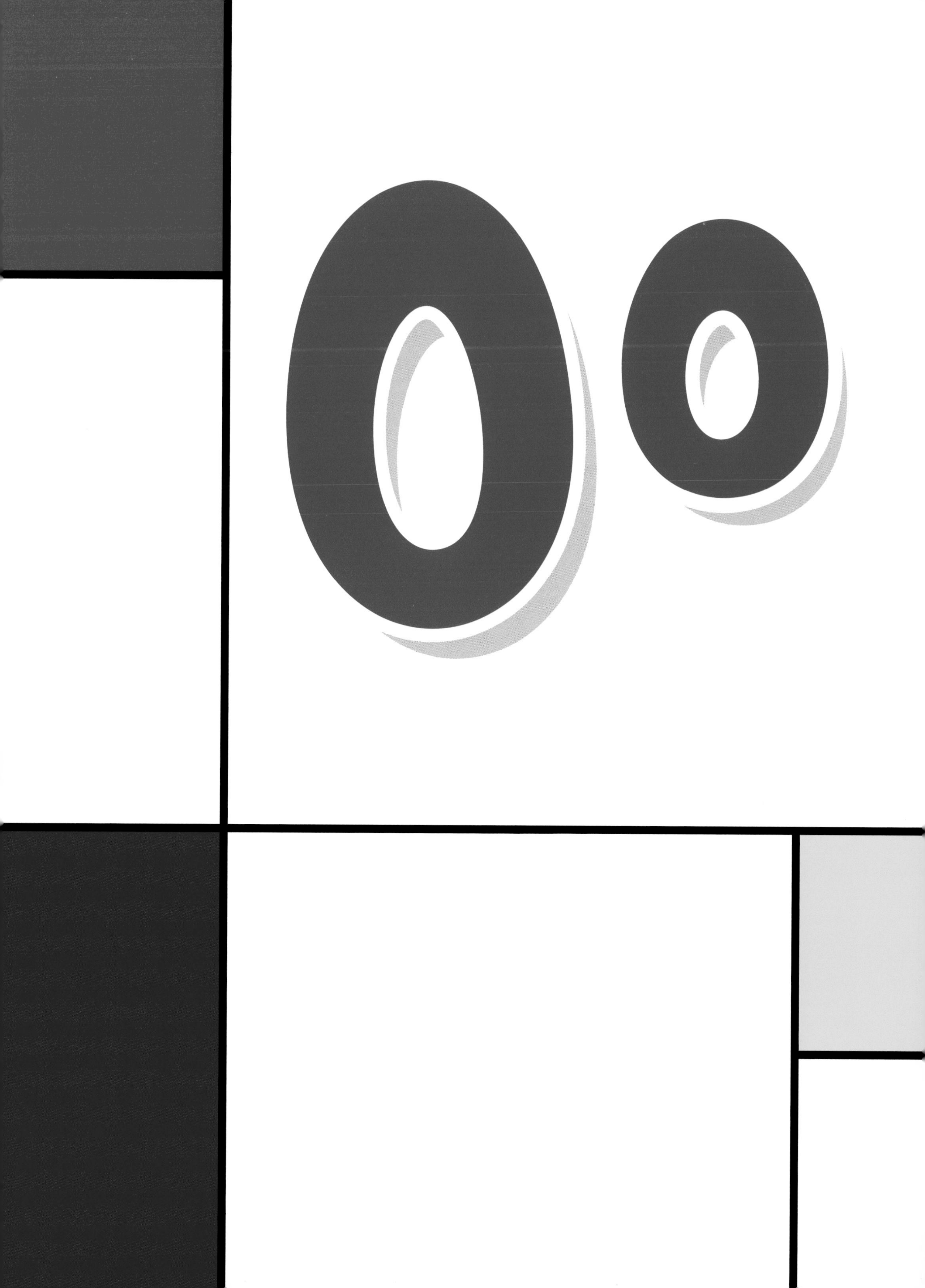

Obadiah

(OH buh DIGH uh)
Means "Yahweh's servant."
1. Israelite prophet who preached against Edom. He lived at the same time as Jeremiah. He preached against the Edomites who acted proud before God and hurt His people.
2. Fourth book in the division of Minor Prophets of the Old Testament. This book teaches that God will punish those who give His people trouble.
Obadiah 1:1,15

The rugged mountains of Edom, the nation against which the prophet Obadiah preached

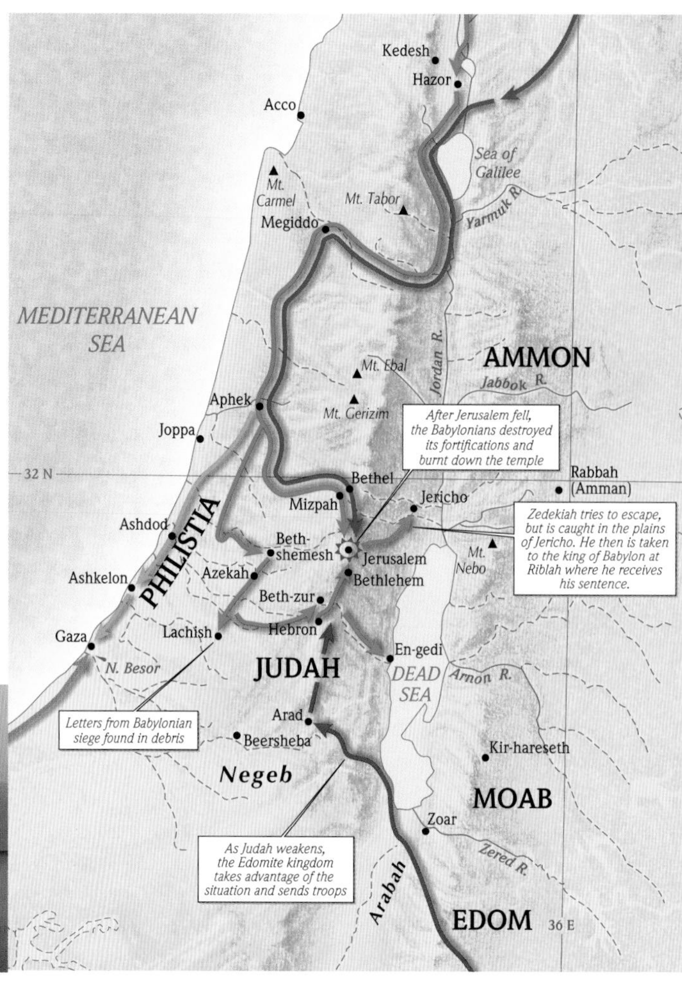

Edom was Judah's neighbor to the southeast. The Edomites and the people of Judah were related. They had numerous conflicts throughout history.

Odor

Scent or fragrance. When God sent plagues on Egypt because Pharoah would not let the Israelites leave, He sent frogs that covered the land. When they died, they were piled in heaps and the odor was terrible.
Exodus 8:1-14

Offering

Gift people give God. Some biblical offerings were money or valuable items such as jewelry. Burnt offerings, fellowship offerings, and peace offerings were animals or parts of animals. They were sacrificed and given to God. Grain and bread could also be given as offerings.
2 Chronicles 31:2,10

Obed

(OH bed)
Son of Boaz and Ruth, father of Jesse, and grandfather of King David. Jesus was a descendant of Jesse. (See *Line, family.*)
Ruth 4:13-17;
Matthew 1:4-6,16

Obey/ obedience

To hear God's Word and act on it. In the Old Testament the word for obey means "to hear." In the New Testament the word translated "obey" means "to hear" or "to listen" and "to trust." When a person hears or reads God's Word, he needs to obey what he hears or reads. To really hear God's Word is to obey God's Word. Peter and John told the Jewish leaders that they needed to obey God rather than men.
Exodus 19:5;
Jeremiah 7:23;
Acts 5:29

Peter and John before the Sanhedrin

Oholiab
(oh HOH lih ab)
Craftsman, designer, and embroiderer from the tribe of Dan who assisted Bezalel in supervising the construction of the tabernacle and its equipment.
Exodus 31:6; 35:34; 36:1-2; 38:23

God gave Bezalel and Oholiab the ability to teach others the skills required to build the tabernacle. The skills included cutting gems and doing embroidery with yarn and fine linen.

Old Testament First part of the Bible. Tells the history of the nation of Israel and God's dealings with them. For Jews it is the complete Bible. Christians believe it shows that Jesus Christ fulfills many of the Old Testament prophecies. The Old Testament has five divisions: Law, History, Poetry, Major Prophets, Minor Prophets.

Oil Made from olives and used for food, medicine, fuel, and religious rituals. Oil was considered a blessing given by God. Samuel used oil to anoint Saul and David as kings. Elijah helped a widow have plenty of oil to make bread during a time of no rain.
Deuteronomy 11:14; 1 Kings 17:8-16

Olive oil and bread

DIVISIONS OF THE OLD TESTAMENT

LAW
Genesis
Exodus
Leviticus
Numbers
Deuteronomy

HISTORY
Joshua
Judges
Ruth
1 and 2 Samuel
1 and 2 Kings
1 and 2 Chronicles
Ezra
Nehemiah
Esther

POETRY
Job
Psalms
Proverbs
Ecclesiastes
Song of Songs/
Song of Solomon (KJV)

MAJOR PROPHETS
Isaiah
Jeremiah
Lamentations
Ezekiel
Daniel

MINOR PROPHETS
Hosea
Joel
Amos
Obadiah
Jonah
Micah
Nahum
Habakkuk
Zephaniah
Haggai
Zechariah
Malachi

Aa Bb Cc Dd Ee Ff Gg Hh Ii Jj Kk Ll Mm Nn Oo Pp Qq Rr Ss Tt Uu Vv Ww Xx Yy Zz

Olives Fruit from the olive tree. Olive trees grow best in warm weather with cool winters and hot dry summers. Olives are pressed to create yellow oil. The oil used in the lampstand in the tabernacle was from olives. **Exodus 27:20-21**

Olive press

Omnipotent (ahm NIP uh tuhnt) Being all-powerful, which is true only of God. The Bible tells that all power belongs to God, that God does whatever He pleases. With God, all things are possible. He can do far more than people ask or think. **Psalm 147:5; Luke 1:37; Ephesians 3:20**

Omnipresent (ahm nih PREH zunt) Being present everywhere at once, which is true only of God. **Psalm 139:7**

Omniscient (ahm NIH shunt) Having all knowledge, which is true only of God. God knows people better than they know themselves and better than any other person knows them. **Psalm 139:1-6**

Onesimus (oh NESS ih muhs) Slave for whom Paul wrote his letter to Philemon. Onesimus had run away from Philemon but became a Christian after Paul told him about Jesus. Paul encouraged Philemon to be kind to Onesimus. Later, Onesimus went with Tychicus to take a letter to the Colossians. **Colossians 4:7-9; Philemon**

Paul prepares a letter for Onesimus to take to Philemon.

Oracle/oracles Messages from God. Sometimes a person asked God a question and God answered it. Other times God spoke to a person and gave him a message to deliver to God's people. The messages could be about future events or about decisions related to a present event. **Zechariah 9:1**

Ordinance Church event which Jesus commanded His followers to do. The two ordinances are the Lord's Supper and baptism. **Matthew 26:29; 28:16-20**

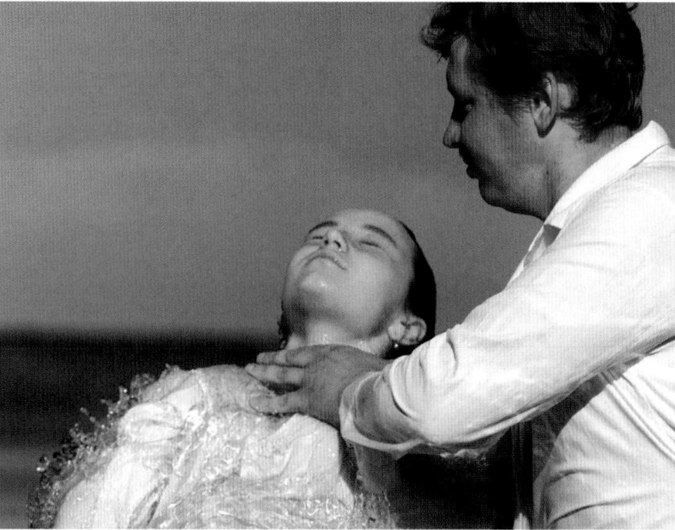

A new believer is baptized.

Ordination/ ordain Recognizing that God has called people in the church to special service. Usually church leaders lay their hands on the heads of the chosen people and pray for them. The church at Jerusalem ordained seven men to help with the work of the church. The apostles "prayed and laid their hands on them." The leaders of the church at Antioch prayed and laid hands on Paul and Barnabas whom the Holy Spirit had called as missionaries. **Acts 6:1-6; 13:1-3**

Barnabas and Saul are set apart to take the gospel to other parts of the Mediterranean world.

Oven Place for baking food, especially bread. Ancient ovens were made of clay and were two to three feet in diameter. **Exodus 8:3**

Large domed oven

Overseer Person in charge of a group to make sure the work gets done. **Exodus 5:1-14; 1 Timothy 3:2**

Pp

Palace

Home of a king or pharoah. The Pharaoh of the Exodus lived in a palace in Egypt. David and Solomon both built themselves a palace in Jerusalem.
Exodus 7:23;
2 Samuel 5:11
I Kings 7:8

A portion of the northern palace complex built by Herod the Great at Masada on the western shore of the Dead Sea. According to the Jewish historian, Flavius Josephus, Herod built this palace between 37 and 31 B.C.

Pallet (PA leht)

small mattress, usually straw-filled, light enough to be carried. **Acts 5:15**

Papyrus
(puh PIGH ruhs)
Bulrush (KJV)

Reed plant. Moses' mother used papyrus to make a basket for her son. She place him in the reeds, at the edge of the Nile River, to protect him from Pharoah's command that every male Hebrew child should be drowned. The papyrus plant was also used to make writing paper. The core of the papyrus stalk was cut into strips, soaked in water, dried, beaten, and glued together to make a scroll. (See *Reeds.*)
Exodus 2:1-4

A modern variety of the ancient papyrus plant from whose stalks writing paper was made first in Egypt and then in other countries around the Mediterranean Sea.

Palestine

(PAL uhs tighn) Land of the Bible. The land west of Jordan River that God gave to the Israelites. God promised the land to Abraham, and it was called Canaan. When God spoke to Moses, He called it "the land I promised." The area was called Israel during the reigns of David and Solomon. When the kingdom was divided, the land of ten tribes was called Israel and the remaining two tribes were called Judah. By New Testament times, the land had been divided into three areas: Judea, Samaria, Galilee.
Genesis 12:5;
Deuteronomy 34:4;
2 Samuel 5:1-2;
1 Kings 12:20-21

Parable

(PAR uh buhl) Story Jesus told to help people understand the kingdom of God. Jesus told parables about a man who sowed seed, a woman who lost a coin, and a son who left home. (See *Parables of Jesus* chart.)
Matthew 13:3-9;
Luke 15:8-32

One of Jesus' best known parables is about four different kinds of soil.

PARABLES OF JESUS

PARABLE	OCCASION	LESSON TAUGHT	REFERENCES
The speck and the log	Sermon on the Mount	Do not judge others	Matthew 7:1-6; Luke 6:37-42
The two foundations	Sermon on the Mount	Build your life on a solid foundation	Matthew 7:24-27; Luke 6:47-49
Children in the marketplaces	Jesus to the crowds	A fault-finding disposition is evil	Matthew 11:16-19; Luke 7:32
Two debtors	Dinner with Simon the Pharisee	Much forgiveness results in much love	Luke 7:41
An unclean spirit's return	Jewish leaders demand a sign	Unbelief hardens the heart	Matthew 12:43-45; Luke 11:24-26
The rich fool	Dispute of two brothers	Storing up treasures is futile	Luke 12:16-21
Barren fig tree	Report of executed Galileans	Unbelief is dangerous	Luke 13:6-9
The sower	Jesus taught from a boat	Hearers respond to preaching in various ways	Matthew 13:3-8; Mark 4:3-8; Luke 8:5-8
The wheat and the weeds	Jesus taught from a boat	Good and evil will be separated at the harvest	Matthew 13:24-30
The seed	Private teaching	Hearers respond to preaching in various ways	Matthew 13:19-23; Mark 4:14-20; Luke 8:11-15
The mustard seed	Jesus teaching	The kingdom will start small but grow much larger	Matthew 13:31-32; Mark 4:30-32; Luke 13:18-19
The yeast	Jesus teaching	The kingdom will spread throughout the world	Matthew 13:33; Luke 13:20-21
Using your light	Jesus teaching	Spreading the kingdom news (or, the gospel should be shared)	Matthew 5:15; Mark 4:21; Luke 8:16; 11:33
The large net	Teaching the disciples	Evil people will go to hell	Matthew 13:47-48
The hidden treasure	Teaching the disciples	The kingdom is valuable	Matthew 13:44
The priceless pearl	Teaching the disciples	The kingdom is priceless	Matthew 13:45-46
The storehouse of truth	Teaching the disciples	Kingdom instruction includes old and new	Matthew 13:52
A question about fasting	To John's disciples and the Pharisees	Christ's companionship brings joy	Matthew 9:15; Mark 2:19-20; Luke 5:34-35
The patched garment	To John's disciples and the Pharisees	Christianity replaces Judaism	Matthew 9:16; Mark 2:21; Luke 5:36
Wine in wineskins	To John's disciples and the Pharisees	Christianity replaces Judaism	Matthew 9:17; Mark 2:22; Luke 5:37
Your adversary	Sermon on the Mount	Forgive your adversaries (or, be reconciled with God)	Matthew 5:25; Luke 12:58
The unforgiving slave	Teaching the disciples	The forgiven must forgive	Matthew 18:23-35
The good Samaritan	Testing Jesus	Love your neighbor	Luke 10:30-37
The three loaves	Disciples ask about prayer	Be persistent in prayer	Luke 11:5-8
The good shepherd	Pharisees reject miracle testimony	Jesus is the only way to God	John 10:1-16

PARABLES OF JESUS

PARABLE	OCCASION	LESSON TAUGHT	REFERENCES
The narrow way	Jesus is questioned about who is saved	Follow the road to life	Matthew 7:13-14; Luke 13:24
The guests of the banquet	Teaching on humility	Choose to be humble	Luke 14:7-11
The great banquet	Teaching the Pharisees	God invites guests; when some reject the call, others will be invited	Matthew 22:2-9; Luke 14:16-23
The wedding clothes	Teaching at the temple	Necessity of purity	Matthew 22:10-14
The tower	Teaching the crowds	Calculate the cost of following Jesus	Luke 14:28-30
The king going to war	Teaching the crowds	Calculate the cost of following Jesus	Luke 14:31-32
The lost sheep	Responding to Jewish leaders' intolerance	Rejoice in recovering what was lost	Matthew 18:12-13; Luke 15:4-7
The lost coin	Responding to Jewish leaders' intolerance	Rejoice in recovering what was lost	Luke 15:8-9
The lost son	Responding to Jewish leaders' intolerance	Rejoice in recovering what was lost	Luke 15:11-32
The dishonest manager	Teaching the disciples	Prepare for the judgment day	Luke 16:1-8
The rich man and Lazarus	Rebuttal to the Pharisees	Value the kingdom more than money	Luke 16:19-31
The slave's duty	Teaching the apostles	Do not boast in mere obedience	Luke 17:7-10
The vineyard workers	Teaching the disciples	All believers receive the complete reward	Matthew 20:1-16
The talents	Teaching the disciples	Be faithful with what you have been given	Matthew 25:14-30; Luke 19:11-27
The persistent widow	Teaching the disciples	Do not be discouraged in praying	Luke 18:2-5
The Pharisee and the tax collector	Teaching the Pharisees	Self-righteousness and humility contrasted	Luke 18:10-14
The two sons	Jesus' authority challenged	Obedience is better than words	Matthew 21:28
The vineyard owner	Teaching in the temple complex	Jewish unbelievers are rejected	Matthew 21:33-43; Mark 12:1-9; Luke 20:9-15
The fig tree	Teaching the disciples	Signs indicate when Jesus will return	Matthew 24:32; Mark 13:28; Luke 21:29-30
The homeowner and the thief	Teaching the disciples	Be prepared for Jesus' return	Matthew 24:43; Luke 12:39
A man on a journey	Teaching the disciples	Be alert for Jesus' return	Mark 13:34
Comparison of two managers	Teaching the disciples	The faithful leader will be blessed	Matthew 24:45-51; Luke 12:42-46
The 10 virgins	Teaching the disciples	Stay alert and prepared for Jesus' return	Matthew 25:1-12
The alert people	Teaching the disciples	Those who are ready for Jesus' return will be blessed	Luke 12:36-38
The vine and the branches	Night before the cross	Jesus is the source of life	John 15:1-6

Paralyzed, Withered

(KJV) To be unable to move one's body or one part of the body. Jesus healed a man with a paralyzed hand. He healed another man who was paralyzed and could not walk. **Mark 3:1-5; Luke 5:18**

Jesus heals a man whose hand was paralyzed.

Pastor

(PAS tuhr) Person God chooses to lead a church. A pastor preaches and teaches God's Word, tells people about Jesus, visits the sick, and cares for the people in his church. **Ephesians 4:11**

Patience

(PAY shuns) One of the nine qualities of the fruit of the Spirit. Patience is being able to keep on doing what is right even when times are difficult. **Galatians 5:22-23**

Parchment

(PAHRCH muhnt) Writing paper made from animal skins. **Isaiah 8:1; 2 Timothy 4:13**

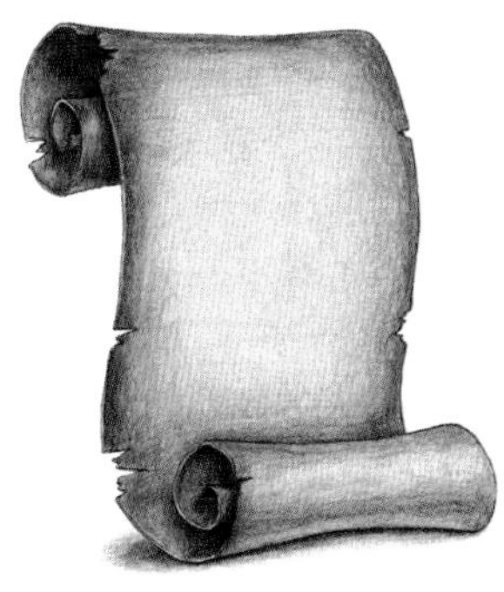

Ancient parchment scroll

Passover

(PASS oh vuhr) Hebrew feast to remind the Israelites of how God delivered them from slavery in Egypt. An angel passed over the Hebrews' houses but killed the Egyptians' firstborn sons. Passover was celebrated by Jesus and His disciples and is still celebrated by Jewish people today. (See *Jewish Festivals and Feasts* chart, p. 59.) **Exodus 12:1-32**

A Jewish girl enjoys matzah ball soup as a part of her celebration of Passover. Matzah is made without yeast or leaven just as the bread that was eaten with the first Passover.

Patriarch (PAY trih ahrk) Ancestor who may have been the founding father of a family, a clan, or a nation. Israel's founding fathers were Abraham, Isaac, Jacob, and the 12 sons of Jacob (Israel). When God called Moses to lead the Israelites out of bondage in slavery, He called Himself "the God of Abraham, the God of Isaac, and the God of Jacob."
Exodus 3:6

Abraham, Israel's patriarch, built a stone altar at Shechem. **Genesis 12:4-7**

Paul (PAWL, PAHL) Roman name of the Hebrew "Saul." Outstanding missionary and writer of the early church. He wrote 13 letters that make up almost one-fourth of the New Testament. Paul was a Jew and a Roman citizen. He grew up in Jerusalem as a student of Gamaliel and as a Pharisee. At first Paul persecuted Christians, but later he became a Christian himself. He was a Christian missionary to Asia Minor, Greece, and other countries around the Mediterranean Sea. Paul was arrested because Jewish leaders did not want him to preach about Jesus. He continued to preach and write letters from prison in Rome. **Acts 22:3,28; Philippians 3:4-6; Acts 9:1-22**

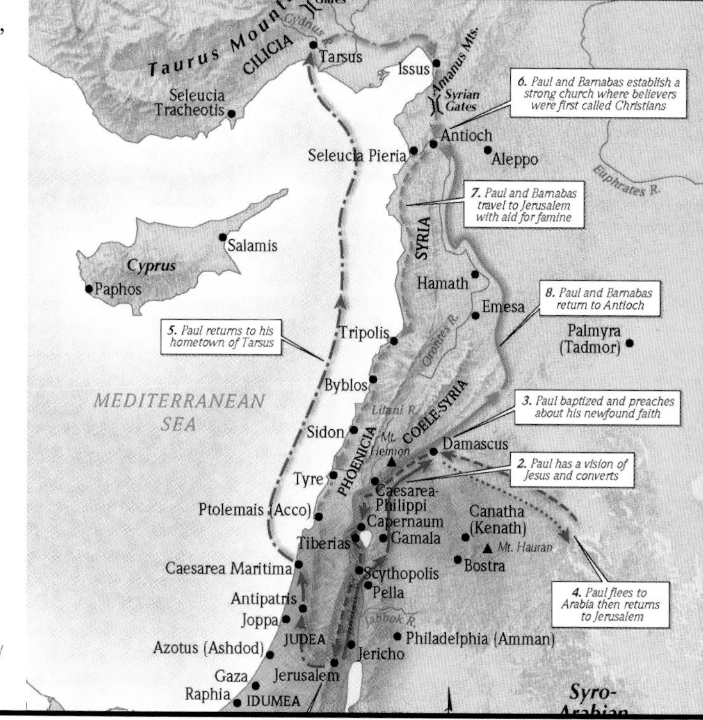

Places of Paul's conversion and early ministry

Peace One of the nine qualities seen in the fruit of the Spirit. A feeling of being safe and secure. Trusting God to take care of one's needs in any situation. **Galatians 5:22-23; Ephesians 1:2**

Pentateuch

(PEN tuh tyook) Word means "five containers." Refers to the first five books of the Old Testament: Genesis, Exodus, Leviticus, Numbers, and Deuteronomy. This division of Scripture is also called *Torah* which means "instruction" or "law."

Thirteen-year-old girl reads from ancient Hebrew Torah (Pentateuch) on her bat mitzvah at a Jewish temple

Pentecost (PEN tih kawst) Major Jewish feast, also called the Feast of Weeks. From the Greek word meaning "fifty," it is held seven weeks (50 days) after Passover to celebrate the grain harvest. During this festival, the Holy Spirit came to believers in Jerusalem. (See *Jewish Festivals and Feasts* chart, p.59.) **Leviticus 23:15-16; Acts 2:1-21**

Peter tells good news about Jesus on Pentecost.

Perfume
Good smelling oils. Many perfumes are mentioned in the Bible including aloes, balsam, cinnamon, frankincense, gum, henna, myrrh, nard, and saffron. **Ecclesiastes 7:1**

An ancient alabastron or jar that contained fragrant ointments

Perga
(PUHR guh) Ancient city in the province of Pamphylia, about eight miles from the Mediterranean Sea. Paul, Barnabas, and John Mark traveled to Perga from Paphos. Young John Mark left the team in Perga to return home. **Acts 13:13**

The south Hellenistic gate of the ancient city of Perga in Pamphylia (modern Turkey)

Perish
To die. If a person has not confessed and trusted Jesus as Savior, death means being separated from God forever. **John 3:16**

Persecution
Hurting or killing people because their faith, culture, or race is different from the people in power. People are persecuted because someone wants to silence, punish, or even kill them. Jesus was persecuted and killed by the religious leaders and government officials of His day. First Peter, Hebrews, and Revelation were written to encourage Christians in times of persecution. **Matthew 27:15-54; Mark 3:6; Luke 4:29; John 5:16; 1 Peter 3:13-18; Hebrews 10:32-39; Revelation 2:8-11**

The Colosseum at Rome, under construction from A.D. 72-80. During times of persecution, many Christians died in the Colosseum.

Perseverance
Continuing to trust God and believe in Him even when life is difficult. **Ephesians 6:18**

Peter
(PEE tuhr) Name means "rock." 1. Apostle of Jesus. Also known as Simon Peter, he was a fisherman who lived in Capernaum and worked with his brother Andrew. He was a member of Jesus' inner circle and a leader and spokesman for the apostles. Peter identified Jesus as the Messiah. He denied Jesus, but after Pentecost he preached and taught boldly.

2. First and Second Peter are the third and fourth books in the General Letters division of the New Testament. Peter wrote these letters to encourage Christians who were being persecuted and to warn them about false teachers. **Matthew 16:18; 26:69-75; Mark 3:16; 9:2; Acts 4:18-20; 1 Peter 1:1-2; 2 Peter 1:1-2**

Andrew introduces his brother, Peter, to Jesus.

Persia
(PUHR zhuh) Old Testament nation that is now the nation of Iran. Babylon conquered Jerusalem and destroyed the temple in 586 B.C. Later Cyrus of Persia conquered Babylon. He allowed the Jews to return to Judah and encouraged them to rebuild the temple. Both Ezra and Nehemiah were official representatives of the Persian government. Daniel was taken into exile by the Babylonians, but his work continued into the time of the Persians. Esther is a story of God's rescue of His people during the rule of the Persian emperor, Ahasuerus (also known as Xerxes I). **Ezra 1:1-4; 7; Nehemiah 10:1; Esther 1:1; Daniel 1:6**

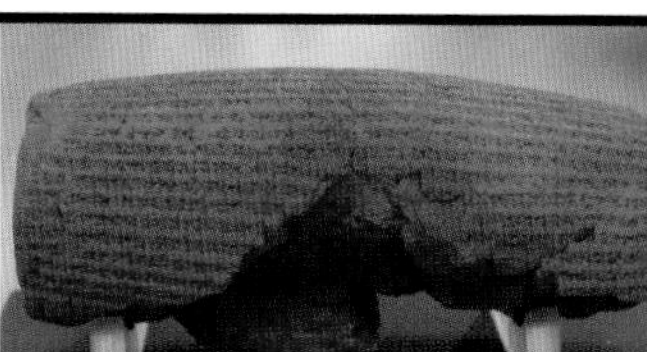
The Cyrus Cylinder, inscribed with the famous Edict of Cyrus the Great in 538 B.C. (2 Chronicles 26:23; Ezra 1:2-3). The Cyrus Cylinder was discovered in 1879 in Nineveh, Iraq, by Hormuzd Rassam. It is currently located in the British Museum.

Pharaoh

(FEHR oh)
Means "great house." Title for an Egyptian king.
Exodus 5:1-2

The funerary mask of King Tut (Pharaoh Tutankhamun) of Egypt

Philemon

(figh LEE muhn)
1. Christian who received a letter from Paul asking him to be kind to his runaway slave, Onesimus, who had become a Christian. 2. Thirteenth book in the division of Paul's Letters in the New Testament. Written to the man of that name who lived in Colossae. Paul encouraged him to forgive his runaway slave Onesimus and treat him as a brother in Christ. (See *Onesimus*.) **Philemon**

The mound marking the site of ancient Colossae, the home of Philemon. Paul sent his letter to Philemon by Tychicus and Philemon's slave, Onesimus.

Philip

(FIL ip) Name means "fond of horses." 1. One of Jesus' twelve apostles. From Bethsaida Philip called Nathanael to "come and see" Jesus. Before Jesus fed the 5000, He asked Philip where they could buy food for all the people. 2. A member of the church at Jerusalem who was chosen as one of the first seven deacons. Philip went to Samaria to tell people about Jesus. An angel of the Lord told him to go to the Jerusalem-Gaza road where he met an Ethiopian, told him about Jesus, and baptized him.
Matthew 10:3; John 1:43-45; John 6:5-7; Acts 6:5; Acts 8:5-8,26-40

Philip, the deacon, explains the Scriptures to the Ethiopian official.

Pharisees

(FEHR uh see) Means "separated." In New Testament times, religious leaders who taught the law. Most of the Pharisees did not like Jesus and His teachings. They looked for a way to arrest Jesus. Two Pharisees, Joseph of Arimathea and Nicodemus, helped take Jesus' body from the cross for burial.
Matthew 21:45-46; John 19:38-42

The Pharisee and the tax collector
Luke 18:9-14

Philippi

(FIH lih pigh) City in Macedonia where Paul met Lydia, who became a Christian. While Paul was starting a church there, he was beaten and put in prison. Later Paul wrote a letter to the church thanking them for all their help. **Acts 16:11-40; Philippians 1:1**

Ruins of the marketplace in the ancient city of Philippi

Aa Bb Cc Dd Ee Ff Gg Hh Ii Jj Kk Ll Mm Nn Oo Pp Qq Rr Ss Tt Uu Vv Ww Xx Yy Zz

Philippians (fih LIP ih uhnz)

Sixth book in the division of Paul's Letters of the New Testament. Was written to the church in Philippi to thank the believers for their kindness to Paul and to explain that true joy comes only from knowing Jesus. **Philippians 1:1-2**

Site of ancient Philippi

Pilate, Pontius

(PIGH luht, PAHN chuhss)
Roman governor of Judea. The Jewish leaders handed Jesus over to him for crucifixion.
Matthew 27:1-26

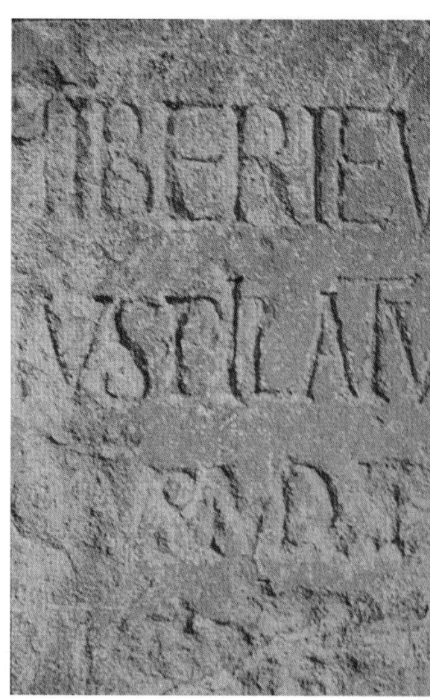

An inscription on a building at Caesarea Maritima bearing the name Pontius Pilate. Pilate dedicated the building to his emperorer, Tiberius Caesar. This important stone slab is in the Israel Museum in Jerusalem.

Philistines

(fih LISS teenz)
One of Israel's enemies as they settled in the land of Canaan. During the time of the Judges, they were a real threat to Israel. King Saul could not defeat the Philistines and was killed while fighting them at Mt. Gilboa. David finally defeated them.
Judges 13–16;
1 Samuel 31:1-13;
2 Samuel 5:17-25

Ekron was one of the five key cities of the Philistines. Picture is a reconstruction of an olive press at Ekron.

Phylactery

(FIH LAK tuh rih)
Also called "frontlet." Small box that contained Old Testament verses. Jews strapped them to their foreheads and left arms when they prayed. Jesus said the scribes and Pharisees loved to be seen doing religious things like wearing their phylacteries.
Deuteronomy 6:8;
Matthew 23:1-7

An orthodox Jewish man praying at the Wailing Wall in Jerusalem. He wears a frontlet or phylactery that contains Scripture passages on small scrolls. These leather containers are worn both on the forehead and the left arm.

Pillar

Stone monuments or standing structures, sometimes used to hold up the roofs of buildings. Solomon's temple in Jerusalem used two free-standing pillars named Jachin and Boaz.
1 Kings 7:15-22

The pillars on Solomon's temple: Jachin and Boaz.

Pinnacle Highest point of a structure or building. The devil took Jesus to the pinnacle of the temple for one of His three temptations. **Matthew 4:5-7**

The traditional pinnacle of the temple in Jerusalem

Pitch Dark-colored mixture used for waterproofing boats. Noah covered the ark with pitch to make it waterproof. Jochebed, Moses' mother, coated the basket she made for him with pitch. **Genesis 6:14; Exodus 2:3**

Plagues (PLAYGZ) Usually refers to the 10 plagues that God brought on the Egyptians. The plagues were mighty works of God that showed His power. After the tenth plague, the death of the firstborn, Pharaoh told Moses to take the Israelites out of Egypt. (See *Jewish Festivals and Feasts* chart, p. 59.) **Exodus 7:14–12:30**

10 PLAGUES OF EGYPT

1. WATER TO BLOOD
The waters of the Nile turned to blood. **Exodus 7:14-25**

2. FROGS
Frogs infested the land of Egypt. **Exodus 8:1-15**

3. GNATS
Small stinging insects infested the land of Egypt. **Exodus 8:16-19**

4. FLIES
Swarms of flies infested the land of Egypt. **Exodus 8:20-32**

5. PLAGUE ON THE CATTLE
A serious disease infested the cattle belonging to Egyptians. **Exodus 9:1-7**

6. BOILS
A skin disease infected the Egyptians. **Exodus 9:8-12**

7. HAIL
A storm destroyed the grain fields of Egypt but spared the land of Goshen where the Israelites lived. **Exodus 9:13-35**

8. LOCUSTS
An infestation of locusts stripped the land of Egypt of plant life. **Exodus 10:1-20**

9. DARKNESS
A deep darkness covered the land of Egypt for three days. **Exodus 10:21-29**

10. DEATH OF THE FIRSTBORN
The firstborn male of every Egyptian family died. **Exodus 11:1–12:30**

Plain Flat area of land. Sometimes a valley, such as the Jordan Valley. **Genesis 19:29; Joshua 13:23**

The Plain of Jezreel with the Carmel Mountain range in the background

Plan, God's God's plan for a person's life is what God wants him to do with his life. God created each person for a purpose. **Psalm 139:14-16; Jeremiah 29:11**

Cedar Tree grown in Lebanon and used as building material. King David used cedar from King Hiram of Tyre for his royal palace. King Hiram sent King Solomon all the cedar and cypress timber he needed to build the temple. **2 Samuel 5:11; 1 Kings 5:10**

Fig Fig trees have short stout trunks with thick branches and twigs with rough leaves. Round fruit ripens in the summer. Adam and Eve used fig leaves as clothes after they sinned in the Garden of Eden. **Genesis 3:7**

Date Palm Among the earliest cultivated trees. Five-thousand-year-old inscriptions from Mesopotamia give instruction for their care. Palms are characteristic of oases and watered areas. Jericho was known as the city of palms. Deborah sat under a palm tree as she judged the people. When Jesus entered Jerusalem, people waved palm branches to welcome Him. **Judges 1:16; 4:5; John 12:13**

Flax Plant used to make linen. The fibers from the stem of flax. The stems were dried on rooftops. After removing seeds and soaking the fibers, they were spun into thread for weaving. When the king was looking for the spies Joshua had sent to Jericho, Rahab hid them under flax on her rooftop. **Joshua 2:1-21**

Grape Vines Grape vines grow in vineyards and have long flexible stems with tendrils and leaves. Short flowers grow among the new leaves in early summer and the tiny flowers develop into clusters of sweet grapes. When the spies returned to Moses, they carried a bunch of grapes on a pole. **Numbers 13:23**

Hyssop Small bushy plant that has small white flowers in bunches. Moses told the Israelites to use hyssop to sprinkle blood on their doorposts as part of their celebration of Passover. A branch of hyssop was used to offer Jesus vinegar at His crucifixion. **Exodus 12:22; John 19:29**

Lilies Many types of lilies grew in Bible times. When Jesus preached His Sermon on the Mount, He probably spoke of a wildflower that grew in the spring. **Matthew 6:28**

Pods Dry coverings of beans and similar plants. The pods that the prodigal son wanted to eat were likely the pods of the carob tree, which served as a common feed for livestock. These sweet-tasting pods can be one foot long. **Luke 15:16**

Ripe carob pods

Poor (POOR) People who have no jobs or money are poor. In Bible times, sometimes poor people were forced to become slaves or servants. Jesus was concerned for the poor and preached a message of hope to them. **Luke 4:18**

Beggar at the Damascus Gate in Jerusalem

Poor in Spirit Person with a humble attitude who depends on God. In Jesus' Beatitudes, He said, "Blessed are the poor in spirit, because the kingdom of heaven is theirs." **Matthew 5:3**

Portion Share or part of something that belongs to someone. Used to describe a share of food, clothing, or property. When Joseph was second in command in Egypt, his brothers came to buy grain. Joseph knew who they were, but they did not recognize him. The brothers met with Joseph, and Benjamin, the youngest brother, was given a portion of grain five times larger than the other brothers received. **Genesis 43:34**

Potiphar (PAHT ih fuhr) Egyptian captain of the guard who bought Joseph from the Midianite traders. He put Joseph in charge of his household. Joseph refused to have an affair with Potiphar's wife, so she lied and told her husband that Joseph tried to hurt her. Potiphar had Joseph thrown into prison. **Genesis 37:28; 39:1-20**

Potter's Field Land in the Hinnom Valley outside Jerusalem used as a cemetery. The field was bought with the money that the priests had paid Judas for betraying Jesus. Judas returned the money after Jesus' death, but the priests said that because the money was used to bring about bloodshed, it could not be returned to the temple treasury. **Matthew 27:3-10; Acts 1:18**

Pottery Jars and pots made from baked clay and heated in an oven. The jars and pots were used as bowls for food and water. When David left Jerusalem in the war with his son Absalom, people brought beds, basins, and pottery to him along with food. Job scraped the sores on his body with potsherds, which are broken pieces of pottery. **2 Samuel 17:27-29; Job 2:8**

A Middle Eastern potter making pottery in the same manner used in biblical times

Joseph was a faithful manager in the house of Potipher. God blessed Potipher because of Joseph.

Praetorian Guard (pri TAWR ih uhn) Roman military group who guarded the royal family. The term "Caesar's household" often described the Praetorian guard. Units of guards were sent all over the Roman Empire. *Praetorium* refers to the headquarters where Jesus was taken before His crucifixion. The Praetorium in Jerusalem was the palace of the Roman governor at the Tower of Antonia, located next to the temple.
Matthew 27:27; Mark 15:16; John 18:28,33; 19:9

Antonia Fortress in a model of first century Jerusalem. This was the Praetorium in Jerusalem.

Praise One way people can respond to God. The Bible tells people to praise the Lord. People can praise the Lord through giving offerings, praying, and telling what God has done for them. People can praise God with music as they sing hymns, psalms, and choruses. They can also praise God by playing songs and hymns on musical instruments.

David wrote many psalms as praise songs to God. The Levites sang hymns of praise to God when Solomon dedicated the temple in Jerusalem. Paul told the church at Ephesus that they should speak to "one another in psalms, hymns, and spiritual songs, singing and making music to the Lord in your heart."
Psalm 8:1-9; 2 Chronicles 7:6; Ephesians 5:19

A young woman raises her arms in praise to God.

Pray/prayer Talking to God and listening to Him.

1. When the people of Israel were slaves in Egypt, they cried to God for help. He heard their prayers and sent Moses to bring them out of slavery (Exodus 3:7).
2. Moses prayed for the people when they had sinned by worshiping the golden calf (Exodus 32:11-13).
3. God worked miracles through the prayers of Elijah and Elisha (1 Kings 17:19-22;18:20-49; 2 Kings 4:32-35).
4. The book of Psalms teaches that when people pray they can praise God and ask for healing and forgiveness (Psalm 41;51;105).
5. Daniel and his friends prayed for God's help when the king wanted to kill all the wise men (Daniel 2:17-23).
6. In the New Testament, Jesus set the example of prayer by praying to His Father (Mark 1:35).
7. When the disciples asked Jesus to teach them to pray, He gave them an example of prayer (Matthew 6:9-13).

Daniel and his friends pray to God.

Preach

To speak to a group of people and help them understand the Word of God. Pastors preach each week, helping church members know how to live in ways that please God. **Romans 10:14-15**

A pastor proclaiming God's Word

Prison

Place where people accused or convicted of a crime are kept. Joesph was in prison in Egypt. Peter was put in prison in Jerusalem. Paul and Silas were put in prison in Philippi. **Genesis 39:19-20; Acts 12:6-19; 16:23-33**

Interior of the Mamertinum in Rome. This is the prison where both Peter and Paul were probably held before they were executed when Nero was emperor.

Priest

In Bible times, priests led people to worship God through sacrifices. Aaron the Levite and his descendants were priests. Ezra the priest read the law to the people who had returned from exile in Babylon. **Exodus 28–29; Nehemiah 8:1-12**

Ezra reading the Law to those who returned from Babylon.

Priscilla

(prih SIL uh) Wife of Aquila and friend of Paul. (See *Aquila and Priscilla*.) **Acts 18:1-3**

Proclamation

Announcement to a group of people. After the Israelites brought offerings to build the tabernacle, Moses ordered that a proclamation be given to tell the people to stop bringing the offerings, because they had brought enough. **Exodus 36:6-7**

Proconsul

(proh KAHN suhl) Office in the Roman government. Proconsuls led the work of civil and military matters in a country. They were responsible to the senate in Rome. The New Testament refers to two proconsuls: Sergius Paulus in Cyprus and Gallio in Achaia. **Acts 13:7; 18:12**

The tribunal where Paul stood before Gallio, the proconsul in Corinth

Profane

Treating God as less than He deserves. **Leviticus 22:2**

Promise

To make a statement that you will do what you say you will do. The Bible often tells how God promised the Israelites that He would give them land and provide for them. God always keeps His promises. **Deuteronomy 9:5; Joshua 23:14-16**

Promised land

The land of Canaan which God promised to Abraham and his descendants. (See *Palestine*.) **Exodus 33:1**

Prophecy

Word from God to a group of people. In Old Testament times, God spoke to the people through many prophets. Prophets told people about the coming Messiah, encouraged them to obey, warned them of punishment, and told them to repent of sin. Isaiah spoke prophecies about the coming Messiah many years before Jesus' birth. **Isaiah 7:14**

Prodigal Son

(KJV) Jesus told the parable, or story, of the prodigal son. The young man asked for his part of his father's property. He took the money and left home. The young man made wrong choices and spent all his money. He got a job feeding pigs. He decided that his father's servants had better food and went home. As his father saw him coming down the road, he ran to his son and welcomed him home. Jesus told this parable to help people know that God the Father loves them and wants to have a relationship with them. God offers to forgive people even though they sin and make wrong choices. **Luke 15:11-31**

The prodigal son was forced to feed pigs in order to survive. According to Moses' Law, pigs were unclean, and those who took care of them were not allowed to come to the temple.

Aa Bb Cc Dd Ee Ff Gg Hh Ii Jj Kk Ll Mm Nn Oo Pp Qq Rr Ss Tt Uu Vv Ww Xx Yy Zz

Prophet/ prophetess

Persons who spoke God's words of prophecy to the nations of Israel, Judah, Edom, Nineveh, and others. God told prophets to deliver His message. Miriam, the sister of Moses, was a prophetess who praised God when the Israelites crossed the Red Sea. The prophet Elijah faced the prophets of the idol Baal and proved with God's fire from heaven that the Lord is God.
Exodus 15:20;
1 Kings 18:20-40

Elijah speaks for God on Mount Carmel.

Proverbs

(PRAHV uhrbs) Third book in the division of Poetry of the Old Testament. Proverbs contains godly wisdom, much of which was written or spoken by King Solomon. The book calls people to live in ways that please God; it gives practical advice, and it makes wise observations.
Proverbs 3:5-6

Cistern at Gibeon, the place where young King Solomon prayed for wisdom above everything else. Solomon's prayer pleased God (1 Kings 3:4-15).

Providence

God's taking care of His creation and giving people everything that they need.
1 Corinthians 2:9

Prostitute, Harlot (KJV)

Woman who sleeps with a man for money. Rahab was a prostitute in Jericho who is listed as an ancestor of Jesus (See *Rahab*.)
Joshua 6:25;
Matthew 1:5

Province Roman political regions such as Judea. These territories were originally military regions governed by generals. The Romans often divided provinces into smaller territories so that no governor would have too much power. **Acts 19:21-27**

Rome divided its territory into two kinds of provinces: senatorial and imperial. Imperial provinces were the most difficult to govern or were recognized as being important to the well-being of the empire.

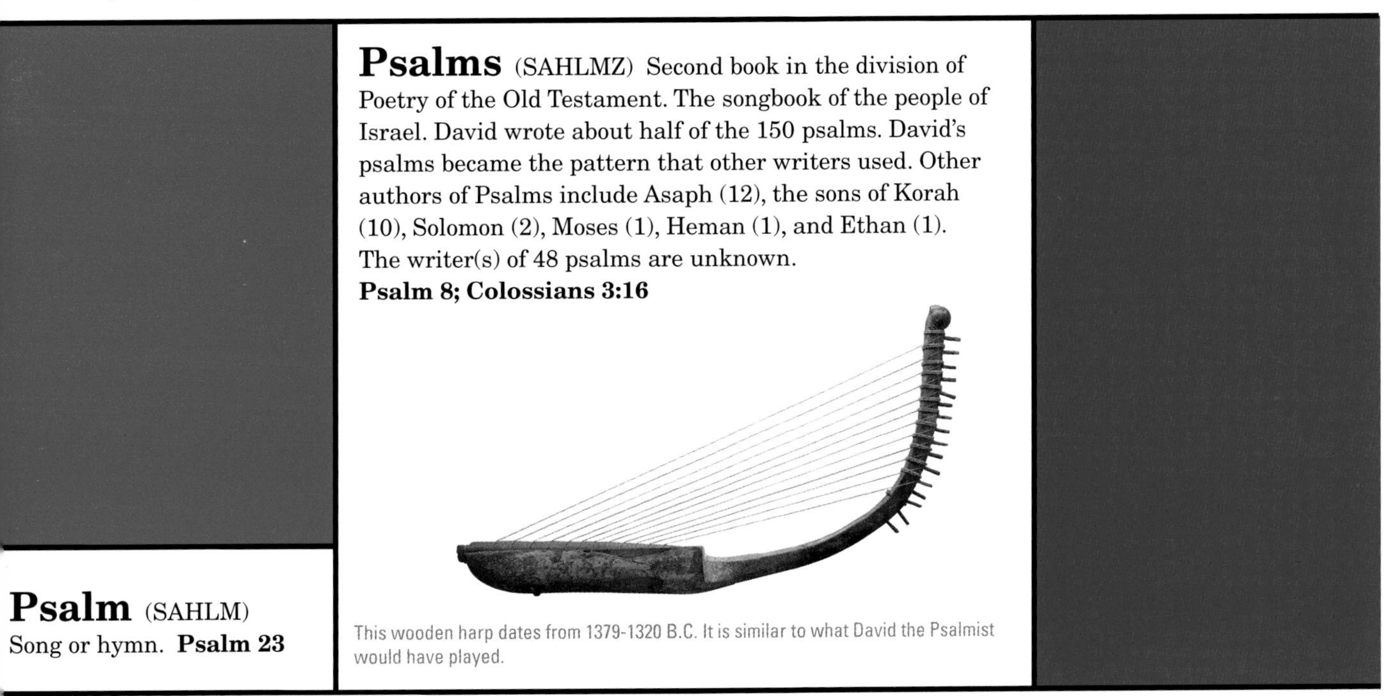

Psalms (SAHLMZ) Second book in the division of Poetry of the Old Testament. The songbook of the people of Israel. David wrote about half of the 150 psalms. David's psalms became the pattern that other writers used. Other authors of Psalms include Asaph (12), the sons of Korah (10), Solomon (2), Moses (1), Heman (1), and Ethan (1). The writer(s) of 48 psalms are unknown. **Psalm 8; Colossians 3:16**

This wooden harp dates from 1379-1320 B.C. It is similar to what David the Psalmist would have played.

Psalm (SAHLM) Song or hymn. **Psalm 23**

Pulpit (KJV)
1. In churches today the pulpit is a high desk behind which the pastor stands to preach. The pulpit is usually on a raised platform, or stage.
2. Raised platform on which a speaker stood. Ezra stood on a pulpit to teach God's Word to the people who had returned to Jerusalem from exile. **Nehemiah 8:4**

A contemporary pulpit with video monitor

Purify To make one's self clean. In the Old Testament when the people wanted to worship God, they needed to clean themselves and then sacrifice an animal to atone for their sins. Because God is pure, they could not come into His presence with sin in their lives. In the New Testament, Jesus came to earth to die for the sins of all peoples. His death made possible a right relationship with God and purifies people from their sin. (See *Sacrifice*.)
2 Timothy 2:21-22

Purim (PYOO rim) Festival that celebrates the deliverance of the Jewish people in the time of Esther. The celebration includes reading the Book of Esther aloud. When the name Haman is mentioned, the congregation boos, hisses, stamps their feet, and uses noisemakers. Also during Purim the people send gifts of food, give to the poor, and enjoy a feast together. (See *Jewish Festivals and Feasts* chart, p. 59.)
Esther 9:29-32

Eating Hamentaschen, cookies made in the shape of Haman's hat, is part of the celebration of Purim.

Purple In Bible times, purple cloth was expensive; and only kings or wealthy people could buy it. Purple yarn was used in building the tabernacle, and in the special clothing that priests wore. Lydia, who was from Thyatira, made and sold purple cloth.
Exodus 28:1-5; 36:8;
Acts 16:11-15

The ruins of Thyatira in ancient Asia Minor. Thyatira was the home of Lydia, a dealer in purple cloth who came to faith in Christ in Philippi.

Pyramids (PEER uh mid) Burial places of the pharoahs of Egypt and their family members.

Three pyramids at Giza, Egypt, architectural wonders of the ancient world

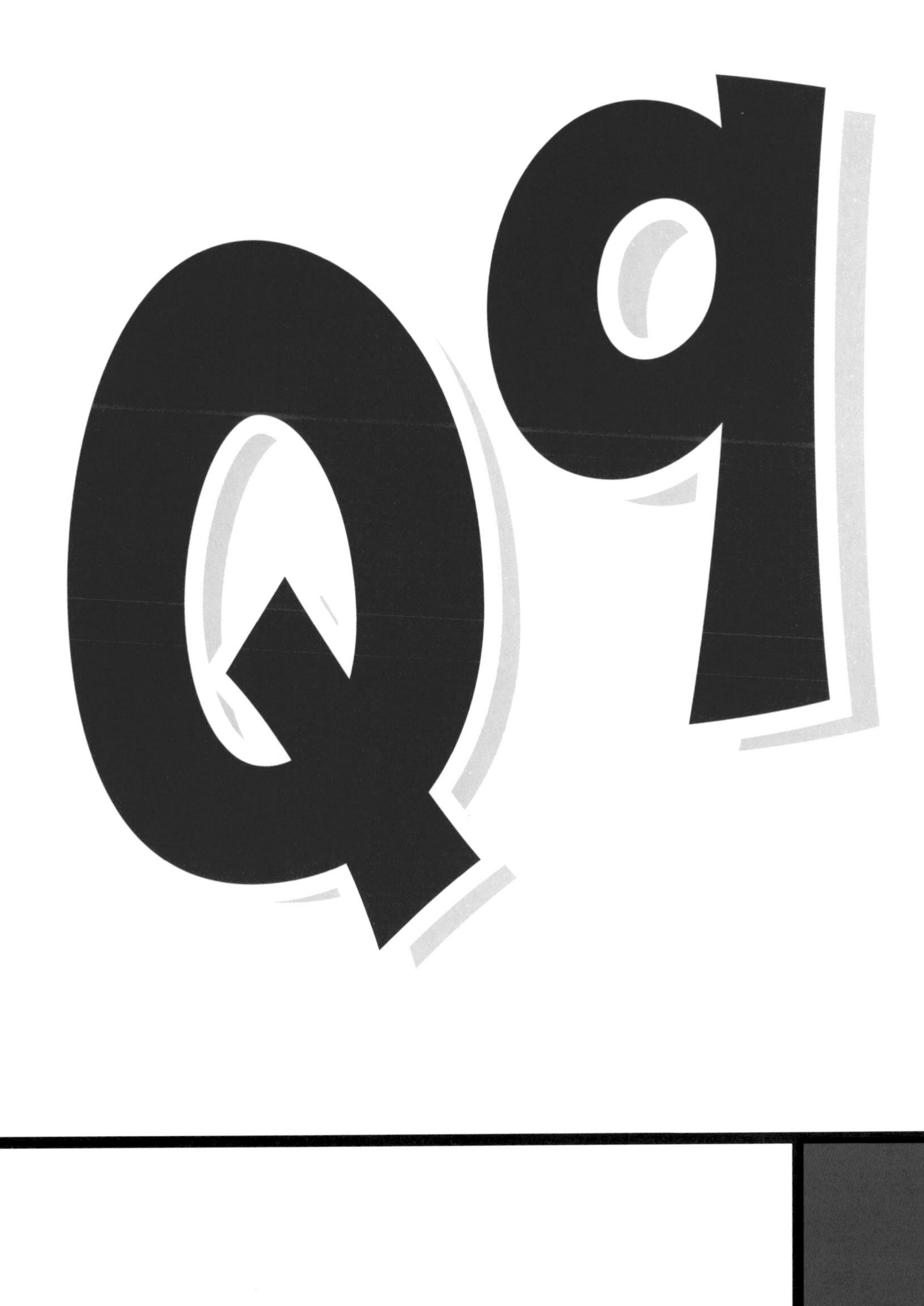
Qq

Quarrel

To argue or fuss. **Proverbs 20:3**

Quarry

Place where stones are cut and removed to be used for a building. King Solomon commanded the builders of the temple to cut large stones for the temple's foundations. **1 Kings 5:17-18**

Solomon oversees the gathering of materials for building the temple.

Queen

Wife or widow of a king. Female ruler of a country. "Queen mother" refers to the mother of a reigning king. Esther was a queen in Persia, married to King Ahasuerus. **Esther 5:1-5**

King Ahasuerus presents his new queen, Esther.

Quiver

Leather case, hung over one's shoulder, for carrying arrows. **Jeremiah 51:11**

Qumran

(KOOM rahn) Archeological site near the caves where the Dead Sea Scrolls were discovered.

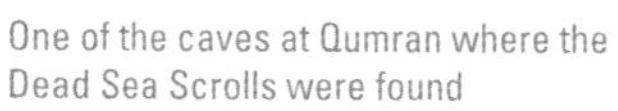

One of the caves at Qumran where the Dead Sea Scrolls were found

Rr

Rabbi (RAB igh)
Title meaning "my master," applied to Jewish teachers and other religious leaders. In the New Testament, a rabbi was an expert in the law of Moses. Some people called Jesus "Rabbi" because He taught with authority. Nicodemus called Jesus "Rabbi" when Jesus told him how to have eternal life. **John 3:2**

Rachel (RAY chuhl) Younger daughter of Laban, the second wife and cousin of Jacob, and the mother of Joseph and Benjamin. Running away from his brother Esau, Jacob met Rachel when she brought the sheep to drink water. Jacob immediately liked Rachel. **Genesis 29:1-12; 35:24**

Jacob meets Rachel.

Rahab (RAY hab)
Prostitute in Jericho. She hid two Hebrew spies that Joshua sent to find out the strength of the city of Jericho. When the king of Jericho heard about the spies, he wanted Rahab to give them up. She hid them among stalks of flax on the rooftop of her house. She asked the spies to save her when Joshua came to take the city. They agreed and Rahab and her family were saved. Rahab was an ancestor of King David and Jesus. **Joshua 2:1-24; Matthew 1:5-6,16**

Rahab talks with the spies.

Rainbow Caused by the reflection and refraction of sunlight by droplets of rain, a rainbow often appears after a thunderstorm. The bow is colored by the division of sunlight into its primary colors. God created the rainbow to remind all future generations of people of His covenant with Noah to never again destroy the earth with a flood. **Genesis 9:8-17**

"I have placed My bow in the clouds, and it will be a sign of the covenant between Me and the earth."
Genesis 9:13

Ramah

(RAY muh) Birthplace, home, and burial place of Samuel.
1 Samuel 1:19-20; 1 Samuel 7:15-17; 25:1

Ramah, Samuel's birthplace, home, and burial place

Ram's horn (KJV)

(See *Shophar.*)
Joshua 6:5

Reconcile

1. To bring together two people or groups that are arguing or fighting.
2. Salvation is the result when Jesus brings God and man together.

Acts 7:26; Colossians 1:20

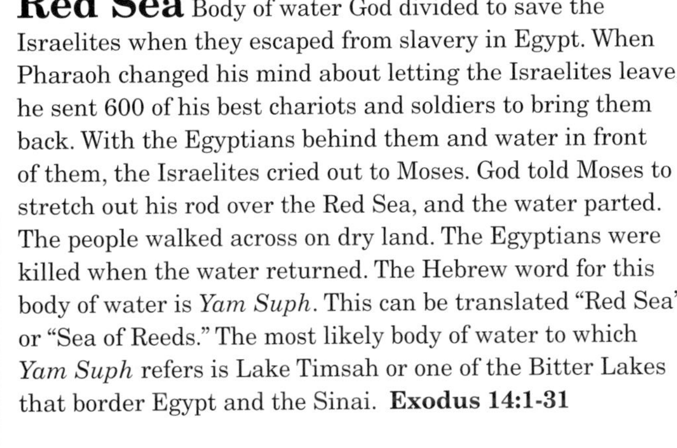

Red Sea

Body of water God divided to save the Israelites when they escaped from slavery in Egypt. When Pharaoh changed his mind about letting the Israelites leave, he sent 600 of his best chariots and soldiers to bring them back. With the Egyptians behind them and water in front of them, the Israelites cried out to Moses. God told Moses to stretch out his rod over the Red Sea, and the water parted. The people walked across on dry land. The Egyptians were killed when the water returned. The Hebrew word for this body of water is *Yam Suph*. This can be translated "Red Sea" or "Sea of Reeds." The most likely body of water to which *Yam Suph* refers is Lake Timsah or one of the Bitter Lakes that border Egypt and the Sinai. **Exodus 14:1-31**

Lake Timsah, one of the possible locations for Yam Suph, "Sea of Reeds"

Rebekah

(reh BEK uh) Daughter of Bethuel, Abraham's nephew. Rebekah was Isaac's wife, and mother of Jacob and Esau. Abraham sent his servant to find a wife for Isaac. The servant prayed that the woman who would offer to water his camels would be the one to marry Isaac. Rebekah offered to water the camels, so she was the answer to his prayer.
Genesis 24:1-67; 25:19-26

Rebekah, wife of Isaac and mother of Esau and Jacob

Redeemed

To have paid a price in order to get something back from someone else. In the New Testament, the word often means to pay what is required in order to free someone from oppression or enslavement. Jesus' death on the cross provided redemption from sin for people who confess Him as Savior and Lord.
Luke 24:21

Reeds

Reeds Three types of reeds are mentioned in the Bible. One grows in shallow water or wet, salty sand. Pens were made from the bamboo-like stems. Another type grew in shallow water in hot places like the Nile River. The stems were used for making rafts, making baskets, and writing paper. The third type is known as a cattail and may have been the one in which Moses was hidden.
Exodus 2:3; 3 John 13

A hippopotamus among the reeds on the banks of a river

Regiment

Tenth of a legion, as many as 600 men. Cornelius, a centurian of the Italian Regiment, sent for Peter who told him about Jesus.
Acts 10:1-8,17-43

The helmet and armor of a Roman centurion

Rehoboam

Rehoboam (REE huh BOH uhm) One of Solomon's sons. He became king after Solomon's death. While at Shechem for his crowning ceremony as king over Israel, the people asked Rehoboam if he would remove some of the tax burden and labor laws which his father had placed on them. Instead of taking the advice of the older men, he acted on the advice of those who wanted more taxes. The Northern tribes revolted and made the rebel Jeroboam their king. Rehoboam was left with only the tribes of Judah and Benjamin. **1 Kings 11:43; 12:1-24**

The Divided Kingdom. Solomon's son, Rehoboam, was king of Judah, the Southern Kingdom. Jeroboam was king of Israel, the ten tribes that made up the Northern Kingdom.

Refuge

Refuge Place to hide in safety from an enemy. When David was in hiding from King Saul, he hid in the cave of Adullam. Later David wrote Psalm 62 and said God was his refuge. **1 Samuel 22:1-2; Psalm 62:7**

The east face of the Mount of Transfiguration showing caves where people of the area sought refuge

Repent

Repent To turn or change from disobeying God to obeying Him. When a person repents, he changes his behavior. When Peter preached at Pentecost, he told people to repent and be saved.
Acts 2:38

Reputation
What people think about other people based on their actions and the choices they make. The men who became helpers at the Jerusalem church had to be men of good reputation.
Acts 6:3

Respect
To treat people with kindness and honor, especially parents and other people in authority.
Romans 13:7

Restitution
Returning something that has been taken or replacing something that has been damaged. **Exodus 22:6**

Zacchaeus, the tax collector, told Jesus he would provide restitution beyond what the Scriptures required to those from whom he had stolen (Luke 19:8). Shown in the bowl are coins of the kind Zacchaeus would have collected for the Roman government and for himself.

Resurrection
Historical event when Jesus came back from physical death to life with a glorified body, never to die again. The resurrection of Jesus is one of the central truths of the Christian faith. His resurrection shows that He was God in human form and that by His death on the cross people who trust Him have forgiveness of sin. The four Gospels tell about the resurrection of Jesus. In 1 Corinthians, Paul told about a group of 500 people who had seen Jesus after His resurrection.
Matthew 28:1-10; Mark 16:1-8; Luke 24:1-12; John 20:1-18; 1 Corinthians 15:1-11

Mary Magdeline saw the stone had been removed from the tomb where Jesus was buried. **John 20:1**

Reuben (RHOO ben) First son of Jacob, born to Leah. Reuben was the ancestor of the tribe of Reuben. When Joseph's brothers threw him in the cistern, Reuben felt sorry for young Joseph. He was willing to be responsible for Benjamin when Joseph commanded that the youngest brother be brought to Egypt.
Genesis 29:32; 37:21-22; 42:37

The tribe of Reuben

Revelation (REV uh LAY shuhn) Only book in the Prophecy division of the New Testament and last book of the Bible. Written by the apostle John on the Island of Patmos. In beautiful, symbolic language John encouraged and warned Christians about events leading up to the end of time and the coming of a new heaven and a new earth. **Revelation 21:1**

The Island of Patmos, a small island in the Aegean Sea about 37 miles off the southwest coast of Asia Minor. The Romans used such barren places for political exiles.

Reverence
Respect or honor given to God, to God's place of worship, and to God's commandments.
Hebrews 12:28

Righteous
To do what is right or to be someone who does what is right. God is righteous because He always does what is right and good. God helps people make right choices and live in ways that please Him when they become Christians.
Psalm 11:7; Galatians 3:11

Robe Long, sleeveless outer clothing. Royalty, priests, prophets, and rich people wore robes of blue or purple fabric. Jacob gave Joseph a robe of many colors. Jesus took off His robe when He washed the feet of the disciples. When the prodigal son returned from the far country, his father ordered his servants to bring the best robe for his son.
Genesis 37:3; John 13:4; Luke 15:22

Rod Straight, slender stick growing on or cut from a tree. "Staff" is another word for rod. Rods and staffs were used as walking sticks or for defense. God caused Moses' rod to turn into a snake. He also used it to turn the water in the Nile River to blood. God also told Moses to strike a rock with a rod he used to strike the Nile and water would come out.
Exodus 4:1-5; 7:8-10; 14-21; 17:5-11; Psalm 23:4

Shepherd in Israel taking care of his sheep. He carries a rod to defend the sheep against enemies.

Roman Empire (ROH muhn) Rome ruled most of the Mediterranean and beyond after 27 B.C. The first several emperors of the Roman Empire ruled at the time of the beginning of the Christian movement.

DISTRIBUTION OF ROMAN LEGIONS IN THE TIME OF TIBERIUS

- City
- X Gemina Roman legions
- Roman Empire
- ------ Provincial boundaries

HIBERNIA
BRITANNIA
London
I Germana
V Alaudae
XX Valeria Victrix
XXI Rapax
GERMANIA
BELGICA
GALLIA (GAUL)
Lutetia
II Augusta
XII Gemina
XIV Gemina
XVI
LUGDUNENSIS
Loire R.
NORICUM
VIII Augusta
IX Hispana
XV Apollinaris
PANNONIA
DACIA
Danube R.
AQUITANIA
Lyons
Rhone R.
Alps Mts.
Vercellae
Po R.
Bordeaux
NARBONENSIS
ILLYRICUM
VII
XI
MOESIA
IV Scythia
V Macedonia
BLACK SEA
Caucasus Mts.
CASPIAN SEA
Massalia
Corsica
Tiber R.
ITALIA
ADRIATIC SEA
Rome
Cannae
MACEDONIA
Philippi
THRACE
Byzantium (Istanbul)
BITHYNIA AND PONTUS
TARRACONENSIS
LUSITANIA
V Macedonia
VI Victrix
X Gemina
Tagus R.
Merida
Corduba
BAETICA
Balearic Is.
Sardinia
Cagliari
TYRRHENIAN SEA
Thessalonica
EPIRUS
AEGEAN SEA
ASIA
Pergamum
Ancyra (Ankara)
Halys R.
ARMENIA
CAPPADOCIA
ADIABENE
GALATIA
Athens
Ephesus
Sardis
PHRYGIA
COMMAGENE
ACHAIA
Corinth
Sparta
Miletus
PISIDIA
CILICIA
III Gallica
VI Ferrata
X Fretensis
XII Fulminata
Hippo (Bone)
Carthage
Sicily
SICILIA
Syracuse
Malta
Rhodes
Antioch
SYRIA
Ecbatana
Tingis (Tangier)
NUMIDIA
III Augusta
MAURETANIA
Crete
Fair Havens
Salamis
Cyprus
Tripolis
PHOENICIA
Palmyra
Tigris R.
MESOPOTAMIA
PARTHIA
MEDITERRANEAN SEA
Tyre
Damascus
Babylon
Leptis Magna
Cyrene
TRIPOLITANIA
CYRENAICA
Alexandria
JUDEA
Jerusalem
Euphrates R.
Pelusium
NABATEA
Memphis
III Cyrenaica
XXII Deiotariana
EGYPT
Nile R.
RED SEA
ARABIA (PETRAEA)
PERSIAN GULF
Sahara Desert
0 250 500 750 Miles
0 250 500 750 Kilometers

The Roman Empire during the reign of Tiberius Caesar (A.D. 14-37)

Rome (ROHM) Capital city of the Roman Empire. Paul made the trip to Rome as a prisoner and was under house arrest there for two years. **Acts 28:11-16**

1. Forum of Augustus
2. Forum of Julius
3. Temple of Vespasian
4. Theatre of Marcellus
5. Forum of Peace
6. Basilica Julia
7. Colossus of Nero
8. Flavian Amphitheatre
9. Temple of Cybel
10. Temple of Apollos
11. Temple of Hercules
12. Tiber River
13. Claudian Aquaduct
14. Domitian Hippodrome
15. Circus Maximus
16. Temple of Diana

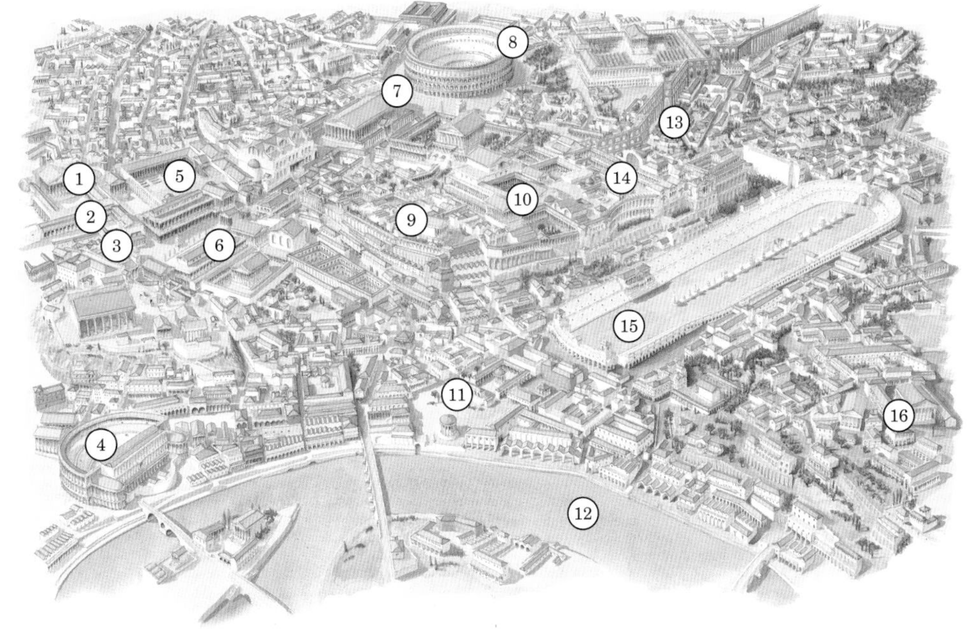

Reconstruction of first-century Rome.

Romans

(ROH muhnz) First book in the division of Paul's Letters of the New Testament. Romans was written to Christians in Rome. It is about living in ways that please God because of faith in Him. **Romans 1:1-7**

Roof Outside covering of a house or building. Large wooden beams were laid across the walls to support the roof. Smaller pieces of wood or reeds were placed in between the beams and then covered with a layer of mud. Roofs were flat. Sometimes people slept on the roofs in hot weather. **Luke 5:19**

Ruth

(ROOTH)

1. Daughter-in-law of Naomi, wife of Boaz, and mother of Obed. After her husband died, Ruth traveled with her mother-in-law to Bethlehem. She gathered grain for food and met Boaz, who became her husband.
2. Third book in the History division of the Old Testament. Tells the story of God's care for Naomi and her daughter-in-law Ruth. The book tells how Ruth met and married Boaz and had a son named Obed, King David's grandfather, and one of Jesus' ancestors. **Ruth 1–4**

Ruth and Naomi

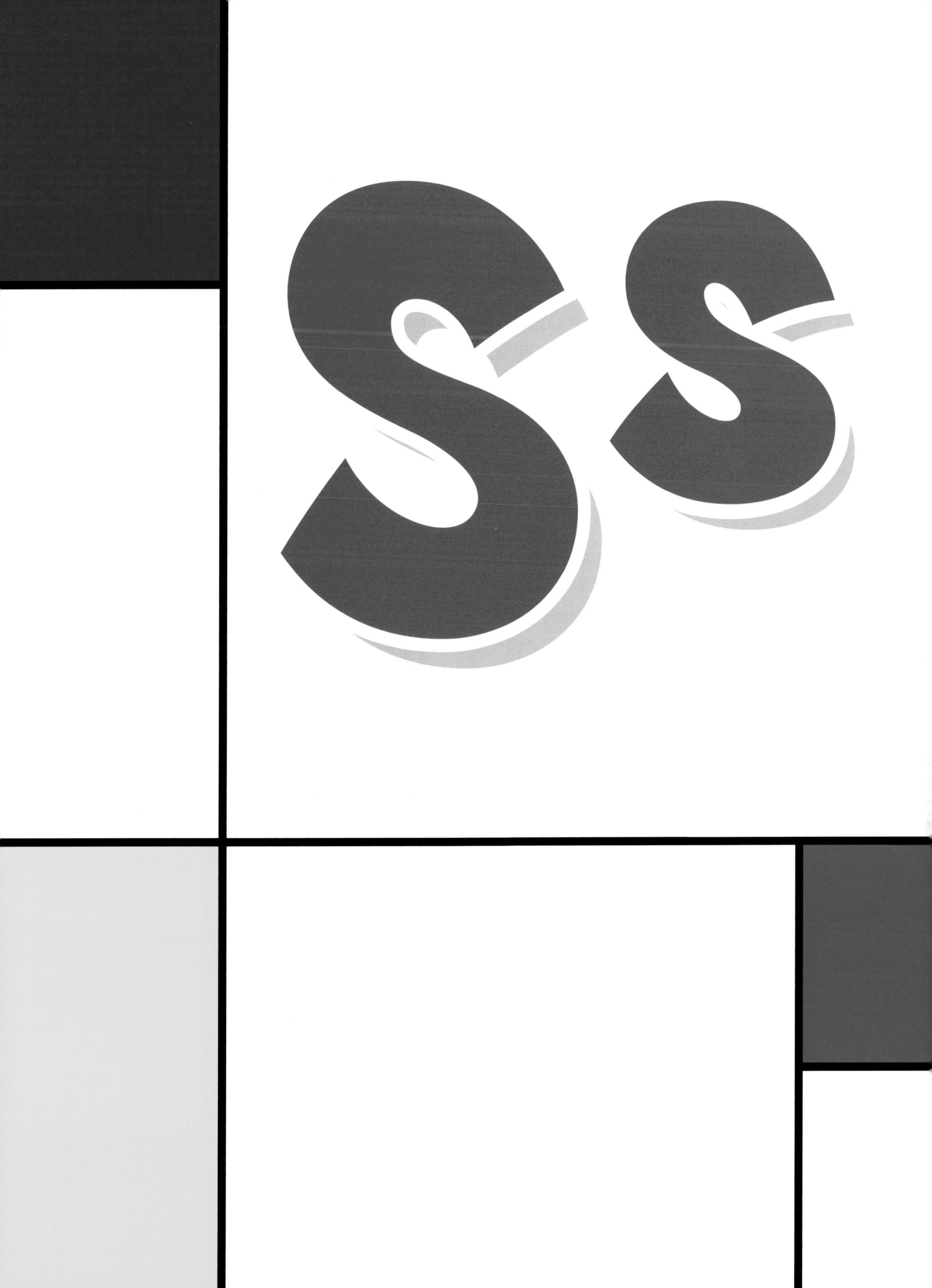
Ss

Sabbath

(SAB uhth) Day of rest, considered holy to God because of His rest on the seventh day after creation. Sabbath became a time for the Israelites to gather together and worship. The Sabbath began at sundown on Friday, and ended at sundown on Saturday.

In the New Testament, the Pharisees had strict rules about what could and could not be done on the Sabbath. The Pharisees said that Jesus broke the law by healing people on the Sabbath, but Jesus told them that doing good things on the Sabbath is allowed.

At first, Christians also met on the Sabbath with the Jews in the synagogues to proclaim Jesus. However, for Christians, Sunday, the first day of the week, the day of Jesus' resurrection, became their day of worship and rest.
Genesis 2:2-3; Exodus 20:8-11; Leviticus 23:1-3; Matthew 12:1-14; 28:1-10; Mark 2:23-28; John 5:1-18; Acts 13:14

Sacrament

Religious ceremony that some people believe provides salvation from sin. However, the Bible teaches that salvation comes only through confessing Jesus as one's Savior and Lord. People cannot do anything to earn eternal life. In this sense, baptism and the Lord's Supper are ordinances, not sacraments. (See *Ordinances, Baptism, Lord's Supper.*)
Ephesians 2:8-9; 2 Timothy 1:9

Sacrifice

What the worshiper brings to God to express love, thanksgiving, or the need for forgiveness. Cain and Abel brought offerings to the Lord. After the flood, Noah built an altar and offered burnt sacrifices. Sacrifices continued throughout the Old Testament. In the New Testament, Jesus' death provided the one and only sacrifice that removes sin. However, Christians are still instructed to sacrifice, or give up their own desires, in order to follow Jesus. **Genesis 4:1-5; 8:20; Romans 12:1-2; Hebrews 9:26; 10:4, 11-18; Hebrews 13:15**

Saint

Holy people, a title for all God's people. In the New Testament and today, saints are people who confess Jesus as Savior and Lord and who obey His teachings. The New Testament refers to all believers as saints.
1 Corinthians 1:2; Ephesians 2:19

The cross is a symbol of the greatest sacrifice ever offered. Jesus gave His life to provide forgiveness for sin, freedom from sin, and eternal life to those who trust Him.

Sadducees

(SAD joo seez) Religious leaders who came from the wealthy and high priestly families. They were in charge of the temple and its services. Unlike the Pharisees, they wanted to keep the practices of the past. They opposed the oral law, accepting the Pentateuch as the ultimate authority. They did not believe in life after death or rewards or punishment beyond this life. They denied the existence of angels and demons. The Sadducees supported the Roman rulers by keeping the Jewish people quiet. By cooperating with the Romans, they were able to maintain their positions of leadership. The Sadducees opposed Jesus because they felt threatened by Him.
Matthew 16:12; Acts 23:6-8

Salem

(SAY luhm) Shortened name for Jerusalem. (See *Jerusalem.*)
Genesis 14:18

Salvation

Rescue from sin and death. After Adam and Eve disobeyed God in the garden of Eden, sin entered the world and separated all people from God. This separation results in physical and spiritual death. However, God provides salvation from sin and spiritual death through the death and resurrection of His Son, Jesus. The Holy Spirit convicts a person of sin and brings about salvation.

The word *conversion* describes when a person turns from sin (repents) to God and trusts Jesus as Savior and Lord. Salvation is a free gift from God that rescues the believer from sin and its consequences, renews the believer to a holy life, and restores the believer to a right relationship with God for all eternity.
(See *Conversion.*)
Genesis 3:22-24; Mark 1:15; Luke 19:9; Acts 4:10-12

Samaria/Samaritan

(suh MEHR ih uh)/(suh MEHR ih tuhn) Means "mountain of watching." 1. The city of Samaria was founded by Omri, the sixth king of Israel, when he purchased the hill of Samaria for his royal residence. Later, Samaria included the region surrounding the city, or the tribal territories of Manasseh and Ephraim. Even later, the entire Northern Kingdom was called Samaria.

2. The name *Samaritan* at first was given to the Israelites of the Northern Kingdom. When the Assyrians conquered Israel and exiled 27,290 Israelites, the poorest people stayed in the land. Assyrian captives from other nations also came to live there. Some of the Jews who lived there married the Gentile captives from other countries and began to worship their gods.

3. In the New Testament, the Jews hated the Samaritans because their ancestors were both Jews and Gentiles. Most Jews refused to travel through Samaria and went out of their way to avoid the region. However, Jesus showed love to the Samaritans by healing a Samaritan leper, telling the parable of the Good Samaritan, and talking to a Samaritan woman and her neighbors. Jesus told His disciples to tell everyone about Him, including Samaritans. Philip later preached in Samaria.

2 Kings 17:24,29; Luke 10:30-37; 17:11-16; John 4:4-30,39-42; 8:48; Acts 1:8; 8:5

A Roman defense tower at Samaria

Samothrace (SA muh thrays)
Samothracia (KJV) (sa muh THRAY shuh)

Mountainous island in the Aegean Sea that Paul visited on his second missionary journey. **Acts 16:11**

Remains of a pagan worship site on Samothrace

Samson (SAM suhn) Means "of the sun." Last of the major judges of Israel, about 1100 B.C. Before he was born, Samson's parents dedicated him to God to be a lifelong Nazirite. As a Nazirite, Samson's hair was not supposed to be cut. God made Samson very strong in order to defeat the Philistines, who were enemies of Israel. Samson's strength came from God, not from his long hair. When Delilah tricked Samson and had a man cut his hair, Samson was no longer strong because he had disobeyed God by breaking his Naziarite vow. The Philistines captured Samson. However, God made Samson strong again so that even as a prisoner he could defeat the Philistines. (See *Nazirite*.) **Judges 13:3-7,24; 16:16-31; Hebrews 11:32-34**

As a final act Samson asked God to strengthen him so he could bring down the temple of Dagon, the god of the Philistines.

Sanctuary
A sacred and holy place, especially a place of worship. The tabernacle and the temple in Jerusalem were sanctuaries.
Exodus 25:8; 1 Kings 8:6

Samuel (SAM yoo uhl) Means "name of God." 1. Israelite priest and prophet who was Israel's last judge. Before his birth, Samuel's mother, Hannah, prayed for a son and promised God that she would give her son to Him. When Samuel was a young boy, Hannah took him to the tabernacle in Shiloh, where he lived and helped the priest Eli. As an adult, Samuel followed God's instructions and anointed Israel's first two kings, Saul and David. 2. First and Second Samuel are the fourth and fifth books in the History division of the Old Testament. These two books are about Israel's history from the end of the period of the judges into the time that Israel was a united kingdom led by human kings. The books describe the selection and rule of Israel's first two kings, Saul and David.
1 Samuel 1:9-11,24-28; 2:11; 10:1; 16:13

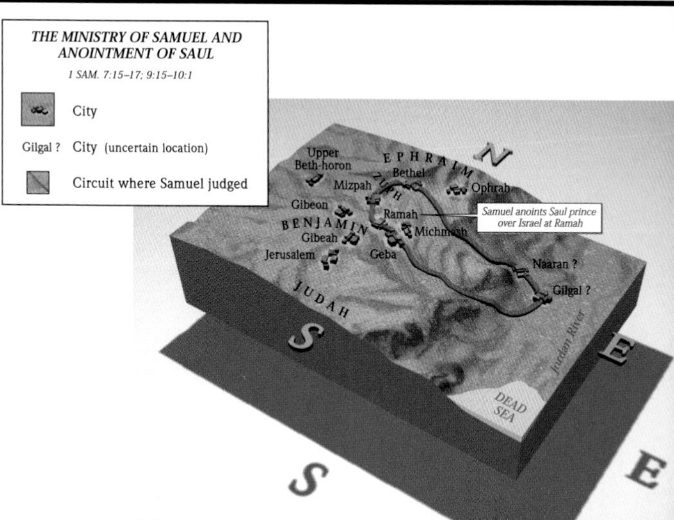

Sandals/shoes

In Bible times two types of shoes existed: slippers of soft leather and the more popular sandals with a hard leather sole. God told Moses to take off his sandals because he was standing on holy ground. Removing the sandals of guests and washing their dusty feet was the job of the lowliest servant. Jesus showed His disciples how to serve others when He washed their feet.

Exodus 3:5; John 13:1-15

Papyrus sandals for a child from Egypt between 1550 and 1300 B.C.

Sanhedrin

Sanhedrin (san HEE drihn) Group of Jewish leaders that acted as a legal council. In the New Testament, the Sanhedrin was the highest Jewish council. It had 71 members and was led by the high priest. The Sanhedrin included Pharisees and Sadducees. It did not have the authority to condemn people to death. However, the Gospels describe the role of the Sanhedrin in the arrest, trials, and condemnation of Jesus. Under the leadership of Caiaphas the high priest, the Sanhedrin plotted to have Jesus killed. After His arrest they brought Jesus into the council and used false witnesses to condemn Him. They sent Jesus to Pilate, the Roman governor of Judea, and pressured him into having Jesus put to death on the cross. Later, the Sanhedrin warned Peter and John not to preach about Jesus.

Mark 14:55-65; 15:1-15; Luke 22:66-71; John 11:47-53; 18:31; 19:1-16; Acts 4:5-21

Sarah/Sarai

Sarah/Sarai (SEHR uh/ SEHR igh) Means "princess." Wife of Abraham. First called *Sarai*, she was Abraham's half sister, since she had the same father as Abraham. Sarai could not have children for many years. When Sarai was almost 90 years old, God changed her name to *Sarah* and promised her a son. A year later, she gave birth to Isaac.

Genesis 17:15-22; 20:11-12; 21:1-3

A son for Abraham and Sarah

Aa Bb Cc Dd Ee Ff Gg Hh Ii Jj Kk Ll Mm Nn Oo Pp Qq Rr Ss Tt Uu Vv Ww Xx Yy Zz

Satan (SAY tuhn) Means "adversary." Another name for the Devil. Satan tempted Jesus in the wilderness at the beginning of Jesus' ministry. (See *Devil*.) **Matthew 4:10**

Satrap (SA trap) Political official who governed a province of the Persian Empire. King Darius chose 120 satraps to govern his kingdom. He also chose three administrators over the satraps. Daniel was one of the administrators. The satraps and other administrators were jealous of Daniel and tried to find a way to get rid of him. **Daniel 6:1-5**

Save/saved 1.To rescue someone from a dangerous situation. 2. When a person admits to God that he is a sinner, believes that Jesus' death on the cross provided forgiveness of sin, repents of his sin, and confesses Jesus as his personal Lord and Savior, that person is saved, or rescued, from eternal separation from God. Only through His Son Jesus, who died and was raised from the dead, does God save people from sin. **Luke 19:10; Acts 2:21; 4:12**

Savior, Saviour (KJV) (SAY vih'awr) One who saves others. 1. In the Old Testament, God is identified as the only true Savior. 2. In the New Testament, Jesus is the Savior. By dying on the cross, Jesus took the penalty for sin and offers salvation from eternal separation from God. **Isaiah 45:15,21-22; John 4:39-42; 2 Timothy 1:10**

Scapegoat On the Day of Atonement, the high priest went into the holy of holies to offer sacrifices for the sins of his family and for all the people. He killed one goat as a sin offering. The high priest laid his hands on a second goat's head to transfer the sins of the people to the goat. This goat was the scapegoat. Then the goat was led away into the desert to symbolize removing the people's sins. **Leviticus 16:8,10**

Saul (SAWL) Name means "asked for." 1. First king of Israel, who ruled about 1050–1010 B.C. At first Saul honored God, but later he disobeyed God. God chose David to replace Saul as king. Before he became king, David played music on his harp for King Saul when he was sad. After David defeated the giant Goliath, Saul became jealous of David and was afraid of him. King Saul wanted to kill David, but David's best friend, Jonathan, King Saul's son, helped David escape. Later, the Philistines killed Saul and his three sons on Mount Gilboa. 2. Hebrew name of the apostle Paul. (See *Paul*.) **1 Samuel 15:7-23; 16:14-23; 18:6-12; 19:1,9-11; 20; 31:1-6; Acts 13:9**

Samuel anoints Saul first king of Israel.

Scepter (SEP tuhr) Official staff or baton of a king that showed he had authority. If a king welcomed a visitor and allowed him or her to approach the throne, the king would extend or hold out the scepter toward the visitor. Queen Esther could talk with the king only if he extended his scepter toward her. **Esther 4:11; 5:2**

Esther approaches King Xerxes (Ahasuerus).

Scribe Person who could write. Baruch was a scribe who wrote the words God gave to Jeremiah. By the time of the New Testament, scribes were a group of Jewish leaders who copied the law of Moses, interpreted the law, and were experts in cases where people were accused of breaking the law. The scribes led in plans to kill Jesus.
Jeremiah 36:32; Mark 2:16; Luke 19:47

The scriptorium at Qumran, the place where the Dead Sea Scrolls were discovered between 1947 and 1960. The scriptorium is the place where scribes copied the scrolls in order to preserve Scripture for future generations.

Scripture (SKRIP chuhr) A collection of 66 books that shows people who God is and how they can have a relationship with Him through His Son, Jesus. Scripture was written by men who were inspired and guided by God. Scripture is true, fully trustworthy, and without error. In the New Testament, the word *Scriptures* was used to describe what is also called the Old Testament. Today, the word *Scriptures* describes the entire Bible—39 Old Testament books and 27 New Testament books. Scripture tells people how to be right with God, to do right, avoid wrong, and be prepared to live a life that pleases God.
Luke 4:16-21;
Acts 8:30-35;
2 Timothy 3:16-17

Scroll Roll of papyrus or parchment used as a writing material. Papyrus was a paper-like material made from a plant by the same name. Parchment was made from specially treated leather from the skins of animals. Jesus read from the scroll of the prophet Isaiah at the synagogue in His hometown of Nazareth.
Luke 4:17

A Torah scroll at a celebration in Jerusalem. The Torah includes Genesis, Exodus, Leviticus, Numbers, and Deuteronomy.

Seal Something with a special mark that represents the authority of the person who owns it. In the Bible some seals were worn around the neck, some were cylinders, and others were rings. Joseph was given the Egyptian pharaoh's ring with his royal stamp of authority, or seal, when Joseph was placed in command of the country. The ring showed that Joseph had the right to act for the king.
Genesis 41:42

Season 1. Period of time. The Israelites "lived in the wilderness a long time," or for a "long season" (KJV). 2. A specific time of the year, such as harvest. Moses sent the 12 spies to Canaan during the season that grapes were ready to be picked (See *Feast and Festivals* chart, p. 59.) **Joshua 24:7; Numbers 13:20**

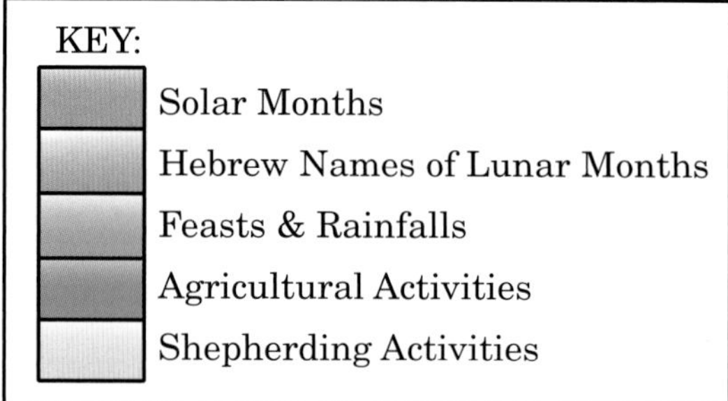

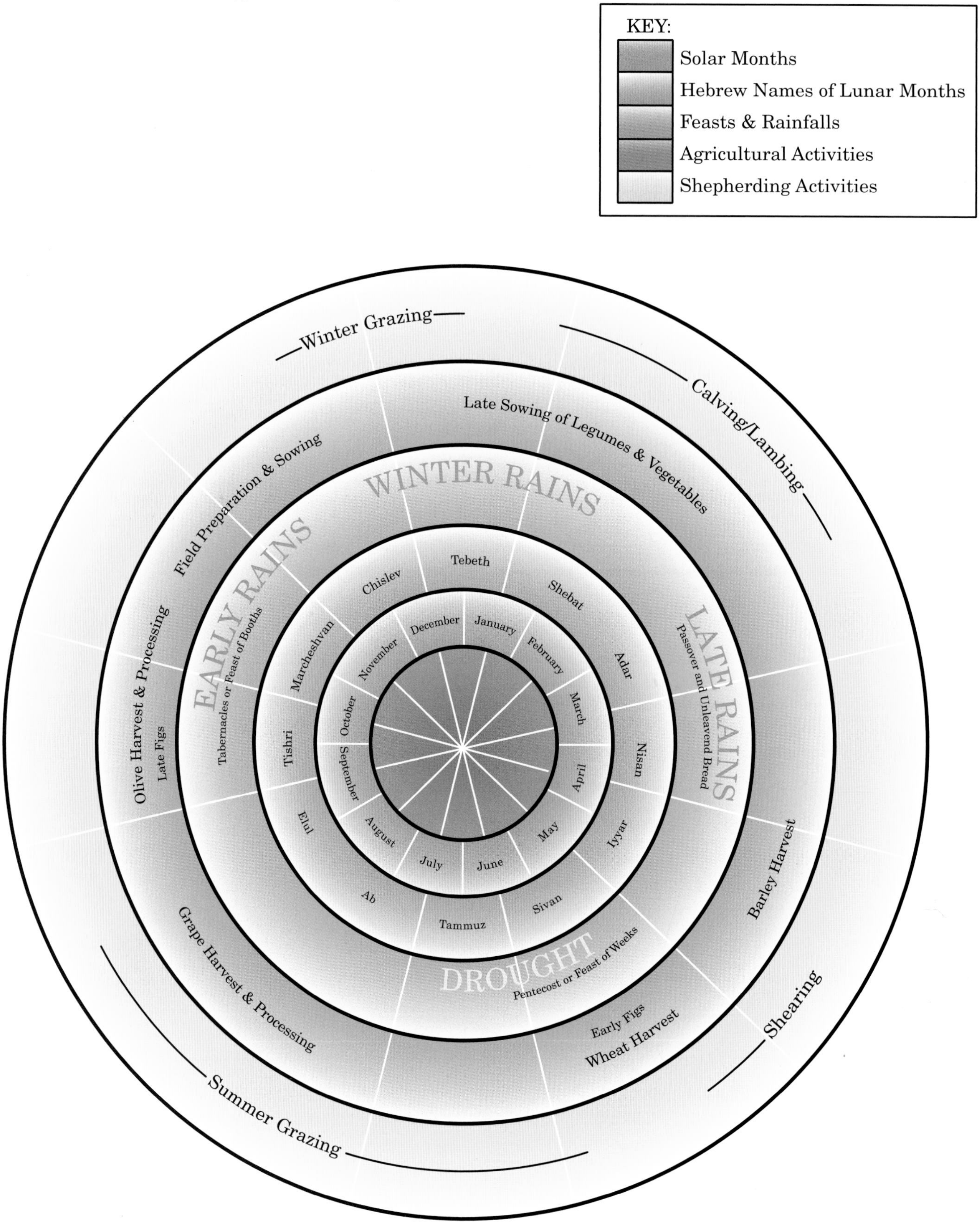
KEY:
Solar Months
Hebrew Names of Lunar Months
Feasts & Rainfalls
Agricultural Activities
Shepherding Activities
Winter Grazing
Calving/Lambing
Shearing
Summer Grazing
Late Sowing of Legumes & Vegetables
Field Preparation & Sowing
Olive Harvest & Processing
Late Figs
Grape Harvest & Processing
Early Figs
Wheat Harvest
Barley Harvest
WINTER RAINS
EARLY RAINS
Tabernacles or Feast of Booths
LATE RAINS
Passover and Unleavend Bread
DROUGHT
Pentecost or Feast of Weeks
Tebeth
Shebat
Adar
Nisan
Iyyar
Sivan
Tammuz
Ab
Elul
Tishri
Marcheshvan
Chislev
December
January
February
March
April
May
June
July
August
September
October
November

Secretary In Bible times, only a few people knew how to write. A secretary wrote words for other people, such as for kings or other important persons. A secretary was also sometimes called a scribe. (See *Scribe*.)
2 Kings 12:10; 22:9-10; 1 Chronicles 24:6

Sect A group, or party, that is part of a larger group. Sadducees and Pharisees were Jewish sects. As a Christian, Paul was accused of being a part of a religious sect.
Acts 5:17; 15:5; 24:5

Self-control, Temperance (KJV) One of the nine qualities seen in the fruit of the Spirit. The Bible encourages Christians to follow Jesus' example in how they live by choosing to do the right thing even when other people make wrong choices.
Galatians 5:22-23

Sennacherib (suh NAK uh rib) Means "Sin (the god) has replaced my brother." King of Assyria (704–681 B.C.) who captured all the fortified cities of Judah except Jerusalem. He then made King Hezekiah of Judah give him a lot of silver and gold. God rescued the Jews living in Jerusalem from King Sennacherib and his men.
2 Kings 18:13–16; 19:32-36

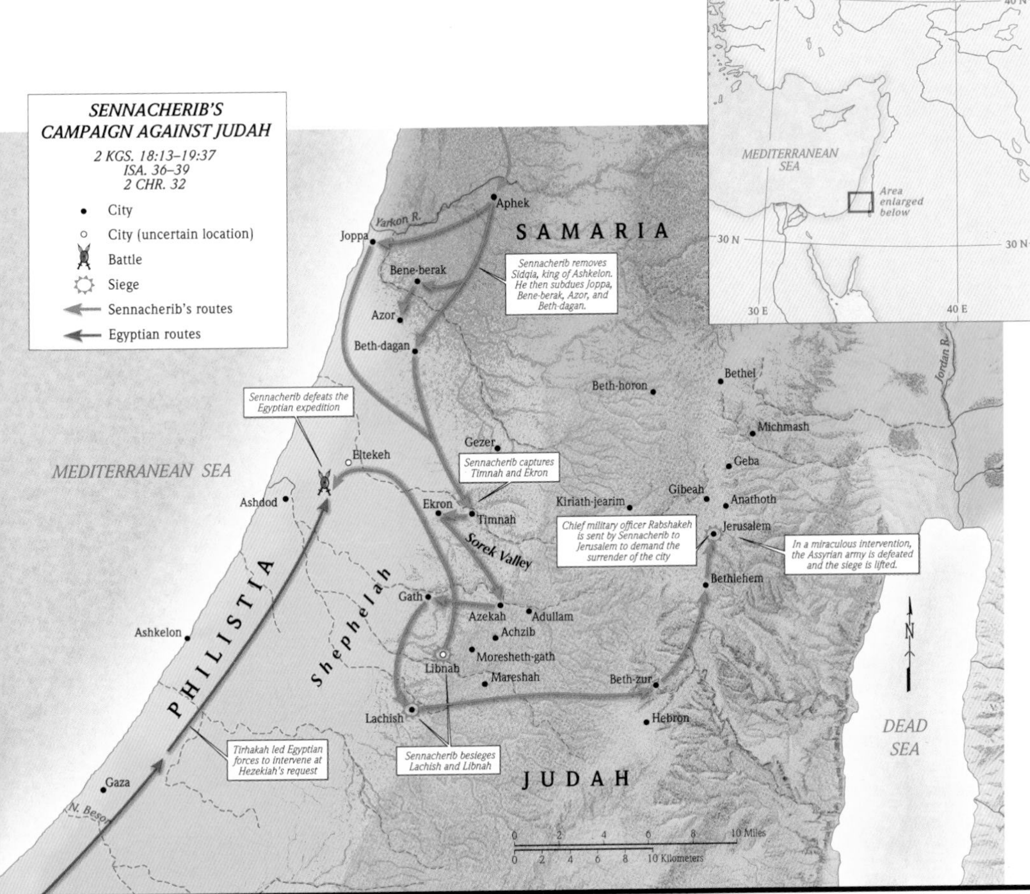

Sentries Men who guarded a military camp, a gate, or a prison. When Peter was in prison, sentries guarded the prison door.
Judges 7:19; Acts 12:6

Sermon on the Mount First of five major teachings by Jesus in the Gospel of Matthew. Jesus spoke mostly to His disciples, but other people listened too. This sermon includes the Beatitudes and the Model Prayer. Jesus also told His disciples to be good examples of how to live, to love their enemies, and not worry. **Matthew 5–7**

In telling His disciples not to worry, Jesus pointed to the beautiful wildflowers that bloomed only a short time and then were used for fuel in furnaces. The flowers didn't have to worry and work at being beautiful. They simply were as God made them. If such short-lived plants were even more beautiful than Solomon's clothing, how much more does God care for human beings made in His image (Matthew 6:28-34).

Serpent One of the words in the Bible for snake. A symbol of evil and of Satan. The serpent in the garden of Eden tempted Eve to disobey God by telling her lies.
Genesis 3:1

Serve/service Work done for other people or for God. In Bible times, service could be slave labor, farm work, or daily labor on the job. Jacob worked for Laban seven years for each of his wives. In the Bible and today, service can also be a way to worship God. Jesus showed His disciples how to serve when He washed their feet and told them to serve others.
Genesis 29:15-30; 2 Chronicles 35:10; John 13:4-17; Hebrews 12:28

Jesus came not be be served but to serve and to give His life for many. **Mark 10:45**

Servant
(See *Slave/servant*.)

Servant of the Lord In the Old Testament, Moses, Joshua, King David, and the nation of Israel were called servants of the Lord. In the New Testament, "Servant of the Lord" is another name for Jesus.
Deuteronomy 34:5; Judges 2:8; Psalm 18:9; Matthew 12:15-21; Acts 3:13

Seth (SETH) Means "He set or appointed" or "replacement." Adam and Eve's third son. Seth was born after his brother Cain killed Abel. He was an ancestor of Jesus.
Genesis 4:25; 5:3; Luke 3:38

Sex God's good gift that is one way husbands and wives express their love for each other, sometimes resulting in the gift of children. Sex between two people who are not husband and wife is called sexual immorality (*fornication*, KJV). The Bible teaches that sexual immorality is outside God's plan for human beings, displeases God, and will have harmful consequences.
Genesis 1:27; 2:22-24; 1 Corinthians 6:18-20; Ephesians 5:3

Shackles, Fetters (KJV) Wooden, bronze, or iron objects that were placed on prisoners' feet so they could not run away. Shackles were placed around each foot of a prisoner and usually were connected with a chain or rope. Samson wore shackles after the Philistines captured him. **Judges 16:21**

Ball and chain

Shadrach (SHAD rak) One of the three Hebrew young men who were taken from Jerusalem along with Daniel to serve in King Nebuchadnezzar's court. God delivered them from the fiery furnace. **Daniel 1:8-16; 3:1-30**

Shechem (SHEK uhm) Means "shoulder" or "back." District and city in the hill country of Ephraim in north central Palestine. When Abram moved to Canaan from Haran, he went to Shechem. When Jacob returned from Paddan-aram, he camped at Shechem and purchased land. Joshua led Israel to renew its covenant with God at Shechem. Rehoboam, King Solomon's son, went to Shechem to be crowned king over all Israel. When the nation divided into two kingdoms, Shechem became the first capital of the northern kingdom of Israel. Later, Samaria became the capital. **Genesis 12:6-7; 33:18-19; Joshua 24:1-18; 1 Kings 11:43–12:1,25**

Shechem stands between Mount Gerazim and Mount Ebal. Here Joshua led Israel to renew their commitment to the law of Moses.

Shema (shuh MAH) The Hebrew word that means "hear." The main statement of the Jewish law that says God is the one true God and His people are commanded to love and obey Him. When Jesus was asked about the greatest commandment, He answered by quoting the Shema. **Deuteronomy 6:4-9; Mark 12:29**

Sheol (SHEE ohl), **Hell** (KJV) The Hebrews thought that Sheol was where people went when they died. Sheol is described as a place deep within the earth and to get there people had to cross a river. Sheol also was thought to be like a city with gates. The Old Testament says that God is there, and people cannot hide from God in Sheol. The King James Version uses the word *hell* for *Sheol*. The New Testament teaches that Christians go to heaven when they die and people who do not confess Jesus as Savior and Lord go to hell. **Amos 9:2; Job 33:18; Psalm 139:8; Matthew 7:2; 19:14**

Shem (SHEM) Means "name." Noah's oldest son. Shem was an ancestor of Abraham and Jesus. **Genesis 5:32; 11:10-26; Luke 3:36**

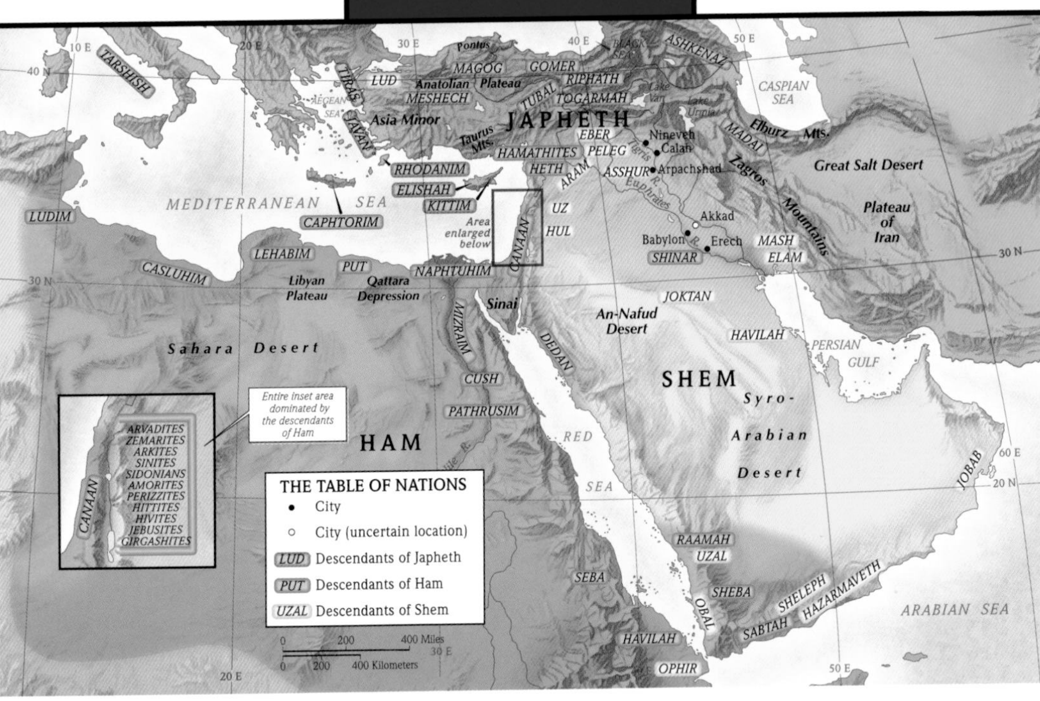

The Table of Nations shows where the descendants of Noah's three sons, Shem, Ham and Japheth, settled.

Aa Bb Cc Dd Ee Ff Gg Hh Ii Jj Kk Ll Mm Nn Oo Pp Qq Rr Ss Tt Uu Vv Ww Xx Yy Zz

Shepherd 1. Person who takes care of sheep. Shepherds in the Bible took sheep to places where they could eat grass and drink water. They protected them from wild animals and carried weak lambs (young sheep) in their arms. Before he became a king, David was a shepherd. Shepherds were the first people to visit Jesus after He was born.
2. In the Bible, the word *shepherd* could be used for a king or leader of Israel.
3. A description of how God cares for His children.
4. Jesus called Himself the Good Shepherd.
1 Samuel 17:34-35; 2 Samuel 5:2; Psalm 23; Isaiah 40:11; Ezekiel 34:2; Luke 2:8-20; John 10:11

A shepherd with his sheep

Shield Used for protection in battle. Some shields were made of leather stretched over wood frames with a handle on the inside. Metal disks could be attached to the leather to make the shield stronger. Shields could be round and would cover about half of a soldier's body. They also could be rectangular and large enough to cover most or all of a soldier's body.

Shield-bearers sometimes carried these larger shields in front of the soldiers. Goliath had a shield-bearer. Gold or brass shields were used for decoration and for ceremonies (See *Armor of God* chart, p. 11.)
1 Samuel 17:41; 1 Kings 14:26-28; Nehemiah 4:16

Old Roman shields

Shiloh (SHIGH loh) Means "tranquil" or "secure." City about 30 miles north of Jerusalem that served as Israel's religious center for more than a century after the conquest of Canaan. At the tabernacle in Shiloh, Hannah promised God that if He would give her a son she would give her son back to God. After Samuel was born, Hannah took him to Shiloh as a way to thank God for her son. Samuel grew up at Shiloh and helped Eli the priest at the tabernacle.
1 Samuel 1:3,9-11,24-28; 2:18; 3:1

Shiloh, about 30 miles north of Jerusalem, was Israel's religious center for over a century after the conquest of Canaan.

Shophar (SHOH fahr) Also known as shofar. Musical instrument made from the horn of a ram. Priests blew the horn to call the people of Israel together. The shophar was also used as a war trumpet. **Exodus 19:16**

Shore Land next to water. After some of Jesus' apostles had fished all night, Jesus stood on the shore of the Sea of Galilee (Tiberias) and invited them to eat the breakfast He was cooking. **John 21:4-14**

After His resurrection, Jesus serves breakfast to His disciples on the shore of the Sea of Galilee.

Showbread, Shewbread (KJV) Also known as "the bread of the Presence." Special bread that was given continually as a sacrifice to God in the tabernacle and temple. The priests ate the old bread after replacing it with new bread. **Exodus 25:30; 39:33-36; Leviticus 24:5-9**

Aa Bb Cc Dd Ee Ff Gg Hh Ii Jj Kk Ll Mm Nn Oo Pp Qq Rr Ss Tt Uu Vv Ww Xx Yy Zz

Shunem

(SHOO nem) The town of Shunem was located southeast of Mount Carmel in the territory of Issachar. A husband and wife who lived in Shunem built a room on top of their house for the prophet Elisha. The prophet stayed often at their home. He prophesied that a son would be born to them, and later he raised that boy from the dead. **2 Kings 4:8-37**

Shur, Wilderness of

(SHOOR) Means "wall." Region on Egypt's northeastern border where the Israelites made their first stop after crossing the Red Sea. **Exodus 15:22**

The wilderness of Shur

Sidon and Tyre

(SIGH duhn) (TIGHR) Phoenician cities located on the coastal plain between the mountains of Lebanon and the Mediterranean Sea. Sidon and Tyre were ancient cities. They were founded long before the Israelites entered Canaan. Stonemasons and carpenters from Tyre built David's palace. They used cedars from Tyre for the palace. Craftsmen and building materials from Tyre were used to build the temple in Jerusalem. **2 Samuel 5:11; 1 Kings 5:1-12,18**

Crusader Castle at the harbor of Sidon, Lebanon

Siege

A city was under seige when an army surrounded it and kept supplies such as food and water from entering the city. The people of the city were usually forced to surrender if they could not get enough food and water. King Nebuchadnezzar of Babylon placed Jerusalem under siege. **2 Kings 24:10**

Above: Lachish was the last fortress to fall before Jerusalem fell to the Babylonians. The small mound to the right was a siege ramp.

Left: Reconstruction of a Roman siege tower with a battering ram

Silas/Silvanus (SIGH luhs/sil VAY nuhs) Leader in the early Jerusalem church, Silas went with Paul on Paul's second missionary journey. In Philippi, Paul and Silas were put in jail. God rescued them, they told the jailer about Jesus, and the jailer and his family became Christians. Silas also did missionary work with Peter. **Acts 16:19-40; 1 Peter 5:12**

Paul and Silas in the jail at Philippi

Silver A precious metal, like gold. In the Old Testament, silver was often more valuable than gold. Some coins were made of silver. Silver was used in building the tabernacle. The Jewish leaders paid Judas "30 pieces of silver" to betray Jesus. Instead of giving silver or gold to a man who could walk, Peter healed him. **Exodus 35:5; Matthew 26:15; Acts 3:1-10**

The solid silver case of a Torah scroll

Silk Expensive cloth made from thread that came from the Chinese silkworm. Silk came to the Middle East from China. **Ezekiel 16:10**

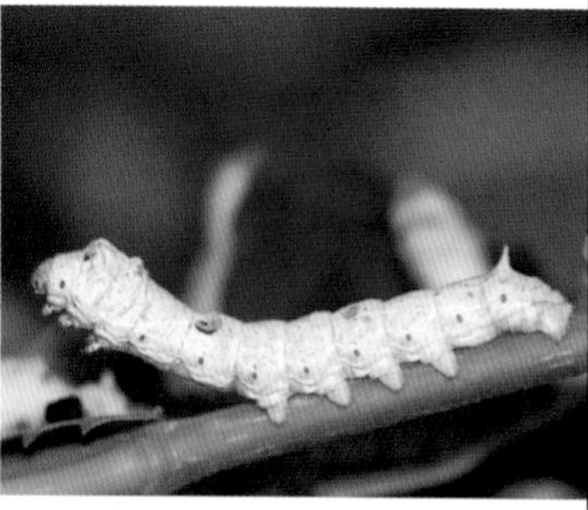

A silkworm on a mulberry branch. Silkworms spin beautiful and highly valued fiber out of their mouths.

Siloam (sigh LOH uhm) The pool of water created by King Hezekiah's tunnel. This tunnel brought water into the walled city to enable the citizens of Jerusalem to better survive attacks by enemies. More than 700 years later, Jesus healed a blind man and sent him to wash in the Pool of Siloam. **2 Kings 20:20; 2 Chronicles 32:30; John 9:1,6-11**

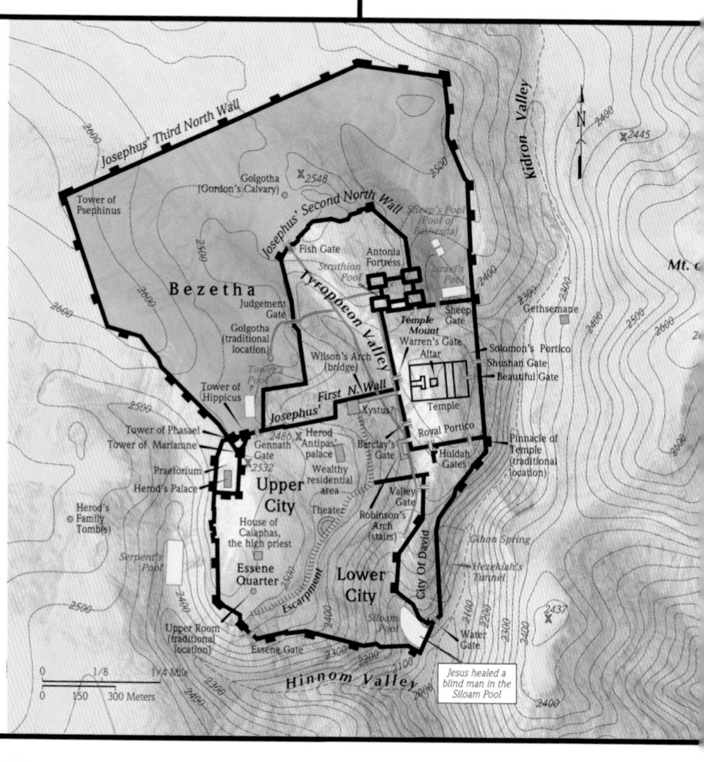

The Pool of Siloam is in the southwest sector of Jerusalem and is still a source of water today.

Simeon (SIM ih uhn) Means "hearing" or possibly "little hyena beast." 1. One of Jacob's 12 sons. Joseph held his brother Simeon as a prisoner to make sure that the other brothers would bring Benjamin to Egypt. 2. Jewish man whom God promised would not die before seeing the Messiah. When Joseph and Mary took Baby Jesus to the temple, Simeon announced God's plan for Jesus. **Genesis 42:24; Luke 2:25-33**

Simeon blesses Jesus.

Simon Means "flat-nosed." 1. One of Jesus' apostles. He was a son of Jonah and brother of Andrew. After Simon confessed Jesus as the Messiah, Jesus changed his name to Peter (Matthew 16:17-18).

2. Pharisee who invited Jesus to eat dinner at his house. Simon learned a valuable lesson about love, courtesy, and forgiveness after a sinful woman anointed Jesus at this event (Luke 7:36-40).

3. A man from Cyrene who was forced to carry Jesus' cross (Mark 15:21).

4. Tanner of animal skins who lived in the seaport of Joppa. While staying at Simon's house, Peter had a vision that caused him to go tell Cornelius about Jesus (Acts 9:43).

5. Jesus' apostle, also called "the Canaanite" or "the Zealot" (Matthew 10:4).

6. Half brother of Jesus (Matthew 13:55).

7. Leper in Bethany at whose house Jesus was visiting when he saw a woman anoint Jesus with expensive oil (Matthew 26:6-7).

8. Magician from Samaria who believed Philip's preaching, was baptized, and then sinned by trying to buy the power to give people the Holy Spirit (Acts 8:9-13,18-24).

Sin Actions, attitudes, words, or thoughts that do not please God. The only person who never sinned is Jesus. Everyone else has sinned. The result of sin is separation from God and spiritual death. God offers to forgive people of their sin through His Son, Jesus, and to give them eternal life. **Romans 3:23; 5:8; 6:23; 10:9-10,13; 2 Corinthians 5:21**

Sisera (SIS uh ruh) Means "mediation." Military leader of Jabin, king of Canaan. Heber's wife, Jael, killed Sisera with a tent peg. **Judges 4:2,21**

Sinai, Mount (SIGH nigh) (See *Mount Sinai.*)

Jebel Musa, the traditional site of Mount Sinai

Sinner Person who has rebelled against God and missed God's purpose for life. According to the Bible, every person is a sinner. In the Old Testament, people who did not obey God's law were considered sinners. In the New Testament, Paul spoke of sinners as people who are separated from God. Jesus died on the cross to forgive sinners and to offer them eternal life. (See *Salvation* and *Sin.*) **Psalm 1; Romans 3:23; 5:8**

Skirt The four corners of a piece of clothing, like a robe. David cut off part of King Saul's skirt while Saul was in a cave. David later felt guilty for his action. **1 Samuel 24:1-7**

Slave/servant

In the first century, one out of three persons in Italy and one out of five in other places were slaves. Some slaves were highly intelligent and held responsible positions. A person could become a slave as a result of capture in war, failure to pay a debt, being sold as a child by very poor parents, committing a crime, or kidnapping and piracy. In the New Testament, Jesus said that He came to earth to be a servant and encouraged His disciples to have the attitude of slaves or servants. Paul told masters to be kind to their slaves. Paul also said that he was a slave or servant of Jesus.
Mark 10:45;
Luke 17:10;
Philippians 1:1;
Colossians 4:1

Sling

Weapon made of two long straps with a piece between them at the end to hold a stone. Shepherds and professional soldiers used slings. David killed Goliath with a sling and a stone.
1 Samuel 17:50

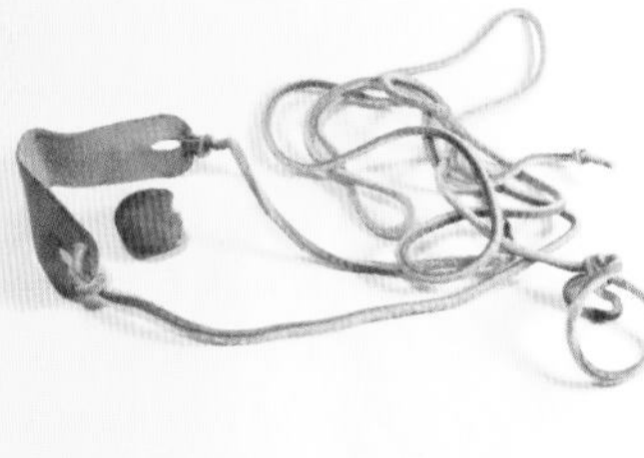

Re-creation of an ancient sling

Snare

Trap for birds and animals. For people snares represented danger and destruction.
Psalm 18:5

Sodom (SAHD uhm) and Gomorrah

(guh MAHR uh) Two cities in Canaan at the time of Abraham that God destroyed because of their wickedness. God rescued Abraham's nephew Lot, who lived in Sodom.
Genesis 19:24-25

View of the Dead Sea and Lisan peninsula. Some scholars believe Sodom and Gomorrah were located here.

Soldier

In early Israelite history, every male was expected to fight when the tribes were threatened. David created a national Israelite army led by 30 special soldiers. In the New Testament, Roman soldiers crucified Jesus. Paul thought of people who helped spread the Good News of Jesus as soldiers.
1 Chronicles 11:10-47;
John 19:23;
Philippians 2:25;
2 Timothy 2:3

Solomon (SAHL uh muhn)

Son of David and Bathsheba. He became king of Israel after David. He is remembered most for his wisdom, his building program—including the temple in Jerusalem—and his wealth. In addition to building the temple, Solomon fortified a number of cities that helped provide protection for Jerusalem. He built store-cities for keeping the materials needed in his kingdom. He built military bases for charioteers. His 700 wives who were princesses and 300 concubines came from many of the kingdoms with which Solomon had treaties. He apparently allowed his wives to worship their own gods and even had altars to these gods built in Jerusalem. After Solomon's death, the northern tribes of Israel rebelled against Solomon's son and made their own nation known as the northern kingdom of Israel.
1 Kings 5–8; 9:15-19; 11:1-3,7-8,29-32; 12:1-19

Solomon's temple

Solomon's Colonnade, Solomon's Porch (KJV)

Raised outer part of the temple in Jerusalem during New Testament times, built by Herod's workers. After healing a man who could not walk, Peter preached to the people there, and then he was arrested. (See *Temple*.) **Acts 3:11-12**

Son of God

Name for Jesus that means He is God's one and only Son. Jesus is the second Person of the Trinity—Father, Son, and Holy Spirit. At Jesus' baptism and transfiguration, God the Father identified Jesus as His Son. After Jesus walked on water, His disciples said, "Truly, You are the Son of God!" As the Son of God, Jesus is the Messiah and provides people salvation from sin (See *Names of Jesus* chart, p. 125.) (See *Trinity*.) **Matthew 3:17; 14:33; 17:5; Romans 1:4**

Son of Man

1. Another name for "man" or "human." 2. What God called the prophet Ezekiel. 3. Another name for Jesus that shows He is fully God and fully man. Jesus often called Himself the "Son of Man." **Psalm 80:17; Ezekiel 2:1; Matthew 9:6**

Song of Songs, Song of Solomon (KJV)

Fifth book in the Poetry division of the Old Testament. Collection of romantic poetry which may have been written by King Solomon or on behalf of him. The book describes the love between a man and a woman.
Song of Songs 1:1

Sorcerer

Person who used magic, sometimes to try to find out what would happen in the future. The Bible warns people not to use sorcery. **Acts 13:6-12; Galatians 5:20-21**

Soul

1. Total person. 2. Emotional part of a person. 3. Spiritual part of a person that lives after the body dies. The Bible says a person should love God with all his soul.
Genesis 2:7; Deuteronomy 6:5; Job 30:25; Psalm 42:11; Ecclesiastes 12:7

Sovereignty of God

God's ability to control all things and accomplish whatever He pleases.
Proverbs 16:9; 2 Timothy 1:8-10

Sow/sower

1. To plant seeds.
2. A person who plants seeds. Jesus told a parable about a sower to help His disciples understand what the kingdom of God is like.
Luke 8:4-18

An Arab farmer near Bethlehem sowing seeds on his land

Sparrow

A small bird. God cares for all of His creation, including sparrows. However, Jesus said that God cares for people more than He does sparrow.s (See *Birds in the Bible* chart, p. 21.) **Matthew 10:29-31**

House sparrow

Spear

Light spear thrown as a weapon. King Saul attempted to kill David by throwing a spear at him.
1 Samuel 18:10-11

Greek soldiers from Sparta armed with spears and shields

Speck, Mote (KJV) Small piece of something. Jesus used the word in His Sermon on the Mount when He talked about how people criticize the wrong choices other people make while they make wrong choices themselves. **Matthew 7:3-5**

Spinning and weaving How people make thread and cloth from raw fibers, such as flax and wool. Raw fibers are pulled into a loose strand and twisted to form a continuous thread. A spindle is a slender stick that can be twirled to twist drawn-out fibers caught in a hook or slot at the top. The finished product can be used for weaving cloth. Weaving is also done on looms.
Exodus 35:25-26,35

A bedouin woman spinning wool into yarn

Spirit 1. The third Person of the Trinity—Father, Son, and Holy Spirit. At the beginning of creation, the Spirit of God hovered over the waters. In His conversation with Nicodemus, Jesus said that the Spirit is like the wind—a person cannot see it but can see what it does. The Spirit of God is everywhere. The psalmist knew that no matter where he was, God's Spirit was with him. Jesus promised the Spirit to His followers as He prepared to leave the world. The Spirit would serve as Comforter and Counselor, continuing to teach Jesus' followers and reminding them of what He had said to them.
2. The part of a person that thinks and understands, and has emotions, attitudes, and intentions. Caleb had a different spirit than most of the other people who were alive during his time because of his obedience to God. A person's spirit can be crushed, steadfast, willing, broken, and arrogant.
Genesis 1:2; Numbers 14:24; Psalm 34:18; 51:10,12,17; 139:7; Proverbs 16:18; John 3:8; 14:26

Spiritual gifts What God gives to Christians so they can serve God through the church. Some of the gifts include teaching, service, administration, helping, and mercy. God has given many different gifts to the church. All Christians have tasks to perform to serve the Lord in the church. **Romans 12:6-8; 1 Corinthians 12:4-11**

Stable Safe place where animals are kept. King Solomon kept large numbers of horses in stalls, or stables. Jesus may have been born in a stable, such as a cave where animals were kept.
1 Kings 4:26; Luke 2:7

Stars 1. Constellations, planets, and all heavenly bodies except the sun and the moon. God created the stars and knows their names and numbers. Probably the most famous of all the stars mentioned in the Bible is the star that led the wise men to Jesus.
2. Jesus is called the Bright Morning Star.
Genesis 1:16; Psalm 147:4; Matthew 2:1-2; Revelation 22:16

Orion, the hunter, is one of the best-known constellations and is mentioned in Job, one of the earliest books of the Bible. **Job 38:31-32; Amos 5:8**

Statute (STA choot) Law or commandment. Moses told the Israelites to obey God's laws.
Exodus 15:26

Stephen (STEE vuhn) Means "crown." One of the seven men chosen to minister to people in the church at Jerusalem. Stephen was full of grace and power. His preaching about Jesus upset some of the Jewish leaders so much that they killed him. Saul, who later became a Christian known as Paul, watched and gave his approval as Stephen was stoned to death.
Acts 6:3-7,8; 7:54-60; 8:1

St. Stephen's Gate (Lion's Gate) in Jerusalem. Many people believe that Stephen, the first Christian martyr, was stoned outside this gate.

Steward The person who takes care of something that belongs to someone else. God owns everything and expects people to use what He provides for His purposes. As stewards of God's creation, people are to take care of it. Christians practice stewardship when they use their things, their money, and their time to serve God and others. **Genesis 1:28-30; 2:15; Genesis 44:1; Colossians 3:17**

Stone Palestine has a lot of stones, or rocks, in the fields. Some stones are expensive; others have little or no value. In the Bible, stones were used to build city walls, houses, Solomon's palace, the temple, pavement in courtyards, and columns. The Israelites often piled up stones to remember what God had done for them. **Joshua 4:20-24; Nehemiah 4:3; Esther 1:6; 1 Kings 6:7; 7:9; Matthew 13:5**

Massive stones at the Western Wall in Jerusalem, the most holy place in the world to which Jewish people have access. This wall was built by King Herod when he began to rebuild the second temple in 20 B.C. Four of the stones in this building are gigantic. The largest of these stones weighs 570 tons and is 44 feet long, 10 feet high and 12-16 feet deep. By comparison, the largest stone in the Great Pyramid weighs 11 tons.

Stocks Wooden frame which secured the feet and hands of prisoners. The Romans often added chains along with the stocks. Paul and Silas were placed in stocks after being arrested in Philippi. Later that night, God used an earthquake to free them from the stocks. **Acts 16:24**

Many people believe that this is the place in Philippi where Paul and Silas were imprisoned until God freed them by means of an earthquake.

Storehouse, storage city Where harvested crops were kept safe. Special sections of Israelite towns were designated as storage areas, with several storehouses lining the streets. Joseph led the Egyptians to store grain so the people would have enough food to eat during the famine. During the divided kingdom period, royal storage facilities were established in regional capitals to collect tax payments made in flour, oil, grain, or wine. **Genesis 41:33-36,47-49,56; Nehemiah 13:12-13**

Storage facilities at Knossos, Crete; oil, wine, and grain were stored here.

Straight Street
Street in Damascus where Paul stayed after he became a Christian. Paul became blind on his way to Damascus when he heard Jesus speak to him. He stayed at a house on Straight Street until God used Ananias to heal his blindness. **Acts 9:3-19**

The traditional street called Straight in Damascus, Syria

Straw
Stalks left after the grain in a field has been stripped. Straw was usually used as bedding for animals. As slaves, the Israelites used straw to make bricks in Egypt. **Exodus 5:6-13**

Submission
Volunteering to follow another person and do what he or she wants to be done. All human beings are required to submit to God. The Bible teaches submission to other Christians, God-appointed leaders, and government leaders. Wives are to submit to their husbands, and husbands are to love their wives. Children should submit to their parents. **Romans 13:1; Ephesians 5:15-25; 6:1-3; Philippians 2:9-11; 1 Peter 5:5**

Succoth
(SUHK ahth) Means "booths." 1. Town whose leaders Gideon punished for not helping him in a military campaign against the Midianites. 2. Place where the Israelites camped after leaving Egypt. **Numbers 33:5-6; Judges 8:5-7,13-16**

Sunday
First day of the week. (See *Lord's Day*.) **John 20:1**

Swaddling clothes
Long piece of cloth used to wrap babies and broken legs or arms. The cloth was wrapped tightly around the body to keep it from moving. Mary wrapped Baby Jesus in swaddling clothes. **Luke 2:7,12**

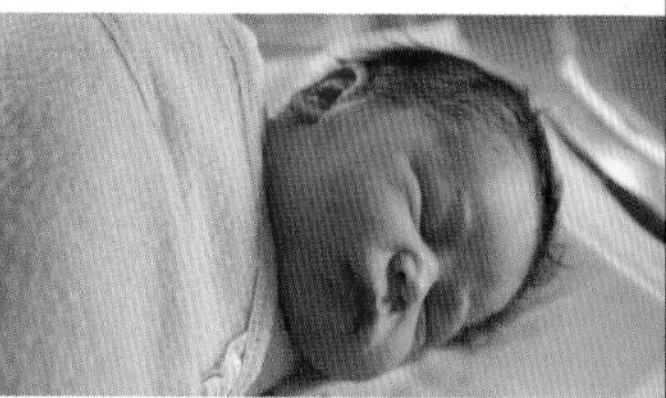

A newborn baby wrapped in swaddling clothes.

Sword
Weapon with a handle and either a short or long blade. Jonathan gave his sword to David to show his friend how much he loved him. **1 Samuel 18:3-4**

Roman soldier with sword drawn in the heat of battle

Sycamore tree
Combination fig and mulberry tree; the fig tree in the Jordan Valley that had leaves like the mulberry tree. The tree's fruit was not as good as the fig tree's fruit. The prophet Amos took care of sycamore figs. Zacchaeus climbed up a sycamore tree to see Jesus. **Amos 7:14; Luke 19:4**

Sychar
(SIGH kahr) Village in Samaria where Jesus talked with the Samaritan woman at Jacob's well. **John 4:4-6**

Synagogue
Special building where Jews met together. After Solomon's temple was destroyed and the people of Judah went into Babylonian exile, the Jews needed a place to pray, worship, and learn about the Scriptures. They built synagogues in different cities. The Jews returned to Jerusalem and rebuilt the temple, but they continued to worship in synagogues. Jesus went to the synagogue in Nazareth and in other towns. Jesus also taught and healed people in synagogues. Paul taught in synagogues in many different cities. A city had to have 10 Jewish men to build a synagogue. **Matthew 4:23; Luke 4:16; 13:10-13; Acts 9:19-20**

Reconstruction of a typical synagogue of the first century A.D. showing the large inner room where the men gathered and its loft above where the women assembled. This drawing is patterned after the synagogue at Capernaum.

Syria
(SIHR ih uh) Term that refers to a geographical region as well as to a series of political groups throughout history. As a geographical term, *Syria* refers to a region that today includes the modern state of Syria, Lebanon, and parts of Turkey and Iraq. In the New Testament, Syria was the name of the Roman province that included Judea. Syria played an important role in the early spread of Christianity. Paul became a Christian on the road to Damascus in Syria and later did mission work in the region. Antioch in Syria was where believers were first called Christians. **Matthew 4:24; Luke 2:2; Acts 9:1-2; 11:26; 13:1-3; 15:41**

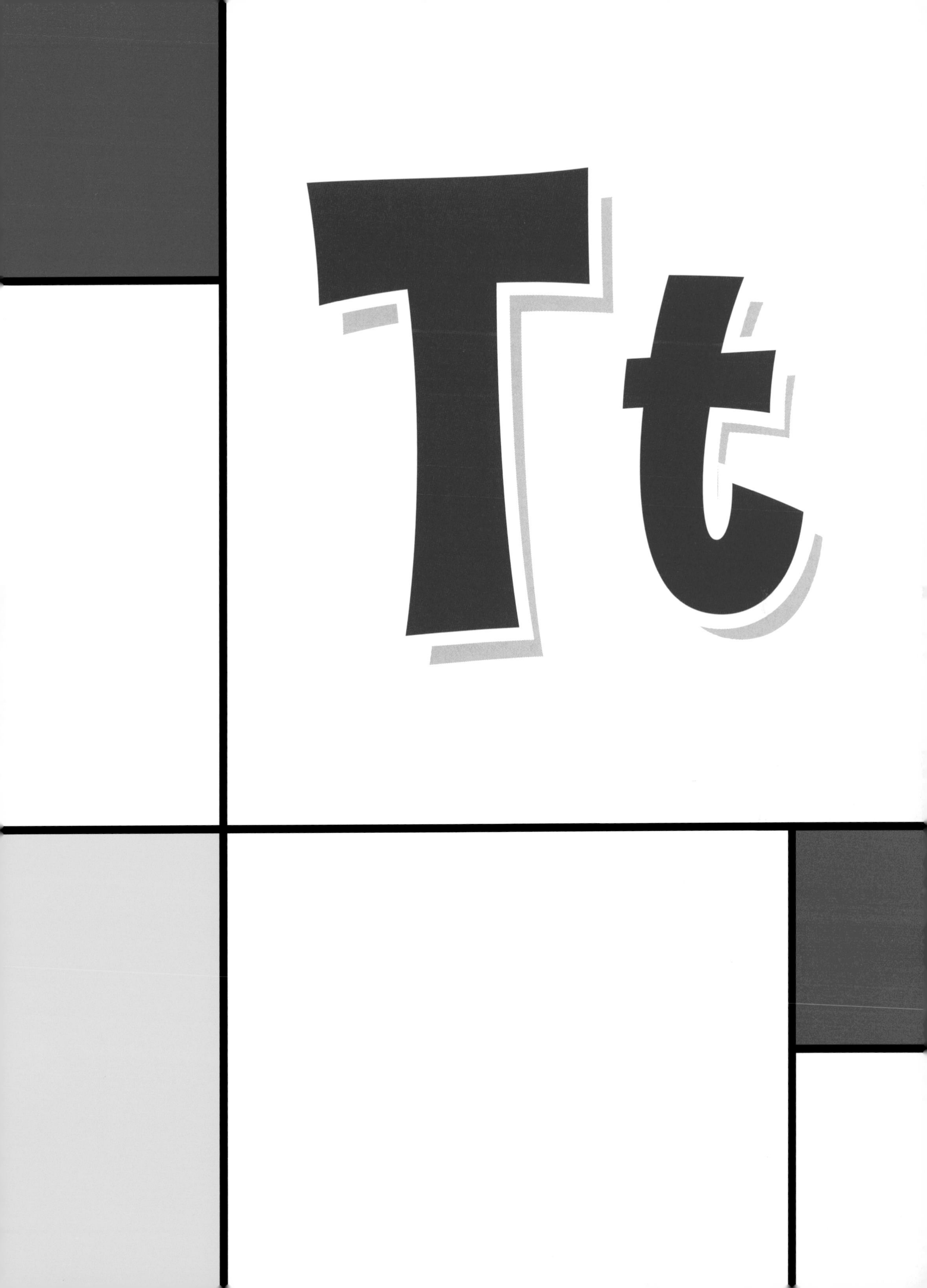
Tt

Tabernacle (TAB uhr NAK uhl) Means "dwelling place." The portable tent where God met with His people. The tabernacle was built from directions God gave to Moses. Also called "the tent of meeting" and "the tent of testimony." **Exodus 25–40; Numbers 17:8**

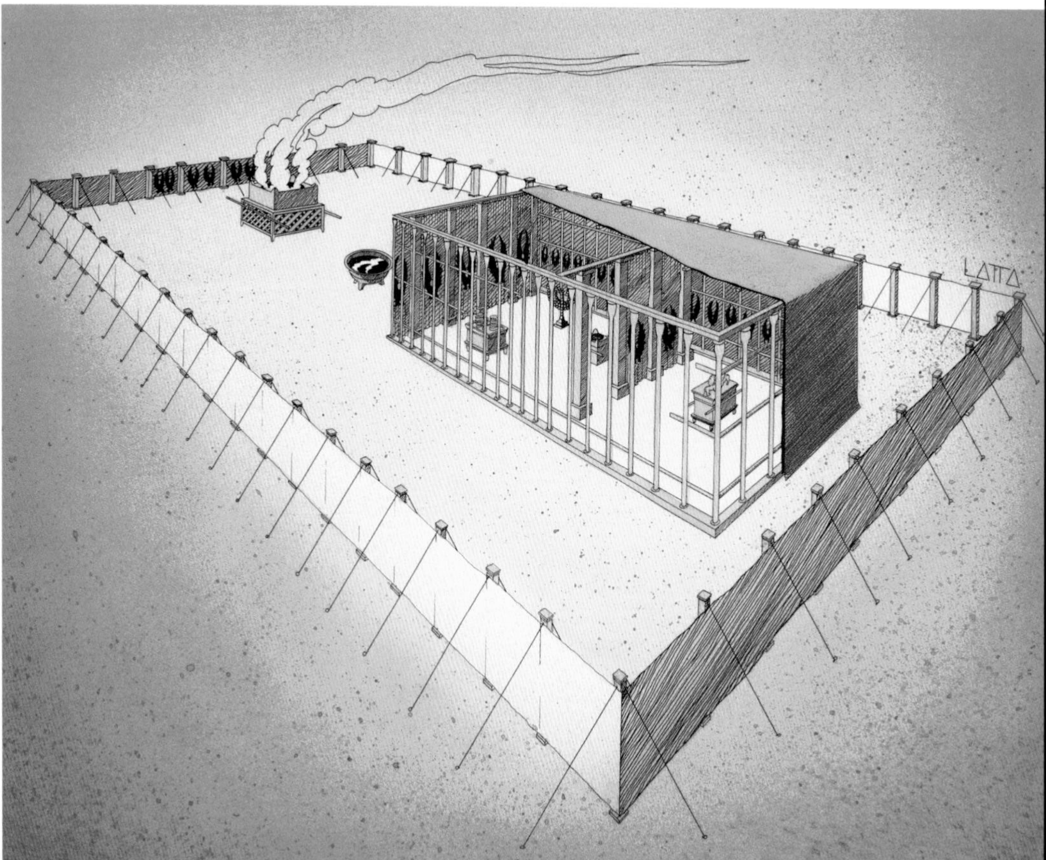

Reconstruction of the tabernacle and its court. The court was formed by curtains attached to erect poles. In front of the tent was the altar of burnt offerings and the laver. The tabernacle always faced east. This view is from the northwest.

Tarshish (TAHR shish) Jonah sailed for Tarshish, the far limit of the western world, from the Mediterranean port of Joppa in his attempt to escape God's call to go to Nineveh. **Jonah 1:1-17**

Reconstructed site of ancient Joppa, the port from which Jonah sailed as he attempted to flee from the Lord

Tablet Flat surface used for writing. 1. Law tablets. The stone objects on which the Ten Commandments were written are known as the tablets (or tables) of the law, testimony, and covenant. These tablets were perhaps small upright stones such as those other nations used to record their laws. 2. Writing tablets. Writing was often done on clay tablets or wood tablets covered with wax.
Exodus 24:12; Exodus 31:18; Deuteronomy 9:9; Ezekiel 4:1; Luke 1:63

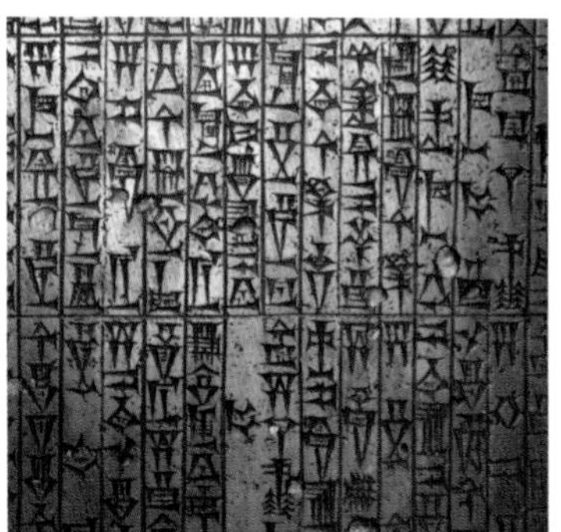

The Code of Hammurabi is one of the most significant legal documents from the ancient world. Hammurabi ruled Babylon from 1792-1750 B.C. Hammurabi's Code is almost completely preserved. It consists of 282 laws arranged in 49 rows.

Tanner Person who works with the skin from animals to make tents and clothing. Peter was staying with Simon the Tanner when he had a vision from God. **Acts 10:1-23**

Tarsus

(TAHR suhs) Birthplace of Paul and capital of the Roman province of Cilicia. **Acts 9:11**

St. Paul's well in Tarsus, believed by some to be on the site of Paul's home

Tax collector, Publican (KJV)

Jobs created by the Romans to help collect taxes in the provinces. Because tax collectors were given their jobs by the Roman officials, they were hated by the Jews. Matthew, one of Jesus' apostles, was a tax collector in Capernaum. Matthew invited Jesus to his home along with other tax collectors and sinners. Zacchaeus was also a tax collector. **Matthew 9:9-13; Luke 19:1-10**

Taxes

Regular payments of money to a nation's government. 1. In the Old Testament, Israel paid taxes to support the tabernacle and the priests. David and Solomon required tribes they had conquered to pay taxes. 2. In New Testament times, Herod the Great charged taxes on what people grew in their fields and items they bought and sold. Taxes were paid to Roman officials. Some taxes at seaports and city gates were gathered by Jews like Zacchaeus and Matthew. The Israelites did not like having to pay taxes to Rome. Some of them thought it was disloyal to God to pay taxes to Rome. When questioned about paying the poll tax, Jesus surprised His questioners by saying that the law should be obeyed.
Matthew 9:9-13; Mark 12:13-17; Luke 19:1-9

Taxation in first-century Israel was a bad experience. It was bad enough that the taxes went to Rome, the country that had conquered and was ruling Israel. Even worse, Jewish citizens were getting rich by being tax collectors for Rome.

Temple Place of worship, especially the temple Solomon built in Jerusalem for the worship of God. There were three temples in Bible times: the first built by Solomon, the one rebuilt by Zerubbabel after the exile, and the temple that Herod built. David planned the first temple and gathered money and items for it. Solomon built it. The temple and the city of Jerusalem were burned by Nebuchadnezzar in 586 B.C. Zerubbabel led the Jews to rebuild the temple and work was completed in 515 B.C. In 17 B.C. Herod the Great began to expand the temple. This big project was not completed until A.D. 63. Three years later, Israel revolted against Rome. As a result, both Jerusalem and the temple were destroyed by the Romans in A.D. 70, only seven years after it was completed. Jesus went there as a boy and later taught there during His ministry. (See *Herod*.)
1 Kings 6–7; Ezra 6:14-16; Luke 2:42-50; John 7:14

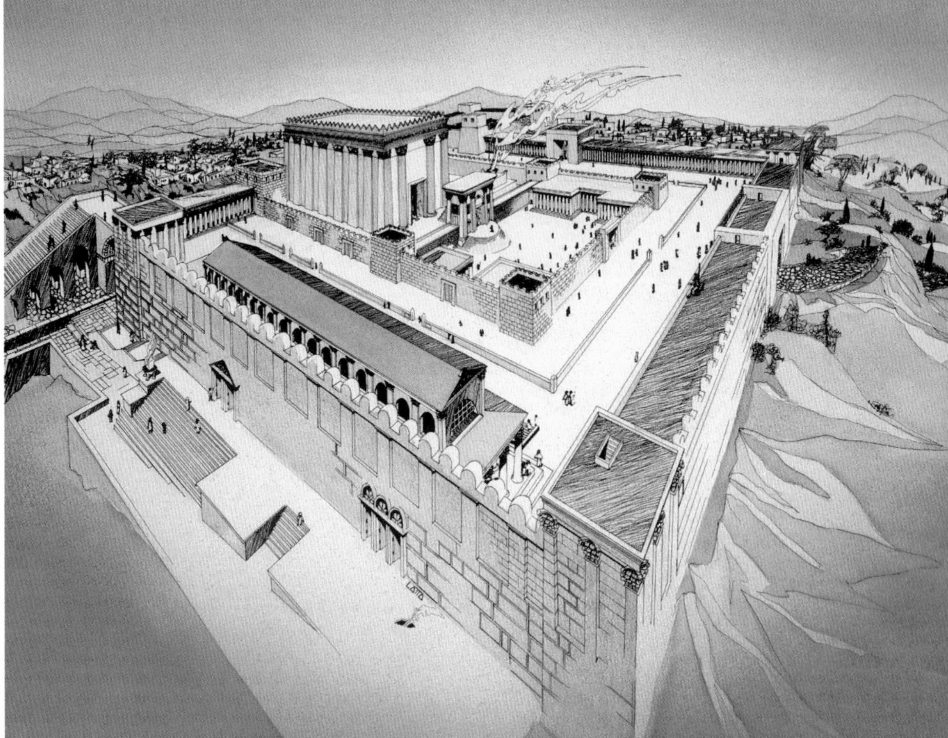

Reconstruction of Herod's temple (17 B.C.–A.D. 70) at Jerusalem as viewed from the southeast. The drawing reflects archaeological discoveries made since excavations began in 1967 along the south end of the Temple Mount platform gateway.

Temples Buildings dedicated to the worship and service of a pagan god or gods. The Parthenon is one of the most recognizable temples in the world, dedicated to the Greek goddess Athena. In Ephesus a silversmith named Demetrius made silver shrines to the goddess Artemis (Diana). Demetrius was afraid that Paul would ruin the business by saying that gods made with hands were not gods. The people of Ephesus would then despise the temple built to Artemis, one of the seven wonders of the ancient world.

The Parthenon was built on the Acropolis in Athens, Greece between 447 and 432 B.C. It housed a large statue of Athena, goddess of wisdom, the arts, industry, justice, and war.

Tempt To try to get a person to make a wrong choice or take an action that is wrong. Satan is the original tempter. Beginning with Eve, Satan tempted Adam, Cain, Abraham, David, and all people to sin. God cannot be tempted by evil, and He does not tempt anyone. When Jesus was in the wilderness, Satan tempted Him to make bread out of stones, to throw Himself from the top of the temple, and to worship Satan. Jesus answered each temptation with verses from Scripture: Deuteronomy 8:3, Deuteronomy 6:16, and Deuteronomy 6:13. The Bible promises that with each temptation God provides a way out. **Matthew 4:1-11; 1 Corinthians 10:13; 1 Thessalonians 3:5; James 1:13**

The Mount of Temptation as seen from the top of Old Testament Jericho

Ten Commandments Laws given to Moses by God on Mt. Sinai. God wrote the laws with His finger on tablets of stone. Moses threw down those stone tablets when he saw the Israelites worshiping a golden calf. When Moses went back up the mountain to talk with God, he took two tablets to replace the broken ones. The first four Commandments tell how to obey God. The last six tell how to get along with people. **Exodus 20:1-17; 32:19; Deuteronomy 5:6-22**

TEN COMMANDMENTS

1. Do not have other gods besides the one true God.
2. Do not make an idol to worship.
3. Do not misuse the name of the Lord your God.
4. Keep the Sabbath day holy.
5. Honor your father and your mother.
6. Do not murder.
7. Keep your marriage promises.
8. Do not steal.
9. Do not lie.
10. Do not want things that belong to someone else.

Tent Outdoor shelter made of cloth or animal skins and held up by poles. Abraham lived in tents. When the Israelites were in the wilderness, they lived in tents. The tabernacle was also called "The Tent of Meeting." **Genesis 13:18; Exodus 16:16; 27:21**

Bedouin tent in the desert of Wadi Rum, Jordan.

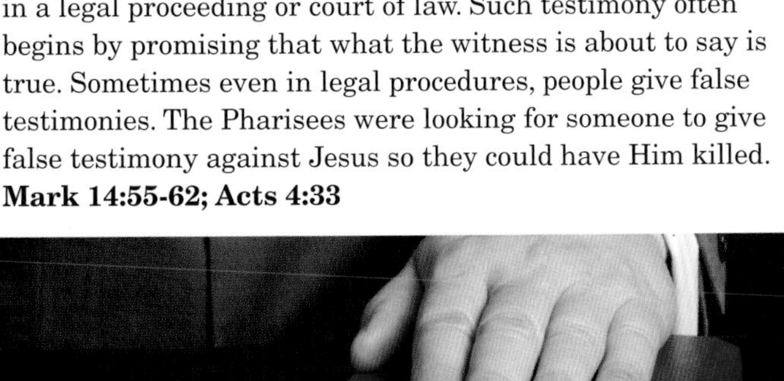

Testimony 1. When someone tells about his experience or about something he has seen. Each person can tell what God has done in his life. 2. Giving a statement in a legal proceeding or court of law. Such testimony often begins by promising that what the witness is about to say is true. Sometimes even in legal procedures, people give false testimonies. The Pharisees were looking for someone to give false testimony against Jesus so they could have Him killed. **Mark 14:55-62; Acts 4:33**

A man places his hand on the Bible and promises that his testimony is true.

Thessalonians, First and Second (THESS uh LOH nih uhnz) Eighth and ninth books in the division of Paul's Letters of the New Testament. Written by Paul to the Christians in Thessalonica. In the first letter Paul praised the church's faithfulness and helped them understand about Jesus' return. The second letter told about events that will happen before Jesus' return. **1 Thessalonians 1:1; 2 Thessalonians 1:1**

Thessalonica (THESS uh loh NIGH kuh) City founded by Alexander the Great in about 315 B.C. Thessalonica was a free city. It had no Roman garrison within its walls, and it made its own coins. Many different groups of people lived in the city. The Book of Acts tells of a Jewish synagogue there. Paul wrote two letters to the Christians who lived there. **Acts 17:1**

The Triumphal Arch of the Roman Emperor Galerius built over the Egnatian Way in Thessalonica

Tiberias, Sea of (tigh BIHR ih uhs) (See *Sea of Galilee*.) **John 6:1**

Thomas (TAHM uhs) Means "a twin." Apostle of Jesus. He wanted evidence that Jesus had risen from the dead. When Jesus appeared to him and showed him the scars in His hands and side, Thomas confessed his faith in Jesus. **John 20:24-28**

Thomas' doubt turns to faith.

Timothy (TIM uh thih) Means "honoring God." 1. Friend and trusted co-worker of Paul. Native of Lystra. Learned the Scriptures from his mother Eunice and grandmother Lois. When Paul was in prison, he sent Timothy to Philippi. 2. Tenth and eleventh books in the division of Paul's Letters of the New Testament. Paul wrote the letters to Timothy to teach the young pastor how to lead his church. The first letter is about church leadership. The second letter gave final instructions and encouragement to Timothy.
Philippians 2:19; 1 Timothy 4:11-16; 2 Timothy 1:5; 4:2

Toll Taxes paid for use of roads and highways. Paul told the Christians in Rome to pay their taxes and tolls.
Romans 13:7

The stones at the right are part of the Via Egnatia, part of the extensive system of roads built by the Romans and funded by taxes. This portion of the Via Egnatia is just outside Philippi and may have been the road that brought Paul and Silas to this city, the place where the first Europeans accepted Christ as Savior and Lord.

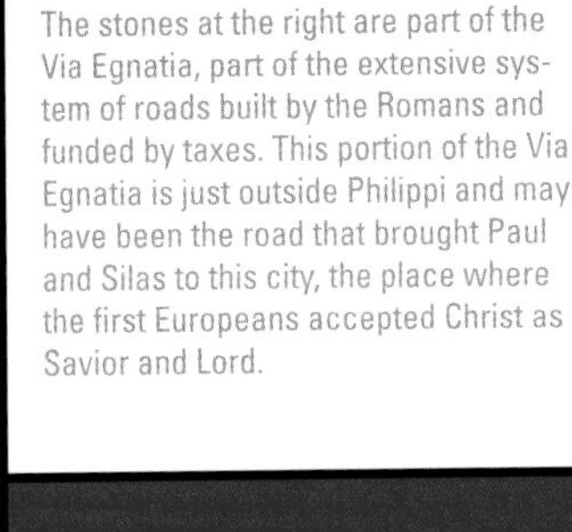

Timothy reads a letter from Paul.

Titus (TIGH tuhs) 1. Gentile friend of Paul. He went with Paul and Barnabas to Jerusalem. In his second letter to the Corinthians, Paul called Titus a co-worker and partner. He worked with the church in Crete. 2. Twelfth book in the division of Paul's Letters in the New Testament. Paul wrote to Titus to encourage him.
2 Corinthians 8:23-24; Galatians 2:3; Titus 1:1-5

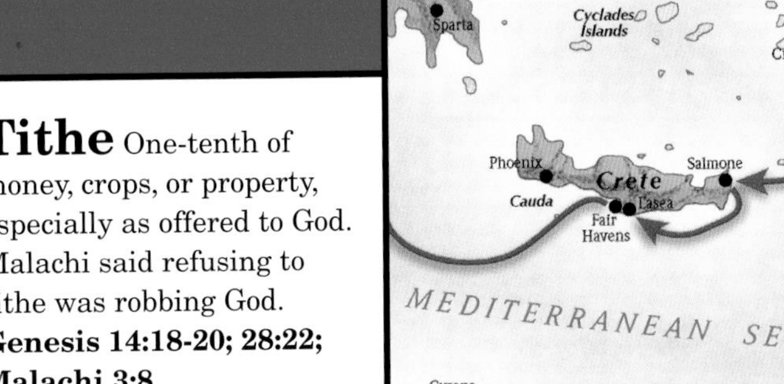

Left: Many believed that after Paul's first imprisonment in Rome, he and Titus planted churches on Crete. Paul left Titus on the island to finish the work they had begun together.

Right: The rugged terrain of Crete. Paul believed Titus was the man to oversee the planting of churches on this Greek island.

Tithe One-tenth of money, crops, or property, especially as offered to God. Malachi said refusing to tithe was robbing God.
Genesis 14:18-20; 28:22; Malachi 3:8

Tomb A place to bury dead people. Jesus was buried in a new tomb that belonged to Joseph of Arimathea. **Matthew 27:57-60**

The Garden Tomb in Jerusalem believed by some to be the place Jesus was buried. The other possible site is where the Church of the Holy Sepulchre is built.

Tool (See *Tools in the Bible* chart, p. 193.)

Torah (TOH rah) Hebrew word for "law." Title given to the first five books of the Old Testament: Genesis, Exodus, Leviticus, Numbers, and Deuteronomy.

A Jewish boy at his Bar Mitzvah with the Torah scroll opened before him

Torch Long pole with cloths dipped in oil wrapped around one end, and used as a light. The soldiers and temple police used lanterns and torches when they came to Gethsemane to arrest Jesus. **John 18:1-3**

A flaming torch

Tower Tall buildings where watchmen could guard pastures, vineyards, and cities. Towers were small one-room structures or large fortresses. Most were made of stones. *Tower* is a word used to describe God's strength. **2 Chronicles 26:9; Proverbs 18:10**

Tower of David in Jerusalem, the highest point in the ancient city including the Temple Mount. The series of fortifications of which the Tower of David is a part protected Jerusalem from the west.

TOOLS OF THE BIBLE

Awl, Aul (KJV) Small tool used for making holes. Made of flint, bone, stone, or metal. **Exodus 21:6; Deuteronomy 15:17**

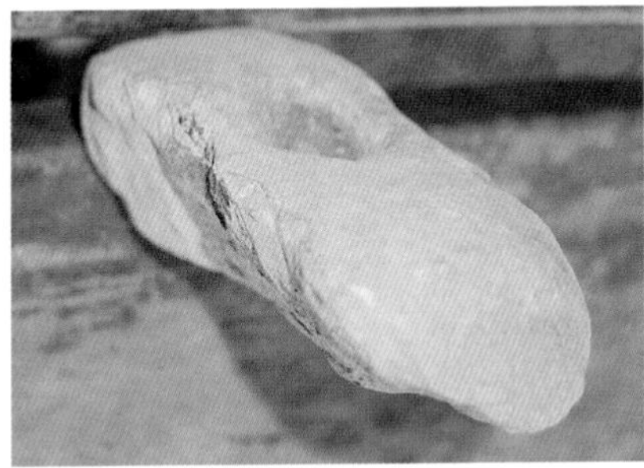

Ax, Axe (KJV) The Old Testament mentions different types of axes. Large axes were used for trees and stone. People used smaller axes for other jobs. The head of the axe was made of iron or stone. Also used as a weapon.
Deuteronomy 20:19; 2 Kings 6:5-7

Chisel Small tool used for finishing work or for rough work. Used with wood or stone.
Exodus 20:25; Isaiah 44:13; Jeremiah 10:3

Hammer Striking tool used in cutting stone, working metal, and for woodworking. **1 Kings 6:7; Isaiah 41:7; 44:12; Jeremiah 10:4**

Hatchet Small, hand-held ax. **Psalm 74:6**

Hoe, Mattock (KJV) Used as a farming tool to dig in the dirt. **Isaiah 7:25**

Knife Blade was made either of flint, a kind of stone, or of metal, such as bronze, copper, or iron. The handle was wooden. Knives were usually 6 to 10 inches long. Often used for killing and skinning animals and for killing sacrificial animals. **Genesis 22:6; Joshua 5:2; Jeremiah 36:23**

Plow, Plowshares Used to cut soil. The blades were made of bronze or iron, and the other parts were wooden. Animals pulled the plows. **1 Samuel 8:12; 13:20; Proverbs 20:4; Luke 9:62**

Plumb Line, Plumbline (KJV) Cord with a weight (usually metal or stone) attached to one end. Dangled beside a wall during its construction to make sure the wall was straight, up and down.
Amos 7:7-8

Mosaic picture of a pruning knife from Italy.

Pruning Knife, Pruning Hooks (KJV) Used to prune and harvest grapevines. **Isaiah 18:5**

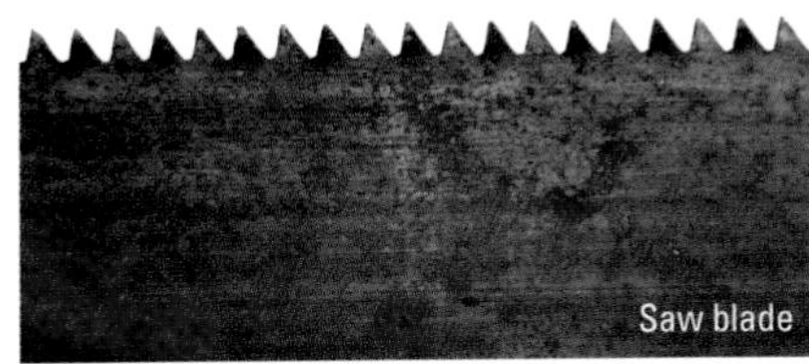

Saw blade

Saw Used to cut wood or stone. At first the blade was made of bronze, but later iron was used.
2 Samuel 12:31; 1 Kings 7:9

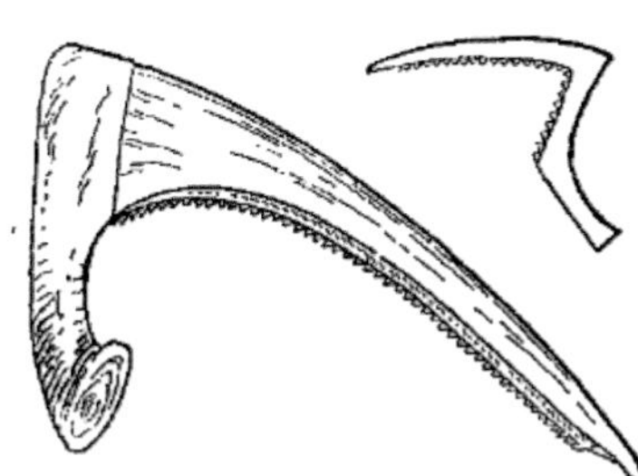

Sickle Used to cut down grain stalks, the sickle had a short handle and curved blade. The blade was made either of flint or metal.
Mark 4:29

TRANSPORTATION IN THE BIBLE

A first century boat, sometimes called "The Jesus Boat," found in the mud of the Sea of Galilee. It can be viewed in a preserving room at Nof Ginnosar, Israel.

Boats Boats like the ones in which Jesus sailed were made of wood with cloth sails and were used for fishing. They could also be steered with oars when there was no wind. Jesus first four apostles were fishermen. Jesus slept during a storm at sea and woke up to still the storm. At another time He walked on the water toward the boat, and Peter got out of the boat and walked to Him.
Matthew 13:22-33; Mark 4:35-42; Luke 5:1-11

Camels Large hump-backed mammals of Asia and Africa used for desert travel to carry burdens or passengers. The camel, called the "ship of the desert," can travel in the desert because of its padded feet, a muscular body, and a hump of fat to sustain life on long journeys. A young camel can walk 100 miles in a day.

When Abraham's servant went to find a wife for Isaac, he traveled by camel and told Rebekah's brother of his master's wealth which included many camels. Jesus said it is easier for a camel to pass through the eye of a needle than for a rich man to enter heaven.
Genesis 32:10-67; Mark 10:23-27

Chariots Two-wheeled land vehicles made of wood and strips of leather and usually drawn by horses. Egyptian chariots are the first mentioned in the Bible. Joseph rode in a chariot to meet his father when Jacob came to Egypt. Pharaoh's horses and chariots went after the Israelites who were crossing the Red Sea on dry land. The water came over the Egyptians and all the horses, chariots, and horsemen drowned. Philistine chariots were fortified with plates of metal that made them stronger than those of the Israelites. In the New Testament the Ethiopian was traveling from Jerusalem to Ethiopia by chariot when God sent Philip to tell him about Jesus.
Genesis 46:29; Exodus 14:23-49; Judges 4:3; Acts 8:26-38

Donkeys Donkeys were the chief means of travel in Bible times. People rode on donkeys, and donkeys carried burdens. When Jesse sent his son David to be Saul's armor-bearer, he sent a donkey loaded with bread and wine. Jesus rode into Jerusalem on the colt of a donkey and fulfilled the prophecy in the Book of Zechariah.
1 Samuel 16:19-23; Zechariah 9:9

Horses Horses are not mentioned in the Bible until David began to use then in battle. Horses were used in battle, officials rode them, and army scouts rode them.
2 Samuel 8:3-42; 2 Kings 7:13-16

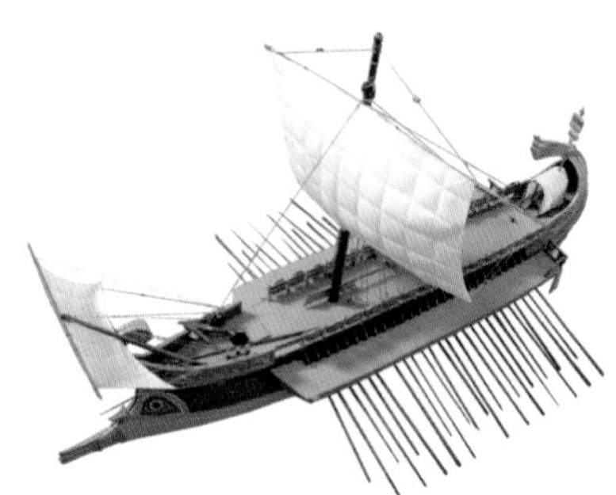

Ships Greek and Roman ships were made of wooden planks and coated with pitch to protect them. Ropes were kept onboard for emergencies. When Paul was taken to Rome to speak before Caesar, he traveled by ship with a Roman centurion. When the ship was in a great storm, the ropes were used to hold the ship together. The ship wrecked near the island of Malta.
Acts 27:1-44

Wagons/carts Made from wood. Large two- and four-wheeled wagons were used in Bible times to move heavy loads and people. Joseph sent wagons to Canaan when his father and brothers moved their families to Egypt. Most wagons and carts were pulled by oxen. **Genesis 45:21-28; 1 Samuel 16:19-23**

Transfiguration Change in Jesus' appearance. Jesus took Peter, James, and John to a mountaintop. His face began to shine like the sun, and His clothes were white as light. Moses and Elijah appeared with Jesus. Peter wanted to build three tents and stay on the mountain. But God spoke and said, "This is my beloved Son. I take delight in Him. Listen to Him!" **Matthew 17:1-13; Mark 9:1-13; Luke 9:28-36**

Jesus' transfiguration before Peter, James, and John

Transportation
(See *Transportation in the Bible* chart, p. 194.)

Tree of Knowledge
Plant in the middle of the garden of Eden. God told Adam and Eve not to eat the fruit of that tree. The serpent tempted Eve to eat the fruit of the tree and to "be like God, knowing good and evil." When Adam joined Eve in eating the fruit, they were ashamed and God made them leave the garden. This was the first sin in the world.
Genesis 2:17; 3:1-22

Tree of Life
Plant in the garden of Eden that represents eternal life.
Genesis 3:22-24; Revelation 22:2

Transformed
To be changed. A caterpillar is transformed into a butterfly. People who admit their sin, believe Jesus is God's Son, and confess Him as their Savior and Lord are transformed. They are changed from nonbelievers to believers.
Matthew 17:1-13; Romans 12:2

A caterpiller becomes a chrysalis, and a chrysalis becomes a butterfly.

Trial Legal event that determines a person's guilt or innocence of a crime. Jesus was tried illegally by several groups:
1. tried before Annas
2. appeared before Caiaphas
3. condemned by the Sanhedrin
4. had a hearing before Pilate
5. was sent to Herod Antipas
6. sent back to Pilate to be sentenced to death

Stephen was tried by the Jewish Sanhedrin who later stoned him. Paul was tried before Felix, Festus, and King Agrippa before being sent to Rome because he appealed to Caesar.
Luke 22:66--23:25; John 18:12-14,19-24; Acts 6:11–7:60; 24–26

Jesus' trial before the Roman governor, Pontius Pilate.

Trinity Term used to describe the three persons of God. The term does not appear in the Bible. In the Bible, God is shown as God the Father, God the Son (Jesus), and God the Holy Spirit.

Tunic Loose-fitting, knee-length garment worn next to the skin. Jesus' tunic was made of one piece of cloth. As He died on the cross the soldiers tossed coins to see who would get it. **John 19:23**

Triumphal Entry Term used for the time when Jesus entered the city of Jerusalem on the Sunday before His crucifixion. Jesus entered the city riding on the colt of a donkey. The people placed palm branches on the road before Him and sang His praises. This event is celebrated on the Sunday before Easter and is called "Palm Sunday." **Matthew 21:1-9; Mark 11:1-10; Luke 19:28-38; John 12:12-15**

Many people believe this is the route of Jesus' triumphal entry into Jerusalem.

Truth Statements that accurately express and describe reality. Lying is the opposite of telling the truth. People who believe in God are to tell the truth. God's Word is truth. His truth is never ending. The Bible is the Word of truth. **Proverbs 12:17; Ephesians 4:25; 2 Timothy 2:15**

Twelve Tribes of Israel Twelve groups of families in Israel who were descendants of the twelve sons of Jacob. Jacob's name was changed to Israel. His twelve sons and their descendants made up the nation of Israel, sometimes called "the children of Israel," or "the sons of Israel." The family of Jacob began when Jacob stayed at Haran with his uncle Laban. The birth of the sons came through Jacob's wives Leah and Rachel and their maids Zilpah and Bilhah. The sons were Reuben, Simeon, Levi, Judah, Dan, Naphtali, Gad, Asher, Issachar, Zebulun, Joseph, and Benjamin. Joseph's sons were Ephraim and Manasseh. They were adopted by Jacob and each one became the father of one of the tribes of Israel. Each tribe except Levi received a portion of the land in Canaan. The tribe of Levi was given cities throughout Canaan. **Genesis 29:31–30:24; 48:1-12**

Uu

Unleavened

Bread baked without using leaven, a yeast that makes bread rise. Unleavened bread was often served to guests. Eating unleavened bread was part of the Feast of Unleavened Bread which was celebrated with Passover. This was done because the Hebrews had to leave Egypt quickly and did not have time for bread to rise. (See *Leaven* and *Yeast*.) **Genesis 19:3; Exodus 12:8**

Jesus celebrates Passover with His disciples.

Upper Room

Upstairs room chosen by Jesus in which He had a final Passover meal with His disciples before His arrest. (See *Guest Room, Last Supper, Lord's Supper.*) **Mark 14:14-15**

Ur

(UHR) Ancient city in lower Mesopotamia where Abraham was born. Ur was an important city in what is now Iraq. **Genesis 11:27-32**

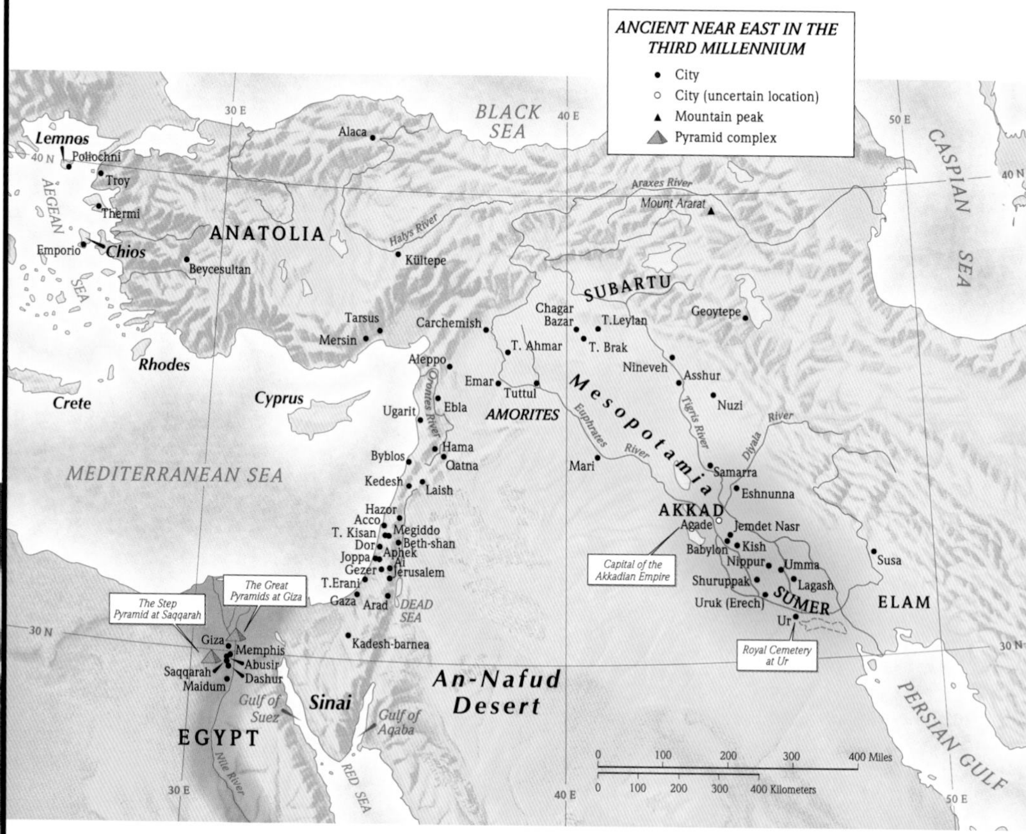

The Middle East at the time of Abraham

Uriah

(yoo RIGH uh) One of David's mighty warriors and one of the group of 30 men close to the king. He was the husband of Bathsheba, the woman with whom David committed adultery. David gave orders for Uriah to be killed in battle. **2 Samuel 11:6-26; 23:39**

Urim and Thummim

(YOO rim) (THUHM im) Objects the high priest used to discover God's will. Little is known about them. They were kept by the high priest in the breastpiece. Later, Moses gave the tribe of Levi responsibility for their care. **Exodus 28:15-30; Deuteronomy 33:8**

Utensils

Items used in the tabernacle and temple for worshipping God. Some of the items were firepans, pots, shovels, basins, and meat forks. **Exodus 27:3; 30:26-29**

Uzziah

(uh ZIGH uh) Means "Yahweh is [my] strength." King of Judah who was 16 years old when he became king. He disobeyed God by going into the temple to burn incense on the altar, a job only a priest could do. God punished him with a skin disease, and he had to live away from all people until he died. **2 Chronicles 26:1-23**

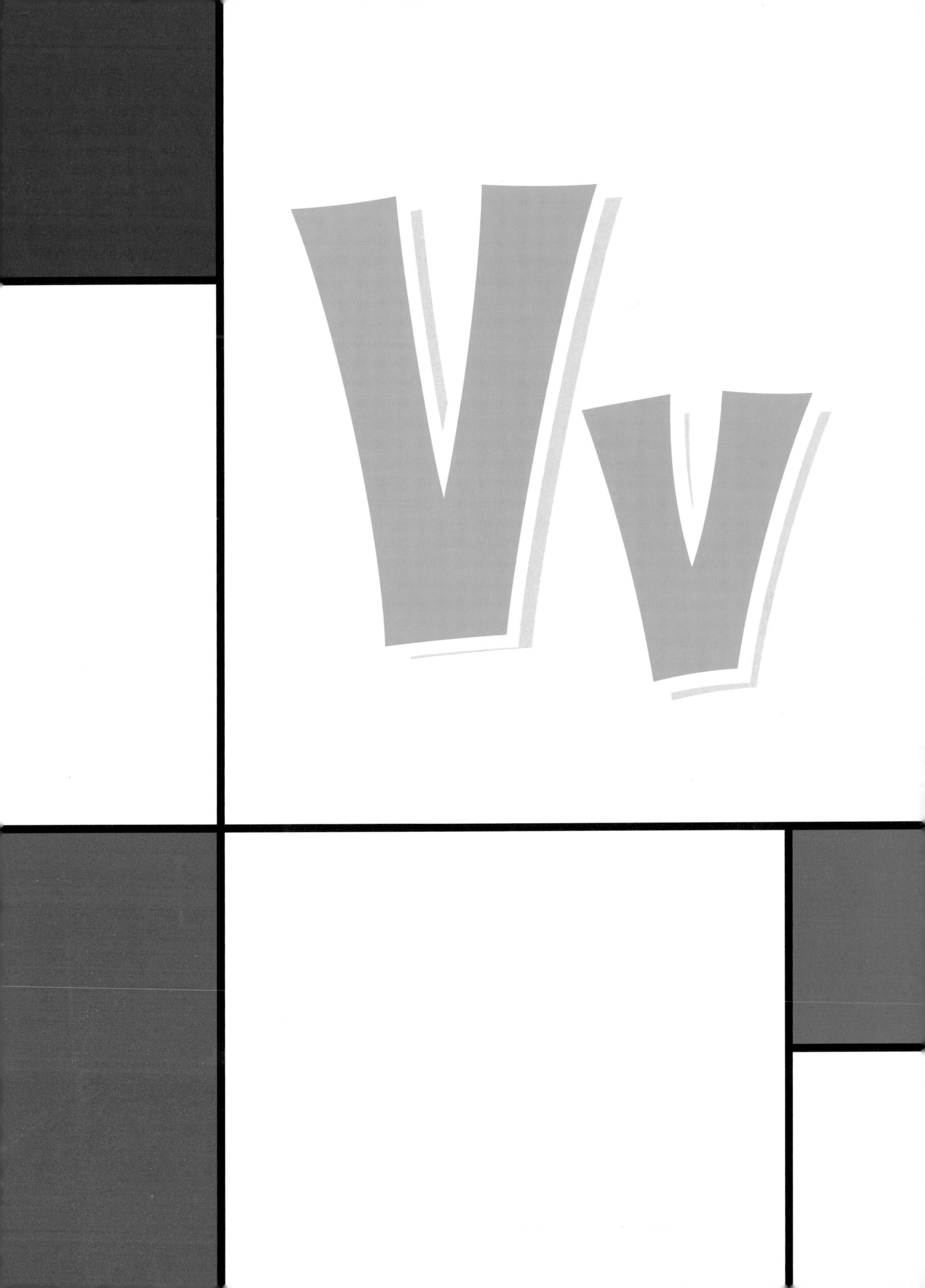
Vv

Veil, Vail (KJV)

Cloth covering. 1. Women's veils. Rebekah veiled herself before meeting Isaac. Her veil was perhaps the sign that she was not married. 2. Tabernacle and temple veil. This curtain separated the most holy place from the holy place. Only the high priest was allowed to pass through the veil and then only on the Day of Atonement. At Jesus' death the temple veil was ripped from top to bottom, illustrating that in Jesus God had abolished the barrier separating humanity from the presence of God.
Genesis 24:65; 2 Chronicles 3:14; Leviticus 16:2; Matthew 27:51; Mark 15:38; Luke 23:45

The temple veil that separated the most holy place (holy of holies) from the holy place

Vengeance

To repay evil with evil. Paul wrote in the Book of Romans that Christians should not pay back someone who hurts them. Vengeance belongs to God. He will decide what happens to people who hurt others.
Deuteronomy 32:35; Romans 12:19-21

Vessels

Bowls, jugs, baskets, and pots used in everyday life. Elisha told prophets to make a pot of stew. Herbs which were poison were added to the pot. Elisha threw meal into the pot to remove the poison. The woman at the well left her water pot at the well when she told the people in her city about Jesus. **2 Kings 4:38-41; John 4:28**

This vessel was found in Lachish, Israel and dates to 1750 to 1650 B.C. Juglets of this kind are found in both Egypt and Canaan. Luxury products such as perfumed oils were transported in these vessels.

Vineyard

Place where grapevines are grown. Naboth owned a vineyard in Jezreel, and King Ahab wanted it.
1 Kings 21:1-16

A vineyard at Birkat Ram in the Golan Heights of Syria.

Virgin

A woman who has not slept with a man. Mary was a virgin when Gabriel came to her and said she would have a son who would be called the Son of the Most High, Jesus. **Luke 1:26-38**

The virgin Mary and Baby Jesus

Vision

One way God communicates with people. In the Old Testament, the prophets Isaiah, Amos, Hosea, Micah, Ezekiel, and Daniel had visions from God. Isaiah saw God in the temple; he knew God was holy and he was a sinful man. In the New Testament, Peter had a vision of a sheet with animals in it. God wanted him to know that nothing God created was unclean. John had a vision from God on the Island of Patmos that led him to write the Book of Revelation.
Isaiah 6:1-8; Acts 10:9-16; Revelation 1:9-20

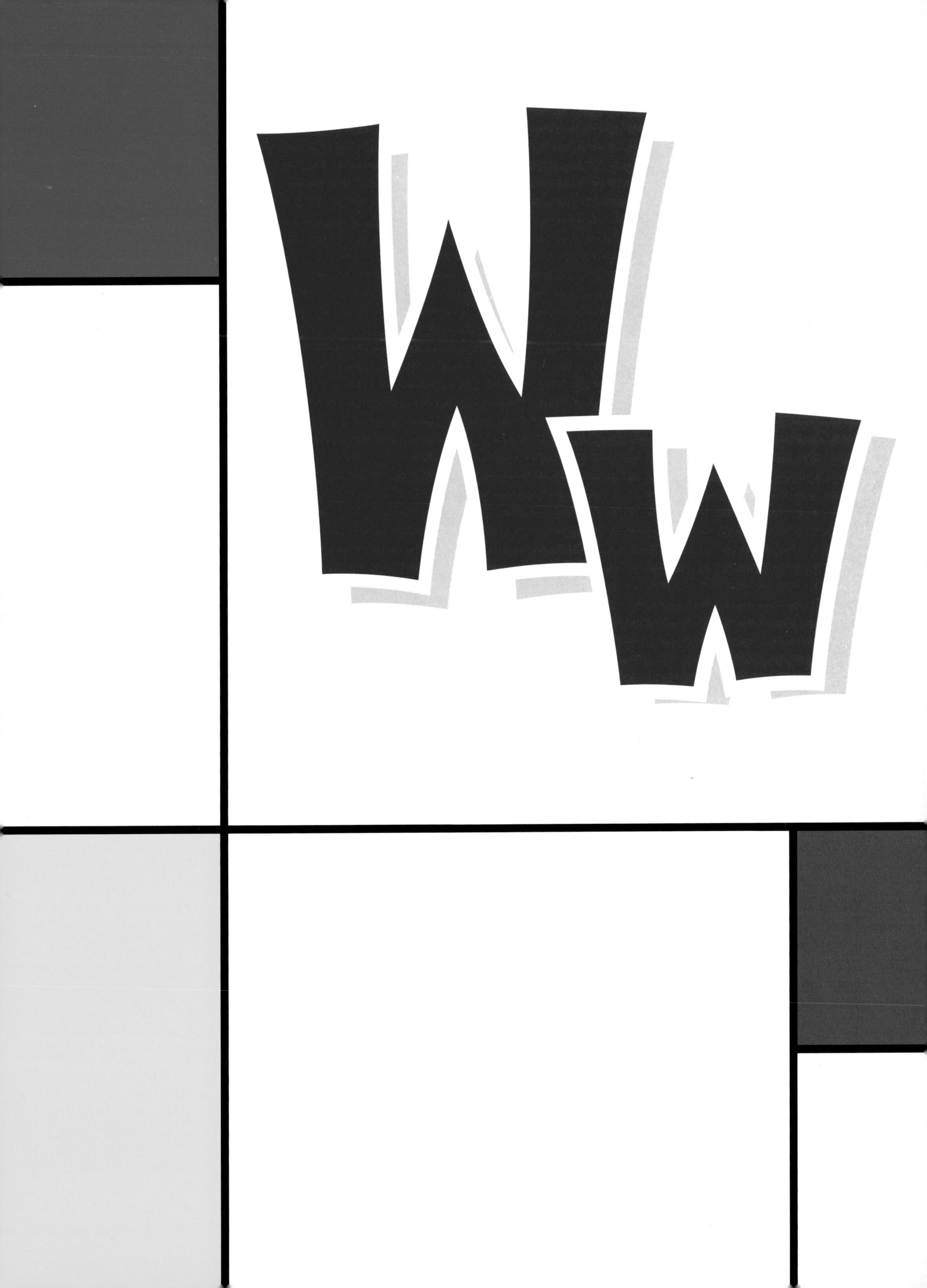

W
W

Wadi (WAH dih), **Brook** (KJV) Stream of water that is dry most of the year. God provided food for the prophet Elijah near the Wadi Cherith. **1 Kings 17:2-7**

The wadi through the limestone cliffs at Qumran near the Dead Sea

Wandering in the wilderness The people of Israel refused to enter the Promised Land after they heard the spies' negative report. God told Moses that no one over the age of 20 would live to enter the promised land, except Caleb and Joshua. For 40 years Israel moved from place to place in the wilderness. **Numbers 14:1-38**

Watchman One who stands guard. 1. Bible times cities had watchmen standing on the walls. Their job was to sound a warning if an enemy approached. 2. Vineyards and fields also had watchmen, especially during harvest. Their job was to guard the produce from animals and thieves. 3. Israel's prophets saw themselves as watchmen warning the nation of God's judgment if the people did not repent. **2 Kings 9:17; Ezekiel 33:2-3**

Watchtower Tower on a high place or built high enough for a person to be able to see for a long distance. The person doing the watching might be a soldier or a servant (See *Tower.*) **2 Kings 9:17; Isaiah 5:2; Mark 12:1**

Wall Outside vertical structures of houses and the fortifications surrounding cities. In ancient times, cities and houses were made of bricks which were made of clay mixed with reeds and hardened in the sun. Archaeologists estimate that the walls of Nineveh were wide enough to drive three chariots together on the top. The walls of Babylon were wide enough to drive six chariots together. Nehemiah led the people of Jerusalem to rebuild the wall of the city in 52 days. **Nehemiah 6:15**

A rabbi prepares to read directly from the open Torah in front of the Western Wall in Jerusalem. The Western Wall was built in 20 B.C. by King Herod when he expanded the temple that Zerubbabel rebuilt (536 B.C.).

Water pot Waterpot (KJV) Container made from clay or stone. Large pots stored water. Women could carry smaller pots on their shoulders. Small pitchers were used for pouring water. Water was also carried in animal skins. Elijah had four water pots filled with water and poured over his sacrifice on Mount Carmel. The disciples who prepared for Jesus' Passover meal with His disciples met a man carrying a water pot. The water in large water pots was turned to wine when Jesus performed His first miracle. Jesus spoke with the woman at the well and she left her water pot to go tell the people of her village about Jesus. **1 Kings 18:33; Luke 22:10; John 2:6; 4:28**

A woman stands before a first century well preparing to draw water.

Weapons
Objects which people, groups, or armies use to hurt, kill, or defeat other people, groups, or armies. In Bible times, armies used chariots and horses, bows, slings, spears, and axes. They protected themselves with swords, shields, armor, and helmets. Armies used towers with battering rams to destroy walls and defenses. David took Goliath's weapons and put them in his own tent after he killed Goliath.
1 Samuel 17:54

Reconstruction of a Roman battering ram (first century A.D.)

Weave
Using a loom to interlace thread to form cloth. An important industry in Bible times. (See *Spinning and weaving.*)
Exodus 35:35

A Middle Eastern weaver operating his loom

Weights
Systems of measurement (See *Table of Weights and Measures in the Bible* chart, p. 117.)

Well
Source of water created by digging in the earth. In the climate of ancient Israel, having enough water was a constant concern. Jesus sat by a well at Sycar when He talked with a woman who had come to draw water.
John 4:1-7

Well at modern Beer-sheba thought by some to be Abraham's Well

Wheat
Grain used to make bread. Hiram, king of Tyre, gave Solomon 100,000 bushels of wheat as food for his household each year (See *Foods of the Bible* chart, p. 63-64.)
1 Kings 5:10-11

Field of dry wheat in the Hachula Valley of northern Israel.

Widow
Woman whose husband is dead. A widow baked a small loaf of bread for Elijah, and neither her jar of flour nor jug of oil ran out until the rains returned to the land.
1 Kings 17:8-16

Wilderness
Holy Land areas with little rainfall and few people. Wilderness is a rocky, dry wasteland. Geographically the wilderness lay south, east, and southwest of the land of Israel. Jesus went into a wilderness after His baptism. He was in a wilderness for 40 days and nights. The devil tempted him there. (See *Wandering in the wilderness.*) **Matthew 4:1-11**

The Negev is one of the areas of wilderness in the Bible. The barren terrain, blue sky, and rippled clouds come together to form a scene of unique beauty. When Mark Twain visited Palestine in 1867, he found the desolation of the Negev beyond imagination. The Negev is not all alike. It is made up of at least five different ecological regions. In recent years innovative land management has made portions of the Negev productive.

Will of God God's plan for His creation and for each person. God does whatever He wants to do. God wants all people do His will. God's will is always good, acceptable, and perfect. Christians can come to know God's will through His written Word, the Bible, through prayer, and through the advice of fellow believers. **Psalm 135:6; Matthew 6:10; Romans 12:2; Ephesians 2:10; Colossians 1:9**

Wine Drink made from fermented grape juice. Grapes grew in Bible times. Wine was made by pressing the juice from the grapes in large stone vats with a small drain at one end. The juice was collected in troughs, poured into large jars, and allowed to ferment while stored in cool, rock cisterns. In New Testament times, wine was kept in skin flasks and often diluted with water. It was also used as a medicine and disinfectant. Jesus' first miracle was turning water into wine at a wedding. The Book of Proverbs offers strong words about the dangers of wine. **Proverbs 20:1; 21:17; 23:30-31; John 2:1-10**

Winnowing Step in the processing of grain when the grain is separated from the chaff, the part people cannot eat. The grain, chaff, and straw are all thrown into the air together. The wind blows away the chaff and the straw, letting the heavier grain fall back to the ground. Boaz and his workmen were winnowing the grain at the threshing floor. Psalm 1 describes wicked people as chaff that the wind blows away. **Ruth 3:2; Psalm 1**

The winnowing process separates the grain from the chaff.

Wisdom Learning how to live each day in a way that is pleasing to God. The books of Job, Psalms, Proverbs, and Ecclesiastes are known as books of wisdom. **Proverbs 3:5-6,13,19; 4:10-14**

Wise men (See *Magi*.)

Witness Someone who tells about what he or she has seen, heard, or experienced. Jesus told His disciples that they would be witnesses to people of their day. Christians today need to be witnesses about their relationship with Jesus. **Acts 1:8**

A woman tells what the Bible says about Jesus.

Wool Thick hair of sheep and some other animals. Wool was made into thread and used to make clothing, blankets, and other articles. Gideon used a piece of wool to know God's will for his life. **Judges 6:36-40**

Basket of fresh and unprocessed sheep wool

Word In the Bible, *Word* may refer to the Law of God, to the gospel message about Jesus, to any part of God's written revelation, or to Jesus Himself. **Psalm 119; John 1:1,9**

World 1. Planet Earth. 2. In the Bible *world* often means the people who live on Planet Earth. In John 3:16, Jesus said "God loved the world in this way: He gave His One and Only Son," to all the humans in the world. 3. The Bible also uses *world* to describe evil and people who do not know Jesus as Savior and choose to do wrong. **Nehemiah 9:6; Colossians 2:20**

Children of the world

Worry To think about an event that may or may not happen, but one that makes you feel afraid, sad, or troubled. A student may worry about a test at school. A child may worry about a parent who is sick. Jesus said not to worry about life, food, or clothes. Instead of worrying, people should be in a relationship with God through Jesus. God will take care of people's needs. Paul said not to worry about anything, but to pray and let God know about the things that cause worry. **Matthew 6:25-34; Philippians 4:6**

Worship Giving honor, reverence, and praise to God. Worship is the response of people to God. God shows Himself to people through the ways He works in their lives. Then people respond to God with thankfulness, praise, obedience, and worship. Two parts of worship in most churches are the Lord's Supper and baptism. **Psalm 29:2; 95:6; Matthew 28:19; Luke 22:19; Acts 2:38,42; 1 Corinthians 11:17-34**

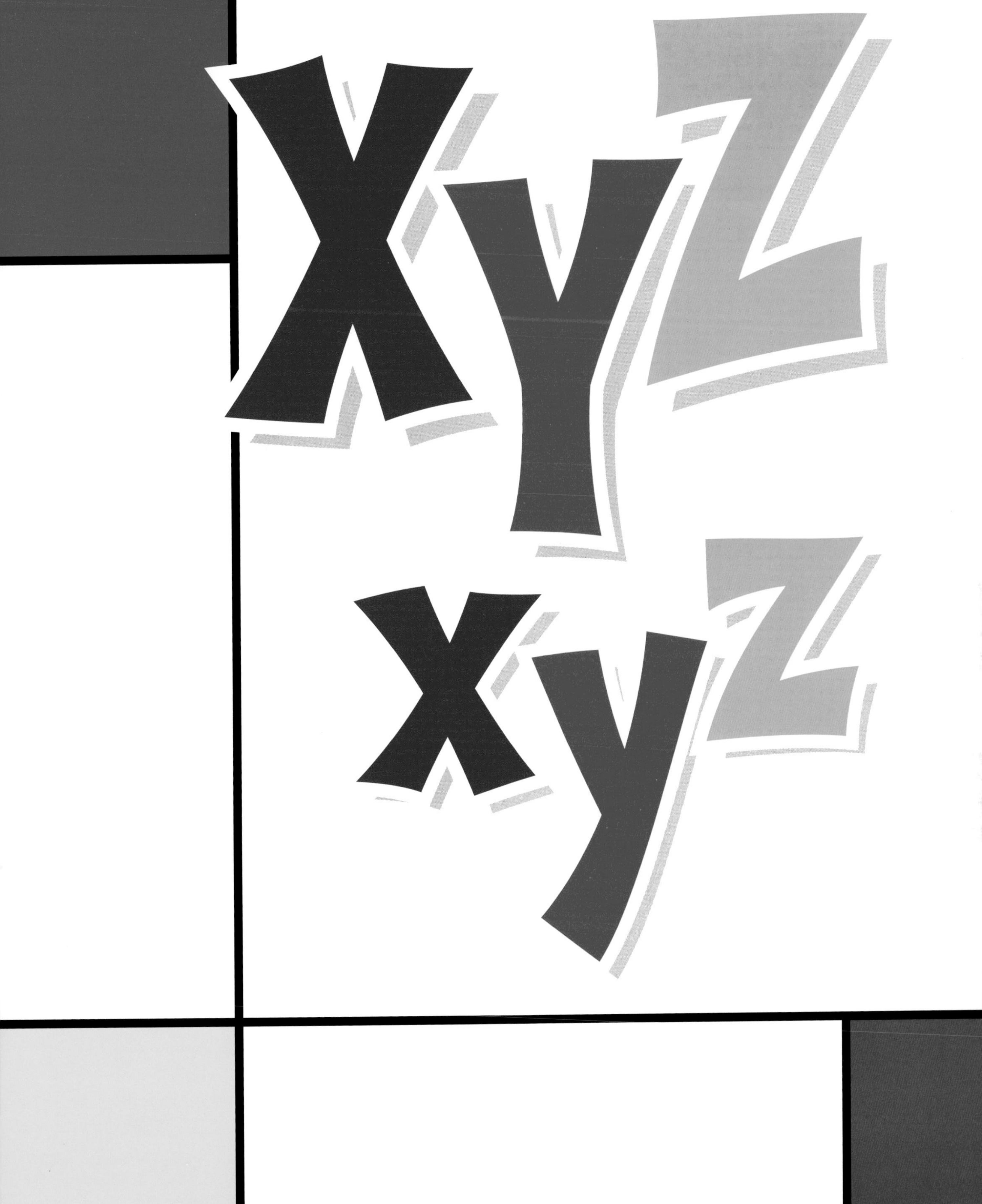
XYZ
xyz

Aa Bb Cc Dd Ee Ff Gg Hh Ii Jj Kk Ll Mm Nn Oo Pp Qq Rr Ss Tt Uu Vv Ww Xx Yy Zz

Xerxes
(ZUHRK seez),
Ahasuerus
(uh hash yoo EHR uhs) (KJV) Persian king who reigned 486–464 B.C. Known in the Book of Esther as Ahasuerus. He chose Esther to be his queen. He was the son of Darius the Great and grandson of Cyrus the Great. **Esther 1:1-2**

A bas-relief carving of a soldier at the 2500 year-old palace of Persepolis in Persia. Originally the home of Xerxes about 500 B.C., the columns and statues are remarkably well preserved.

Yahweh
(YAH weh) God's name. In the Hebrew Bible, Yahweh is written without vowels: YHWH. Since ancient times, Jews have considered it disrespectful to pronounce God's name, so they have been saying Adonai, which means "Lord." Many Bibles substitute the word "Lord" in small capital letters. Since no one knows for sure how to pronounce God's name, some say "Jehovah." **Exodus 3:14-15**

Yeast An ingredient added to flour that keeps bread from being flat. When the Hebrews escaped from Egypt, they had to make their bread dough so quickly that they did not have time to add the yeast and wait for it to make the bread fluffy. God told the Israelites to eat bread without yeast (unleavened bread) during the Feast of Unleavened Bread as a way to remember how He delivered them from Egypt. For other festivals, bread could be made with yeast. (See *Leaven* and *Unleavened*.) **Exodus 12:39**

Challah, traditional braided egg bread, contains yeast. The yeast causes the bread to rise.

Zacchaeus
(za KEE uhs) Tax collector in first-century Jericho. Zacchaeus had to climb a tree to see Jesus. Jesus called him by name and went home with him. During their visit, Zacchaeus announced that he would give half of what he owned to the poor. He would also repay persons four times the amount he had taken from them unjustly. Jesus told those who were listening near by that on that day salvation had come to Zacchaeus's house. Jesus said that seeking and saving those who are lost was His purpose for coming to earth. **Luke 19:2-9**

Jesus loved and forgave Zacchaeus.

Zarephath (ZAR ih fath) Town on the Mediterranean seacoast. At God's command, Elijah fled there after telling the king that a drought would happen in Israel. While in Zarephath he was hosted by a widow and her son. Her supply of meal and oil did not run out during the drought. When her son died, Elijah restored him to life and health. **1 Kings 17:2-23**

A widow provides bread for Elijah.

Zealot (ZEH luht) One who worked for a group or cause. The term came to refer to some of the Jewish people who wanted to overthrow Roman control of Palestine. One of Jesus' apostles was a man called Simon the Zealot. **Luke 6:15**

Zebedee (ZEB uh dee) Means "gift." A fisherman on the Sea of Galilee and father of James and John, two of Jesus' first apostles. Based at Capernaum on the north shore of the sea, Zebedee ran a fishing business which included partners Simon Peter and Andrew. His wife also followed Jesus and ministered to Him. The Bible does not say whether Zebedee ever became a believer, but he did not stand in the way of his sons or wife becoming Jesus' disciples. **Matthew 27:56; Mark 1:19-20; Luke 5:10**

Jesus calls James and John to be His disciples. Their father, Zebedee, is in the boat.

Zebulun (ZEB yoo luhn) Tenth son of Jacob by his wife Leah. Ancestor of the tribe of Zebulun, one of the twelve tribes of Israel. **Genesis 30:20**

Tribal allotment for Zebulun

Zechariah (ZEK uh RIGH uh) Means "The LORD Remembers." 1. Prophet who returned to Judah from the Babylonian exile. 2. Eleventh book in the division of Minor Prophets of the Old Testament. Contains many references to the coming of the Messiah. This gave hope to the Jews who had returned to Jerusalem from exile. Zechariah 9:9 tells that the Messiah would come riding into Jerusalem on a colt of a donkey. Jesus did that when He entered Jerusalem on the Sunday before He was crucified. 3. A priest in Jerusalem and the father of John the Baptist. The angel Gabriel appeared to Zechariah (*Zacharias*, KJV) in the temple and told him that his wife, Elizabeth, would have a son. They were to name the child John. When Zechariah questioned the angel, he could no longer speak. He was silent until his son was born. **Zechariah 1:1; 9:9; Matthew 21:1-9; Luke 1:5-64**

Zechariah, father of John the Baptist. When John was born, the people assumed that he would be named after his father despite Elizabeth's objections that the boy be called "John." When Zechariah confirmed the name by writing it on a tablet, his speech returned.

Zephaniah (ZEF uh NIGH uh) Means "The LORD hides." 1. Prophet from Judah who wrote in 630 B.C. 2. The ninth book in the division of Minor Prophets of the Old Testament. The book tells about the judgment of God on Jerusalem and about God's promise to bring people back to Jerusalem. **Zephaniah 1:1**

Zerubbabel (zuh RUHB uh buhl) Grandson of King Jehoiachin. He was taken to Babylon in the first exile in 597 B.C. by Nebuchadnezzar. He was among the leaders who returned from exile. Zerubbabel and Joshua, the high priest, rebuilt the altar and laid the foundation of the temple. Their work was stopped by people who had stayed in Palestine during the exile. The Persian ruler Darius gave the Jews permission to continue rebuilding the temple, a task that was completed in 516 B.C. **Ezra 2:2; 4:1-6,24; 6:1-12; 2 Kings 24:10-17; Haggai 1:1**

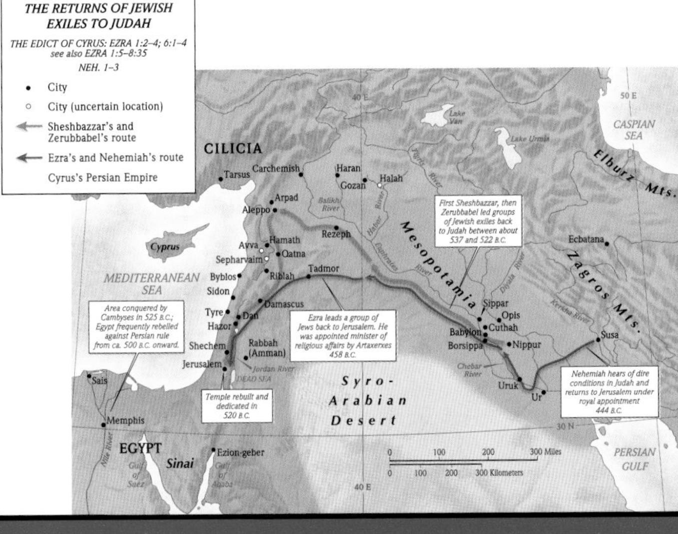

Ziggurat (ZIH guh rat) Stepped building, usually with a temple on the top. Built by placing smaller levels of brick on top of larger layers. Most Bible teachers believe the tower of Babel was a ziggurat **Genesis 11:3-9**

A reconstruction of a ziggurat dating to the Babylonian period (605-550 B.C.)

Zilpah (ZIL puh) Leah's maid given to Jacob as a concubine. Mother of Gad and Asher, who were regarded as Leah's sons. **Genesis 30:9-13; 35:26; 37:2**

Zion (ZIGH uhn) Word that described the fortified hill of Jerusalem before David and his men captured it from the Jebusites. The Jebusites boasted that this stronghold could not be captured. They said even the blind and lame could defend Zion. The temple mount is on Zion. Isaiah called Zion "the city of God." *Zion* is also used to describe the heavenly Jerusalem, the place where the Messiah will appear at the end of time. **2 Samuel 5:6-10; 1 Chronicles 11:4-9; Isaiah 33:5; Hebrews 12:22**

David and his men may have captured Jerusalem, Zion, through Warren's Shaft that runs from the Gihon Spring up to the old city of Jerusalem. This passage was rediscovered in modern times (1876) by the British engineer, Sir Charles Warren.

Zipporah (zi POH ruh) Means "small bird" or "sparrow." Moses' first wife and mother of his children, Gershom and Eliezer. She was one of the daughters of Reuel, (also known as Jethro) a priest of Midian. Zipporah may have stayed with her father until Moses had led the people out of Egypt. **Exodus 2:21-22; 18:2-6**

ART CREDITS

B & H Publishing Group expresses gratitude to the following persons and institutions for use of the graphics in this book. Our intent has been to credit each graphic correctly. If we have not done that, please notify us and we will make the appropriate correction.

Photographs

Museum Abbreviations

IMJ = Israel Museum, Jerusalem
JAC = Joseph A. Calloway Archaeological Museum, The Southern Baptist Theological Seminary, Louisville, Kentucky
MFB = Museum of Fine Arts, Boston
MNY = Metropolitan Museum, New York

Photographers

***Biblical Illustrator*, Nashville, Tennessee:** pp. 18, lower; 24, lower left; 27, middle right; 38, lower center; 61, middle right; 97, left; 114, lower right; 148, lower left; 176, left; 183, lower left; 186, upper right; 193, lower left.

***Biblical Illustrator* (Kristen Hiller, photographer), Nashville, Tennessee:** p. 70, lower.

***Biblical Illustrator* (James McLemore, photographer), Nashville, Tennessee:** pp. 120, upper right (courtesy of **Jerry Vardaman**); 193, middle left; 194, upper left; 196, right.

***Biblical Illustrator* (David Rogers, photographer), Nashville, Tennessee:** pp. 38, lower left (MFB); 55, left; 114, upper left; 121, lower left; 128, upper (JAC); 134, lower right (JAC); 153, lower (MNY); 176, upper right; 203, upper middle.

***Biblical Illustrator* (Bob Schatz, photographer), Nashville, Tennessee:** pp. 6 upper center, middle left; 18 middle; 20, upper left; 26, lower; 52, upper; 61, upper left; 70, middle lower; 73, upper; 80, upper; 81, left; 86, lower left; 96, left; 107, upper; 117; 118, upper middle; 124, lower; 128, lower right; 143, upper right; 144, upper left; 150, upper right; 151, upper left; 152, lower; 159, upper left; 162, lower left; 167, upper right; 171, lower left; 175, left; 177, lower right; 183, lower right; 187, lower middle; 194, lower left; 209, lower right.

***Biblical Illustrator* (Ken Touchton, photographer), Nashville, Tennessee:** pp. 25; 43, lower right; 50, lower; 62, upper right; 72, lower right; 74, right; 121, column two lower; 127, lower right; 142, center column; 143, lower right; 144, middle; upper right (IMJ); 145, left; 149, upper left; 160, lower left; 161, lower left (IMJ); 171 right; 178, middle right; 180, center; 181, upper right; 188, lower right; 190, upper left; 194, lower middle; 202, lower left; 204, middle left.

Brisco, Thomas V., Dean and Professor of Biblical Background and Archaeology, Logsdon School of Theology, Hardin-Simmons University, Abilene, Texas: pp. 106, lower left; 136, upper left; 159, right; 172; 182, lower left; 192, upper left.

Hatzigeorgiou, Karen (http://karenswhimsy.com/public-domain-images): p. 38, lower right.

International Mission Board, SBC, Richmond, VA: p. 120, upper middle; lower middle; 134, upper right.

iStock: pp. iv; v; vi; 4; 5, upper right, middle right; 6 lower right; 7 upper center, upper right; 9; 12; 16; 20, middle center; 21 upper left, upper center, upper right, middle left, middle center, middle right, lower left, lower center, lower right; 22, lower; 24, upper left; 28, upper left, upper right; 35, lower; 38, right center; 42; 43, lower left; 43, upper right; 48, lower left; 52, lower left; 56, right; 58; 61, upper right; 63, upper left; upper right; middle left; middle right; lower left; lower right; 64, upper left; upper right; middle; lower left; lower right; 68, lower; 69, upper left; lower left; lower right; 70 upper left; 74, left; 76, upper middle; 77, upper left; 78, upper left; 78, lower left; 79, lower middle; 79, lower right; 87, upper left; middle left; lower left; upper right; lower right; 88, upper left; middle left; lower left; upper right; lower right; 90; 97, middle; right; 102; 106, upper left; 107, right; 108, lower left; 110, lower left; upper column two; upper column three; 112, upper right; 114, upper middle; 116, upper left; 119, upper left; lower middle; 120, left; 121, column three middle; lower right; 124, right; 126, lower left; lower right; 129, upper left; 130, middle left; 133, middle; 134, upper left; 136, upper right; 139, lower left; lower right; 141, left; 146, upper left; lower left; upper right; lower right; 147, lower left; lower right; 148, upper left; 149, lower left; 150, upper left; 154, upper left; upper middle; 160, upper left; upper center; 166, center; 170, right; 173, lower right; 174, lower right; 176, lower middle; 177, upper middle; 178, lower left; 180, lower left; 181, lower right; 182, lower middle; 183, upper right; 184, center middle; lower middle; 186, lower left; 189, lower left; 189, lower middle; 191, lower right; 192, upper right; lower right; 193, upper left; lower left; upper middle; second row, middle; lower middle; upper right; third row, right; 194, upper middle; 195, lower; 200, lower middle; 202, lower right; 203, lower middle; lower right; 204, lower left, lower middle; upper right; 206, middle left; upper middle.

***Illustrated World of the Bible Library*:** p. 120, lower right.

National Optical Astronomy Observatory /Association of Universities for Research in Astronomy/National Science Foundation: p. 37.

Padfield, David, The Church of Christ in Zion, Illinois, padfield.com: p. 187, upper right.

Scofield Collection, E.C. Dargan Research Library, Nashville Christian Resources, Nashville, Tennessee: pp. 49; 62, lower left; 92, lower left; 107, lower; 115, left; 116, middle left; 121, middle left; 143, upper left; 147, upper left; 148, upper right; 177, lower left; 202, upper left; 203, lower left.

Stephens, Ken: 144, lower left.

Sundayschoollessons.com: 80, lower.

Wallace, Daniel B, Center for the Study of New Testament Manuscripts, Dallas, TX: p. 73, lower.

Wikimedia Commons: pp. 40, upper left; 118, left; 142, upper left; 154; 160; 169, left; 182, lower right; 188, lower left; 193, lower right; 200, upper middle;
Wikimedia Commons, Detroit Photographic Company, p. 184, upper left.
Wikimedia Commons, Giovanni Dall'Orto: p.14.
Wikimedia Commons, Felagund: p. 136, left.
Wikimedia Commons, Fredarch: p. 130.
Wikimedia Commons, Marie-Lan Nguyen: pp. 142, lower right, 193, second row, right.
Wikimedia Commons, Fèlix Potuit: p. 167, lower right.
Wikimedia Commons, Rama, p. 194, lower right.
Wikimedia Commons, Effie Schweizer: p. 156.
Wikimedia Commons, Ian Scott: p. 191, upper right.
Wikimedia Commons, Jeroen Zuiderwijk: p. 193, upper left.

Illustrations and Reconstructions

Answers in Genesis, www.answeringenesis.org: p. 10, upper; 62, upper, left.
***Biblical Illustrator*, Linden Artists, London:** pp. 2; 14-15; 163, lower.

***Biblical Illustrator*, Johnny Shumate:** p. 11.

Commons.wikimedia.org, Martin Heemskerck: p. 127, upper right.
Commons.wikimedia.org, Antonio Ciseri, p. 196, upper left.

Goolsby, Abe, Principal, Officina Abrahae, Nashville, TN: pp. 26, upper; 106, right; 144, lower right; 180, right; 200, lower left.

Latta, Bill, Latta Art Services, Mt. Juliet, TN: 10, lower; 14, upper left; 31, lower; 35, upper; 36; 83; 93, lower; 94; 133, upper; 164, upper; 177, lower middle; 184, lower right; 186, upper left; 188, upper; 203, middle left; 209, lower left.

LifeWay Christian Resources/Sunday School Board of the Southern Baptist Convention: pp. 2 (M-952); 4 (M-753); 16 (G-269); 17 (J-488); 19 (M-798); 20 (B-152); 24 (K-671); 28 (S-996); 29 (K-627); 30 (S-807-A); 31 (H-348); 32 (G-264); 34 (K-635); 38 (G-278); 40 (O-621); 43 (O-628); 44 (G-273); 47 (G-280); 48 (K-578); (G-235); 50 (L-464); 55 (O-608); 56 (M-689); 60 (C-88); 61 (M-983); 62 (M-791); 66 (M-879); 70 (M-760); 71 (S-535); (S-627); 72 (M-911); 76 (C-347); (L-464); 77 (G-276); 78 (T-899); 82 (G-254); 83 (J-363); 84 (S-986); 86 (S-928); 93 (N-160); (L-473); 92 (N-271); 95 (N-225); 96 (S-821); 98; (S-565); 104 (M-755); (S-976); 105 (G-271); 106 (M-398); 108 (G-246); (S-635); 109 (L-439); (G-224); 110 (G-224); 116 (G-255); 117 (N-212); 115 (G-278-B); 118 (T-907); 124 (M-889); 126 (B-183); 128 (S-775-B); 129 (K-602); 130 (G-242); 132 (S-632); 134 (S-883); (L-476); 136 (O-618); 139 (S-579); 140 (K-597); 141 (K-660); 146 (G-240); 143 (K-568); (0-608); 148 (T-872); 149 (M-978); 150 (K-653); 151 (G-281); 152 (L-478); 156 (M-580); (M-980); 158 (M-754); (S-578); 163 (C-81); 161 (M-937); 164 (N-122); 168 (P-610); 169 (T-909); 170 (L-465); 171 (M-891); 174 (L-434); 176 (G-279); 178 (L-444); 179 (N-229); 190 (L-468); 191 (S-875); 195 (S-604); 198 (M-373); 200 (S-857); 206 (G-225); 207 (B-211); 207 (M-934); 208 (S-992).